**W9-DJF-250**

# Stream Control Transmission Protocol (SCTP)

# Stream Control Transmission Protocol (SCTP)

# A Reference Guide

### Randall R. Stewart
### Qiaobing Xie

**ADDISON-WESLEY**

**An imprint of Pearson Education, Inc.**

Boston • San Francisco • New York • Toronto • Montreal
London • Munich • Paris • Madrid
Capetown • Sydney • Tokyo • Singapore • Mexico City

Many of the designations used by the manufacturers and sellers to distinguish their products are claimed as trademarks. Where those designations appear in this book, and Addison-Wesley, Inc. was aware of a trademark claim, the designations have been printed with initial capital letters or in all capitals.

The authors and publisher have taken care in the preparation of this book, but make no expressed or implied warranty of any kind and assume no responsibility for errors or omissions. No liability is assumed for incidental or consequential damages in connection with or arising out of the use of the information or programs contained herein.

The publisher offers discounts on this book when ordered in quantity for special sales. For more information, please contact:

Pearson Education Corporate Sales Division
201 W. 103rd Street
Indianapolis, IN 46290
(800) 428-5331
corpsales@peasrsoned.com

Visit AW on the Web: www.aw.com/cseng/

*Library of Congress Cataloging-in-publication Data*

Stewart, Randall R.
    Stream Control Transmission Protocol (SCTP): a reference guide/ Randall R. Stewart, Qiaobing Xie.
        p.      cm.
    Includes bibliographical references and index.
    ISBN 0-201-72186-4
    1. Stream Control Transmission Protocol (Computer network protocol)   I. Xie,
Qiaobing   II. Title.
    TK5105.5835 S74   2001
    004.6'2–dc21                                                    2001043111

Pearson Education, Inc.
Rights and Contracts Department
75 Arlington Street, Suite 300
Boston, MA 02116
Fax: (617) 848-7047

0-201-72186-4

Text printed on recycled paper

Production Services: TIPS Technical Publishing, Inc.

1 2 3 4 5 6 7 8 9 10—MA—0504030201

First Printing, November 2001

To my parents, Jack J. and Betty M. Stewart. Their guidance, love, and direction throughout my life has shown me that you can do anything you set your mind to!

—Randall R. Stewart

To my parents, Weilie-Zeng and Shaojiang Xie.

—Qiaobing Xie

# Contents

# Foreword

Over the years many people have felt that the widely available transport protocols in the TCP/IP protocol suite were not well matched for their particular applications. Many mechanisms have been proposed to change TCP—even going as far as suggesting a "TCP next generation"—to meet a wider set of requirements. However, the community has a well-founded reluctance to accept significant changes into the standard protocols for a number of reasons (for example, robustness issues and complexity issues). This makes the fact that the Stream Control Transmission Protocol (SCTP) has been developed and standardized even more impressive. SCTP is not simply a valuable technical achievement; it also shows the IETF's ability to work with a particular community to solve problems in standard ways, resulting in a protocol that is general and likely applicable beyond the envisioned applications.

In this book Randall Stewart and Qiaobing Xie provide a valuable resource for those wishing to learn about and understand SCTP. This book presents SCTP on several levels, from the original motivations of the protocol, to the design decisions made, to a discussion of a working implementation. This book can be used for everything from gleaning a high-level overview of SCTP and the design process to gaining a nuts-and-bolts understanding of the interactions present in the protocol and their purpose.

This book can provide a wonderful companion to the SCTP specification for those implementing the protocol. While the specification (Stewart et al. 2000) outlines the exact syntax and semantics of SCTP, this book provides readers with a behind-the-scenes look at why certain features were included and the motivations behind the design decisions that were taken. The additional insights will likely help implementers better understand the protocol and therefore lead to better implementations of SCTP. In addition, the book contains an open-source version of SCTP that readers can reference. The concepts under discussion are not simply abstract; they are also shown in great detail.

Finally, this book strengthens the traditional way the Internet protocols have been documented. Traditionally the community writes a specification for a protocol, which is simply the final result of the design effort. As time passes, the community's memory of that process fades and some of the key issues discussed are lost. This book, on the other hand, offers inside insights (by two of the SCTP designers) into the design of the protocol and discusses why the protocol operates as it does. This insight takes much of the "black magic" out of SCTP and makes the protocol more accessible to those future protocol engineers who may be engaged in using and extending SCTP in the future but were not involved in the original SCTP standardization effort. More generally, the design process involved in writing SCTP and discussed in this book provides a valuable reference to those designing new protocols so they can understand the decision-making process and pitfalls that SCTP went through, and thus avoid them in their own work.

This book represents a significant step forward in the community's documentation of transport protocols and their design.

—Mark Allman
Computer Scientist
BBN Technologies
August, 2001

# Preface

This book describes, from the two primary designers' view, the design and operation of the Stream Control Transmission Protocol (SCTP)—a new general-purpose IP transport protocol recently standardized by the Internet Engineering Task Force (IETF).

For those who are familiar with TCP/IP networking, SCTP can be simply viewed as a "super-TCP," that is, a TCP-like, general-purpose reliable data transport protocol with an enhanced set of capabilities.

SCTP is a key piece of the puzzle for making IP a truly viable technology choice in building the next-generation commercial grade infrastructure for telecommunications and e-commerce. For instance, SCTP has been required by the 3rd Generation Partnership Project (3GPP) to carry call signaling traffic in the third-generation cellular systems, and recommended by the IETF to carry the mission-critical Authentication, Authorization, and Accounting (AAA) messages in any future IP service networks.

*Telecommunications Magazine* selected SCTP as one of the "10 Hottest Technologies of Year 2001" in a cover story in its May 2001 issue.

### Why Do We Need SCTP?

The basic design of TCP/IP has worked remarkably well and remained largely unchanged. All the while the Internet has gone through its exponential growth, from a network of only a few nodes connecting a few university campuses, to a truly global Internet with tens of millions of hosts.

The Internet's explosive growth, witnessed by the nineties, continues into the new millennium. At the same time, IP technology has been steadily transforming itself into a cornerstone of the new information-era economy. One of the most visible results of this transformation is that IP technology is beginning to see more and more commercial uses. This is in sharp contrast to the seventies and eighties, when almost the only mention of TCP/IP was heard in academic and research communities.

It is inevitable that this commercialization process has brought with it new requirements to the technology. The original design of TCP, which was conceived and incubated in a mostly academic and research environment, has started to show its limitations in meeting some of these new commercial requirements.

It is this commercialization challenge on IP technology that has brought on the birth of SCTP.

When we first brought the original idea of SCTP (then called MDTP) to the IETF, we were trying to create a protocol to solve a very particular and practical problem; that is, how to transport telephony signaling messages using IP technology in commercial-grade systems. But, at the end of the process, the success of SCTP has grown far beyond our widest expectations.

### Readers

This book is written with two different groups of readers in mind.

The first group consists of those who want to understand SCTP. These readers may include programmers who need to work with SCTP, managers who want to make informed decisions about SCTP, students who want to learn the basics of SCTP, etcetera. For them, this book can serve as an easy-to-read alternative to the IETF standards specification.

In this book they will find not only detailed explanations of all the basic parts and operations of the protocol, often accompanied by a good deal of examples and diagrams, but also a thorough item-by-item comparison between functions of SCTP and TCP/UDP. Some of the chapters also give this group of readers guidance on which parts of the chapter they can safely skip without hindering their understanding of the general protocol operation.

The second group of readers we have in mind consists of the implementers of SCTP. For them, this book can be used as an annotation to the IETF standards specification. It is our hope that they will find some helpful clarifications of certain complex internal mechanisms of the protocol through the examples and illustrations we put in the book. Moreover, the recounts we have in the book on many important IETF debates and consensus-building processes may give them some insight into the protocol design. This in turn may improve their understanding over the rationale behind those same key design decisions.

### Prerequisites

We assume that the readers have preliminary knowledge about TCP/IP and IP networking. (An excellent book for this is W. Richard Stevens' and Gary R. Wright's *The TCP/IP Illustrated, Volume 1: The Protocols*, published by Addison-Wesley.) Moreover, some experience with C programming and Unix systems will be very helpful, though it is not an absolute requirement.

For those who would like to refresh their knowledge of IP networking, we have a short review of the IP networking basics at the beginning of Chapter 1.

## Coverage

This book covers all aspects of SCTP standards as defined in the IETF's *Request for Comments 2960 (RFC2960)* (Stewart et al. 2000). We also include a preview of the proposed SCTP sockets API (application programming interface) extension, which is a work in progress in the IETF.

A CD-ROM containing the open-source user-space SCTP reference implementation is included in this book. Readers who want to read the reference implementation code can find a chapter at the end of the book explaining the overall design and internal structures of the code. This code has been compiled and tested with FreeBSD 4.2, Linux 2.2.17 and 2.4.1, and Solaris 2.8.1 operating systems. Updates and new releases of this open-source SCTP reference implementation can be found at *http://www.sctp.org*.

For those interested in doing experiments with the SCTP reference implementation, a good tool to use to capture and analyze SCTP traffic is the Ethereal Network Analyzer, which is freely downloadable from *http://www.ethereal.com*.

## Acknowledgments

Never in our estimation did we expect to participate in writing an IETF *Request for Comments (RFC)* and subsequently write a book on SCTP, a major transport protocol of the future Internet.

It has been a privilege and an honor to work with the many fine individuals in the IETF SIGTRAN working group. It is through their comments, thoughts, and opinions that SCTP was crafted and refined. Without all of their input, SCTP would be less. Our sincere gratitude therefore goes out to all of our coauthors of *RFC2960* and to many other individuals who contributed greatly in commenting on and reviewing the design.

A special thanks to the SIGTRAN working group chair, Lyndon Ong, and the IETF Transport Area directors, Scott Bradner and Vern Paxson. They have provided insightful guidance and encouragement to "think of the bigger picture" and look into the future. Their superb management and masterful consensus-building skill throughout the process helped speed the specification through the IETF process.

This is the first time for both of us writing a technical book. Undoubtedly our inexperience does make this book-writing adventure a more challenging one. We especially thank our editing staff, Emily Frey, Karen Gettman, Mary Hart, Robert Kern, Jeannine Kolbush, and Elizabeth Ryan, for their step-by-step guidance and patience.

We also thank greatly our technical reviewers, Lode Coene, Muckesh Kacker, John Loughney, Ken Morneault, Kacheong Poon, Ian Rytina, Hanns Juergen Schwarzbauer, Chip Sharp, and Lars Viklund, for providing their different views on various issues, pointing out our numerous editorial oversights and inconsistencies, and keeping us honest by catching technical mistakes.

R.R.S.: A special note of thanks also to my wife Sandra for putting up with me, my late hours, and my constant "calling in to get e-mail." Dear, you are truly my soul mate, and without you I would be lost.

Q.X.: I would especially like to thank my wife Qing for her understanding and patience throughout the writing of this book.

—Randall R. Stewart
Crystal Lake, Illinois

—Qiaobing Xie
Palatine, Illinois

# 1

# Introduction and Overview

In this chapter we first give a brief tour of some basic concepts of IP networking. Then we introduce the SCTP protocol and discuss the rationale behind its development. In this discussion we will talk about SCTP's various features and its uniqueness to other IP transport protocols such as TCP and UDP. In the rest of the chapter we will recount briefly the history of SCTP's development, and the major issues encountered and decisions made during its development.

As in any other technical book nowadays, throughout this book the reader will inevitably encounter a lot of technical terms, abbreviations, and acronyms that are either general definitions for computer networking or more specific terms related to SCTP. For the convenience of the reader, we provide at the end of the book a list of all used definitions in the Glossary and Abbreviations section.

## 1.1   IP Networking Basics

One basic yet very important kind of communications in an IP network is so-called **connection-oriented communications**. In such a communication session, before any user data can be exchanged between two parties in the IP network, the two parties must go through a communication setup procedure and establish themselves in the appropriate state. Normally one party initiates the communication. This relationship usually starts with both parties confirming their willingness to engage in the communication. The involved parties will also need to agree, up front, upon the protocol or language to be used in the communication, the nature of the communication, etc. Once this state is exchanged, the relationship is established and reliable user data communication can begin.

In this section we will first discuss the basic addressing model used in an IP network, that is, how a message is addressed and how it is delivered to the intended receiver. This is essential to an understanding of how the communication parties find and exchange information with each other. Then we will discuss in detail how the endpoints in a communication, as well as the communication relationship itself, are logically defined.

### 1.1.1   How Messages Are Delivered in an IP Network

#### *1.1.1.1   IP Address and IP Datagram Routing*

In an IP network, application programs running on different machines communicate with each other usually by sending and receiving user messages. These user messages are translated into IP datagrams for transport across the IP network. In order to identify each individual machine, the network administrator assigns a unique IP address[1] to each of the machines connected to the network. This IP address assignment is instantiated in the machines either via manual configuration or via an automated address-management protocol such as the Dynamic Host Configuration Protocol (DHCP) (Droms 1993).

In many cases the assignment of an IP address to a machine is permanent; that is, the machine's IP address will remain unchanged for a significant period of time. An example of such a case is a server providing Web pages on the Internet; its IP address will stay the same until some rare circumstances occur and the network administrator decides to reconfigure the network and assign a new IP address to the server.

However, there are other occasions when the IP address assigned to a machine may change very frequently. An example of such a case is when, using a modem, you dial up to your Internet service provider from your home PC to set up a PPP[2] connection. Your Internet service provider will most likely assign a different IP address each time you dial in. However, once assigned, this IP address will normally stay unchanged for the entire duration of the PPP connection.

When the sender sends a message to the receiver, before the message gets on the network, the communication software inside the sender's machine will pack the message into one or more **IP datagrams**. The packing process includes the prefixing of a tag, called the **IP header**, to each IP datagram. The IP header will contain both the sender's machine's and the receiver's machine's IP addresses.

---

1. In some cases a machine may have more than one IP address assigned, based on various factors the administrator may deem appropriate. *See also* Section 1.1.3.

2. PPP (Simpson 1994) is a line protocol often used by Internet service providers to connect a home computer to the Internet.

Once an IP datagram leaves the sender's machine and gets onto the network, **IP routers**, which are essentially computers in the network that are specialized in forwarding IP datagrams, will take over and move the IP datagram toward the receiver machine. This process is called IP routing.

In its simplest form, IP routing requires each involved IP router to decide to which of its neighbors the IP datagram should be forwarded, based on its knowledge of the network topology and the receiver's IP address carried in the IP header of the IP datagram.[3] This process continues until an IP router eventually passes the IP datagram to the receiver machine.

### 1.1.1.2  IP Transport Port

When the IP datagrams arrive at the receiver's machine, the job of the routers in the network is finished. The rest is left to the communication software on the receiver's machine: to unpack the IP datagrams in order to reconstruct the original message, and finally to pass the message to the intended message receiver.

Since there may be other applications waiting for messages on the receiver's machine, there needs to be a way for the communication software at the receiver's machine to ascertain where the message is destined for before it can pass the message to the right receiver application. This need is solved by associating each message-receiving application on the destination machine with a different **transport port**. This assignment of transport ports is normally governed by the operating system on the machine.

When the sender's communication software packs the message into outbound IP datagrams, in addition to adding the IP header, it also prefixes a transport header. This transport header will contain both the sender's and receiver's transport ports. Once the IP datagrams arrive at the receiver's machine, the communication software there will identify the intended message-receiving application by examining the receiver's port number, which is carried in the transport header of each arrived IP datagram.

In summary, in order to uniquely identify a message receiver in an IP network, we need both an IP address of the machine on which the receiver resides and the transport port assigned to the receiver on the machine. The layered reference model of the IP-based communication application shown in Figure 1–1 is a conve-

---

3.  While most of the time only the receiver's IP address is used for routing, in modern IP networks, sometimes routers may also examine the sender's IP address as well as the transport layer ports carried in the transport header. For example, the sender's address may be used for ingress filtering, while the ports may be used for packet filtering for security and load balancing purposes.

Moreover, in the case of source-based routing, both the sender's and receiver's addresses will be considered in making the routing decision. Source-based routing is still a research topic and is not generally available on the Internet, although it may be used by some Internet service providers for maintenance and troubleshooting.

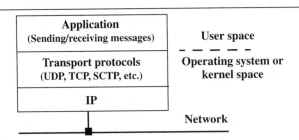

**Figure 1–1** *IP communication application reference model*[a]

a. The transport protocols can also reside in the user space, depending on the specific implementation strategy in use. Moreover, in some special circumstances such as when the platform is built upon a very small device, there may be no separation between the user space and kernel space at all.

nient way of showing this collaboration. The IP address is used in the IP layer to identify the machine (sometimes also called a **communication node** in the network) on which the application is running, and the transport port is used in the transport layer to identify the application on the machine.

Figure 1–2 shows an example of two communicating applications on different machines in a network. In this example, each machine is attached to the network through its network interface (NI). Each network interface has been assigned a unique IP address by the network administrator. Application 1 on machine A has been assigned port number 100 by its operating system; similarly, application 2 on machine B has been assigned port number 200.

When application 1 sends a message to application 2, the IP datagrams that carry the message will have in their IP headers machine A's address (160.15.82.20) as the sender's IP address, and machine B's address (128.33.6.12) as the receiver's IP address. Similarly, the transport header in each IP datagram will indicate 100 as the sender's port and 200 as the receiver's port.

Conceptually, in a simplified view the IP address and port number form a division of labor that accesses the destination application. The IP address serves as the mechanism to route the IP datagrams through the network to the destination machine.[4] The port number serves as a de-multiplexing agent for the destination machine's communication software to use to find the individual receiver application that is to receive the message.

4.  When moving the IP datagram through the network, some special network devices, such as some application-level packet filters, also look at the port information carried in the transport layer header to make routing decision.

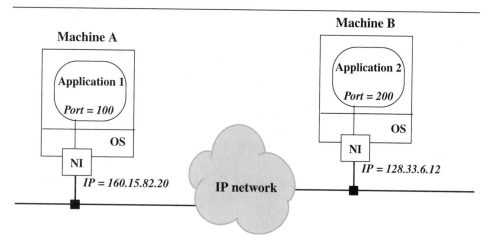

**Figure 1–2** *Example of two communicating applications*

## 1.1.2 IP Protocols

Communication nodes in a network can only communicate with each other if they all follow the same communication rules or conventions. These rules are normally called **protocols** and are defined and maintained by various standardization bodies such as the IETF and the International Telecommunications Union (ITU). For IP networking, the IETF has defined almost all the protocols in use today.

In order to manage the complexity of the modern communication systems better, protocol designers have used a layering principle that divides the communication software design into layers. The behaviors and rules of each of the layers are in turn defined in separate protocols.

For the IP network, the two most important communication layers are the **IP layer** and the **transport layer**, as shown in Figure 1–1.

The IP layer provides a basic connectionless datagram delivery service. The transport layer, which is built upon the IP layer and uses the datagram delivery service provided by the IP layer, provides a more sophisticated end-to-end data transportation service to the application.

Currently, two major IP layer protocols, the IPv4 (Postel 1981a) and IPv6 (Deering and Hinden 1998) protocols, are defined by the IETF. IPv4 has been widely deployed in the field and is the backbone of today's global Internet, while the deployment of IPv6 has just started.

At the transport layer, the best-known and most widely deployed protocols are the Transmission Control Protocol (TCP) (Postel 1981b) and the User Datagram Protocol (UDP) (Postel 1980).

### 1.1.3   IP Multi-homing

Another fundamental IP concept that we will need to understand in order to understand SCTP is **IP multi-homing**.

In the IP terminology, a communication node or host is called **multi-homed** if it can be addressed by (and thus "owns") multiple IP addresses.

Multi-homing is defined in technical detail in Braden (1989). But in a simplified view, multi-homing is usually the result of the host machine (where the communication node resides) being installed with either of the following:

- Multiple network interface cards, with each assigned a different IP address and/or

- A single network card to which multiple IP addresses are assigned[5]

However, for the purposes of our discussion, we will take a simple view in which multiple interfaces are installed and each interface has only one IP address. The example in Figure 1–3 shows such a multi-homed machine.

In the example, machine C has three network interfaces (NI-1, NI-2, and NI-3), each of which is assigned a different IP address. Normally the operating system on the machine is capable of sending and receiving IP datagrams through any of the three network interfaces. The applications running on a multi-homed machine can communicate with the outside through one or more of the available interfaces.

It should be noted that when there are multiple IP addresses on a machine, **there will be a unique transport port number space for each of the IP addresses**. In other words, on a multi-homed machine the transport port number space is defined on a per-IP-address basis, which means that we can have a unique port 100 for each of IP1, IP2, and IP3.

## 1.2   What Is SCTP?

Similar to TCP and UDP, the Stream Control Transmission Protocol (SCTP) is another general-purpose transport protocol for IP network data communications. It was published as *RFC2960* (Stewart et al. 2000) by the IETF in October 2000 as a Proposed Standard.

---

5. This is often the case in IPv6 networks where each network interface card is often assigned with a global address, a site-local address, and a link-local address. It is also allowable for a network card to have more than one of each of these types of addresses. The usefulness of the various addresses in IPv6 multi-homing will only be significant if the additional addresses can be used for path diversity.

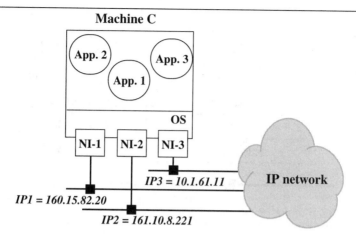

**Figure 1–3** *A multi-homed machine with multiple network interfaces*

The primary purpose of SCTP is to provide a reliable end-to-end message transportation service over IP-based networks.

### 1.2.1 Where Does SCTP Fit in the IP Architecture?

Like TCP and UDP, SCTP belongs to the transport layer in the IP architecture, as shown in Figure 1–4.

Both SCTP and TCP provide a reliable data transportation service between two communication nodes or endpoints that are connected to each other by an IP-based network. However, the SCTP data transportation service is **message-oriented,** while the TCP's is **byte-oriented**.

This means that a sending application can construct a message out of a block of data bytes and then instruct SCTP to transport **the message** to a receiving application. SCTP will not only guarantee the delivery of this data block (message) in its entirety to the receiver; it will also indicate to the receiver both the beginning and end of the data block. This is sometimes also termed **conservation of message boundaries**.

TCP operates very differently in this regard; it simply treats all the data passed to it from the sending application as a sequence or stream of data bytes. It will deliver all the data bytes to the receiver in the same sequential order as they were passed down from the application. However, there will be no conservation of any data block boundaries by TCP.

SCTP is also richer in functionality and more tolerant to network and component failures than TCP. In Section 1.3.3 and in Chapter 12 we will compare TCP and SCTP in more detail.

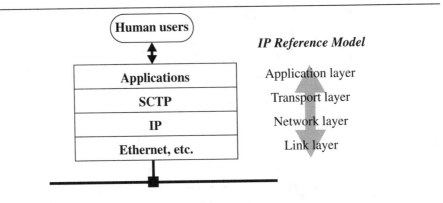

**Figure 1–4** *SCTP in the IP reference model*

## 1.3   Motivation for Developing SCTP

Through its early academic development to its later explosive proliferation into commercial sectors, IP technology has relied successfully on both TCP and UDP as the workhorses of data transfer. However, as the desire of further exploring IP technology for a wider range of commercial applications grows (such as real-time multimedia and telephony applications), some have started to feel that the data transfer services offered by TCP and UDP are inadequate.

One particular application that best exemplifies many of the shortcomings of TCP and UDP and directly motivated the development of SCTP is the transportation of telephony signaling messages over IP networks.

Telephony signaling has rigid timing and reliability requirements that are often set forth through government regulations and must be met in order for the phone service provider to be qualified.

### 1.3.1   TCP Limitations

The following limitations of TCP make it hard to meet the rigid timing and reliability requirements of telephony signaling:

- TCP provides both reliable data transfer and strict order-of-transmission delivery of data. Telephony signaling applications often need reliable message transfer but not a globally strict sequence maintenance. What is often more desirable for telephony signaling is a partial ordering of the data, such as maintaining ordering only within some subflows of the data.

The strict sequence maintenance in TCP not only makes such type of partial ordering of the data impossible, it can also potentially introduce unnecessary delay to the overall data delivery service. Loss of a single TCP segment can block delivery of all subsequent data in a TCP stream until the lost TCP segment is delivered. This is sometimes called **head-of-line blocking**. Excessive delays in telephony signaling may cause various types of service failure and hence must be closely controlled.

- The byte-oriented nature of TCP is often an inconvenience to the message-based telephony signaling. Applications must add their own record marking to delineate their messages, and they must make explicit use of the push facility to ensure that a complete message is transferred in a reasonable time.

- TCP has no built-in support for multi-homed IP hosts. This brings an immense challenge to the system designers who want to build link or path-level redundancy. Without link or path-level redundancy, the data transfer service in a network can become vulnerable to link failures. This is often unacceptable for a telephony signaling network, because providing highly available data transfer capability is one of its primary requirements.

- For telephony applications, especially commercial phone services, security against malicious attacks intended to cause failure or interruptions to the services is often a top priority. But TCP is known to be relatively vulnerable to some denial of service attacks, such as the **SYN flooding** attack.[6]

---

6. A SYN flooding attack is one of a number of denial-of-service attacks (Ferguson and Senie 1998) that have been used on the Internet. It is usually executed by a malicious host (the attacker) sending a targeted host (the victim) a large number of SYN messages. (The SYN message is the first setup message in a TCP connection, similar to SCTP's INIT message, as we will later see.)

The attacker sends each SYN message as if it had come from some other machine; that is, it fakes and keeps changing (often randomly) the source IP address in each SYN message. Each time the TCP stack on the victim machine gets a SYN message for a port that is accepting connections, it allocates some kernel resource in preparation for a new connection and sends back a SYN-ACK message.

The attack takes effect when a great number of such SYN messages flood into the victim machine in a short period of time and eventually deplete its resources. When this happens, the legitimate services provided by the victim machine may be disrupted. In severe cases, the victim machine can be completely knocked out of service by the attack.

It should be noted that some modern TCP implementations do implement methods to make SYN flooding less effective by, for example, enhancing the system resource to sustain attacks with very high connection attempt rates or putting a limit on the number of connection requests that can be attempted over some period of time. Also, Internet providers now do ingress filtering so that invalid IP source addresses are not allowed from the network edge.

### 1.3.2   UDP Limitations

UDP has its own shortcomings when it is being considered for carrying telephony signaling data. First, UDP only provides an **unreliable** data transfer service to the application; in other words, an application using UDP cannot know whether data sent to a peer application is received by the other end or not. Moreover, for those that reach the destination, there is no guarantee on the ordering of the data, and the receiver may get duplicated copies of the same data. Secondly, UDP has no built-in congestion management mechanism to detect path congestion and consequently to throttle back its data transmission. This can have two very undesirable effects:

- Injecting more data into an already congested network is unfriendly to the network; it often will worsen the network congestion and adversely affect other applications communicating using the same network.

- Data sent over an already congested network will likely be discarded by the network. This in turn makes UDP data transfer service more unreliable when the network is congested.

By itself, due to the above shortcomings, UDP cannot meet the data reliability requirements and thus is unsuitable for telephony signaling applications. However, because UDP is message-oriented and generally considered a lightweight protocol that has a relatively small overhead, there have been attempts to make up in the application itself what is lacking in UDP in order to meet more stringent timing and data reliability requirements. This normally means that the application will need to build its own mechanisms to do the following:

- Detect and retransmit any lost messages

- Correct out-of-order and duplicated messages

- Detect and deal properly with network congestion

This may not always be a good solution though, because the added complexity to the application may be considered excessive, and the mechanisms needed are not trivial to design and implement correctly.

### 1.3.3   SCTP Enhancements over TCP and UDP

In order to address the above shortcomings and limitations of TCP and UDP for these types of applications, the Signaling Transport (SIGTRAN) working group in the IETF developed SCTP. While the development of SCTP was directly motivated by the transportation of the Public Switched Telephone Network (PSTN) signaling messages across the IP network, SIGTRAN ensured that the design is also a good match for other applications with similar requirements.

Two major new capabilities are designed into SCTP: the support for multi-homed hosts and the support for multiple streams in a single SCTP association.

The built-in support for multi-homed hosts allows a single SCTP association to run across multiple links or paths, hence achieving link/path redundancy. With this capability, an SCTP association can be made to achieve fast failover from one link/path to another with little interruption to the data transfer service.

The multiple stream mechanism is designed to solve the **head-of-the-line blocking** problem of TCP. This feature gives the user of SCTP the ability to define subflows inside the overall SCTP message flow and to enforce message ordering only within each of the subflows. Therefore, messages from different subflows will not block one another.

Besides the two major new features just described, there are other enhancements designed into SCTP. Table 1–1 gives a more detailed feature comparison between SCTP and TCP and UDP.

## 1.4   A Short History of SCTP Development

SCTP has been formed over a number of years that involved a lot of research and experiments. Some of this research and these experiments the authors of this book were involved with, and much of it we were not. This section details some of the early work that has culminated in the current SCTP protocol.

### 1.4.1   Early Works Before the IETF and MDTP

The work that has become SCTP began quite a number of years ago with the realization that TCP had several key weaknesses in dealing with telephone call control. The first realization came in 1991 when a network broke while testing and many minutes transpired before the TCP socket gave an error indication. This was quite unacceptable and began the quest (at least by the authors) to build something better.

Three consecutive works were started by this incident, each experimenting with methods of putting together reliable communications that used UDP. Each one attempted to escape some of the deficiencies of TCP. One of these early implementations used a continual three-way handshake, while another used a modification of this. Each improved on the other until the last, Multi-network Datagram Transmission Protocol (MDTP), began in 1997. After getting most of the general concepts together and having a working implementation, the authors decided to submit it to the IETF for consideration in 1998.

**Table 1–1** Feature Comparison Between SCTP, TCP, and UDP

| Protocol Feature | SCTP | TCP | UDP |
|---|:---:|:---:|:---:|
| State required at each endpoint | yes | yes | no[a] |
| Reliable data transfer | yes | yes | no |
| Congestion control and avoidance | yes | yes | no |
| Message boundary conservation | yes | no[b] | yes |
| Path MTU discovery and message fragmentation | yes | yes[b] | no |
| Message bundling | yes | yes[b] | no |
| Multi-homed hosts support | yes | no | no |
| Multi-stream support | yes | no | no |
| Unordered data delivery | yes | no | yes |
| Security cookie against SYN flood attack | yes | no | no |
| Built-in heartbeat (reachability check) | yes | no[c] | no |

a. With UDP a node can communicate with another node without going through a setup procedure or changing any state information. This is sometimes called **connection-less**, but in reality each UDP packet has the needed state within it to form a connection so that no ongoing state needs to be maintained at each endpoint.

b. Because TCP treats all the data passed from its upper layer as a formatless stream of data bytes, it does not preserve any message boundaries. However, due to its byte-stream-based nature, TCP can automatically re-size all the data into new TCP segments suitable for the Path MTU before transmitting them.

c. Most TCP implementations do implement a "keep-alive" mechanism. This mechanism is very similar to the SCTP heartbeat, with the main difference being the time interval used. In TCP the "keep-alive" interval is, by default, set to two hours. The goal of this "keep-alive" is long-term state cleanup, which is in sharp contrast to SCTP's much more rapid heartbeat, which is used to aid in fast failover.

The submission of MDTP coincided with another telephony-signaling-over-IP initiative also being started in the IETF. That initiative resulted in the forming of the SIGTRAN working group in the Transport Area. At that time, the goal of SIGTRAN was to move existing telephone signaling protocols, including ISUP, DSSI, etcetera, onto a pure IP-based network.

The requirements for telephony signaling transport and the modular architecture developed by SIGTRAN found a good fit with MDTP's design concept. This began a host of modifications of the protocol in SIGTRAN, improving and refining the original design.

## 1.4.2 IETF Refinements

In the IETF the original MDTP design grew and changed through the input of many on the SIGTRAN mailing list and from the various face-to-face design team meetings that were held between 1998 and 2000. Somewhere along the way the name of the protocol was changed from MDTP to SCTP.

This name change evoked much discussion on the SIGTRAN mailing list as well as within the design team. The name change in many ways was more significant than many thought. It not only symbolized the substantial design improvement that the working group had performed; it signified an expansion of scope and functionality of the protocol. This expansion was what eventually led to SCTP being moved from a protocol running over UDP to one that directly runs over IP.

The following list describes some of the major changes that were invoked by the working group and the Internet Engineering Steering Group (IESG):

- *Multi-stream concept*—The working group made the decision to separate the data reliability function from the message ordering function. This in effect enabled multiple ordered subflows within a single reliable connection and provided a solution to the "head-of-line blocking" problem that the original MDTP design was not able to solve.

- *Congestion control enhancements*—The original MDTP design addressed congestion control incorrectly. The working group corrected this by completely redesigning most parts of the MDTP congestion control function, using both the TCP experiences learned from the past and new research results on TCP congestion control in the IETF and IRTF communities.

- *Four-way secure association initiation sequence*—The original design used a modified three-way handshake initiation sequence similar to that of TCP. This was improved by the working group via the addition of the fourth "leg" to the handshake sequence and the introduction of an encrypted **state cookie** to fend off potential security attacks.

- *Selective acknowledgment (SACK) improvements*—The SACK function was improved and enhanced from its original design so it more closely paralleled the TCP SACK extension.

- *Message bundling improvements*—The original MDTP message bundling was replaced with a very efficient and flexible chunk-based message bundling mechanism by the working group.

- *Path MTU discovery*—This was added to SCTP by the working group as a mandatory function in order to make SCTP more adaptive to various network conditions.

- The large message fragmentation function was redesigned.

- *Extensibility improved*—The chunk-based design and the extension mechanism were introduced to allow the IETF to add new features to the protocol in the future.

- An enhancement was made to allow user data to be piggybacked on the third and fourth legs of the initial opening handshake sequence.

After about two years of designing and reviewing and about twenty revisions on the draft document, SCTP finally became an IETF Proposed Standard in October 2000 and was published as *RFC2960* (Stewart et al. 2000). Since then, the continued work on SCTP has been handed over from SIGTRAN to the Transport Area working group (TSVWG) in the IETF.

If you would like to plumb the history of SCTP and dig through the 4,000+ e-mails that were generated during SCTP's birth, you can consult the IETF Web pages to find the current pointer to the e-mail archives of both SIGTRAN and TSVWG at *http://www.ietf.org*.


## 1.5    Major General SCTP Issues Debated in the IETF

In this section we give a recount of some important architectural discussions that took place in the IETF during the process of developing SCTP. Some of those discussions eventually led to SCTP design decisions of fundamental importance.


### 1.5.1    Do We Really Need a New Transport Protocol?

When the SIGTRAN working group was formed in 1998, one of the first questions it was chartered to find the answer to was whether TCP was good enough for telephony signaling applications. At that time, IP telephony was still a relatively new concept to the IETF, and most of the experience on IP telephony was gained from experiments with personal computers equipped with low-cost sound cards passing sampled speech to each other. However, people quickly realized the potential of providing telco- or carrier-grade telephony services over an IP-based infrastructure on a much larger scale than a few connected PCs with sound cards.

To provide large-scale commercial telephone services, a reliable way of transporting telephony signaling messages across IP networks had to be defined first.

People from the telephone industry, the so-called **Bell heads**, were well aware of the stringent timing and reliability requirements of transporting telephony signaling messages and had specifically created the Signaling System No. 7 (SS7) network to meet those requirements. They had serious doubts about whether TCP, the only reliable data transport protocol in the IP world, was up to the task.

A team led by Telcordia (formerly Bellcore) engineers was formed in SIGT-RAN to investigate the adequacy of using TCP/IP to transport telephony signaling. They came to the conclusion that the main problem with using TCP/IP for providing commercial-grade telephony signaling was the lack of control over the TCP retransmission timers. Some of the working group members quickly pointed out that this lack of user-level timer control was merely an implementation problem of the TCP stack, instead of a limitation on the protocol itself.

However, the analysis also pointed out that the "head-of-the-line blocking" imposed by TCP was also an issue. In high call-volume application scenarios, such as call processing centers, this "head-of-the-line blocking" could become a major problem due to delays imposed on user messages waiting at the receiver for a lost TCP segment to arrive. These delays would impose a domino effect on all calls, escalating the delay to an unacceptable level.

With the submission of MDTP and the ensuing discussions, the working group also quickly agreed on another major shortcoming of TCP: its lack of path-level redundancy support. This was viewed by many telco engineers as a major weakness of TCP/IP compared to SS7, because the latter was designed with full support of link-level redundancy. (For example, in the field, the data connection between two SS7 signaling nodes is often deployed over a set of physical T1 links, commonly referred to as a **link-set**, that may consist of up to 16 separate T1s, thus providing considerable link redundancy.)

Because of its packet-switched nature, a connection in an IP network normally does not confine itself to a specific physical link. Rather, what is equivalent to a link in the circuit-switched SS7 network is a **path** in an IP network. In order to achieve a degree of link-level fault resilience similar to that offered by the SS7 network, the working group reached the consensus that the IP transport protocol for telephony signaling must provide support for path redundancy.

There were also concerns that the three-way handshaking procedure used during the TCP setup might introduce too much delay at call setup.

The option of modifying or enhancing TCP to meet those new requirements was briefly discussed in the working group but was quickly abandoned. The working group was hesitant to take that approach, probably because other similar IETF investigations on transport issues—for example, the Requirements for Unicast Transport/Sessions (RUTS) BOF[7] and the Support for Lots of Unicast Multiplexed Sessions (SLUMS) BOF—had already pointed out the difficulty of modifying TCP.

---

7. BOF (Birds of a Feather) is an informal meeting format used in the IETF to gauge the technical interest of the engineering public on a specific topic prior to the creation of a full working group.

In the end, the working group reached the conclusion that a new transport protocol that would run over UDP was needed. MDTP was adopted as the baseline design of the new protocol. The working group also decided to insert a signaling protocol adaptation layer between the new transport protocol and the telephony signaling protocols. This decision effectively separated the transport function from any specifics of the upper-layer telephony signaling protocols. This separation paved the way for further transformation of MDTP into a generic IP transport protocol.

### 1.5.2   Over UDP Versus Over IP

As stated above, MDTP was designed to run on top of UDP for reasons that include implementation convenience (you do not need to write kernel code) and the desire of having tight control over the retransmission timing. This approach was unchanged after the working group took on the protocol development.

The work on MDTP had been moving forward smoothly and the protocol design was becoming stable when the working group received word from the IETF Transport Area Directorate in December 1999 that some important design decision should be revisited. The TAD had been discussing whether to change the new protocol (renamed SCTP already) to sit directly over IP instead of over UDP.

Soon afterward the IESG and the TAD made the recommendation of moving SCTP to run directly on top of IP. The reason was that the IESG and the TAD saw the value and significance of the new protocol and recognized the great potential of SCTP becoming a major transport protocol. SCTP was thought to be useful to a much wider range of applications than telephony signaling transport. Moving SCTP directly over IP with its own port number space was viewed as the architecturally correct solution.

Initially the working group was very reluctant to accept this recommendation. The main concern was that this change would almost certainly mean that SCTP would have to be implemented in the operating system kernel. It would normally take most operating system vendors a long time, up to several years in some cases, to make a new protocol commercially available in their operating system kernels. It was thought that the telephone industry just could not wait that long for the SIGTRAN protocol. In addition, some were concerned that to have the protocol sitting in the operating system kernel would make it much harder to keep tight control over the retransmission timers. Without this control, the stringent timing requirements of telephony signaling would be difficult to meet.

However, the IESG insisted that the working group should look at the bigger picture beyond signaling transport as well. The long-term benefits of putting SCTP in an architecturally correct position in the IP stack far outweighed the short-term deployment delay the change would incur on the telephony signaling transport applications. Eventually the working group agreed.

## 1.6 Organization of this Book

The authors' intention is to make this book useful for two different groups of people: readers who are seeking an understanding of the protocol and wish to have something easier to read than the protocol specification itself, and serious protocol implementers who are looking for insights into protocol design and detailed discussions on how various protocol features work or should be implemented.

To achieve this goal, we documented some important issues and items of debate that occurred while the protocol was being developed, giving the reader a bird's eye view of how the current protocol took its form in the IETF.

We also provided many examples to illustrate and explain the internal mechanisms and features of SCTP.

Whenever conflicting needs must be accommodated, a designer must make various compromises. SCTP's design is no exception. In this book we try to explain the reasoning behind those compromises, discussing the pros and cons of those features and how best to apply them in various environments.

For implementers we include an annotated version of the open-source userspace SCTP reference implementation. We explain in detail the software architecture and how the overall protocol features are implemented in the reference implementation.

Particularly, in Chapter 2 we provide a detailed analysis of some basic terms and definitions used in SCTP, such as **transport address**, **endpoint**, **association**, etc. Those terms and concepts are essential to understanding the design and operation of SCTP described in the rest of the book.

Chapter 3 describes in detail the SCTP packet formats—the bits and the bytes that appear on the wire. This description is more detailed than you can find in *RFC2960* (Stewart et al. 2000). It will help new readers get a grasp of what is on the wire, and it will provide a valuable reference to protocol developers. Readers whose goal is to gain a basic understanding of the protocol can refer to this chapter as needed but do not need to read it in detail.

Chapter 4 walks the reader through the details of setting up an SCTP association. It gives a high-level overview of the association establishment process, followed by a detailed summary. A reader who only wants to understand the basic concept of and steps for setting up an association can examine the high-level overview and move on, while those who want to implement the protocol may find helpful the detailed information in the rest of the chapter on how and why the protocol reacts the way it does during setup.

In Chapter 5 we discuss how the user data transfer happens within SCTP. For the convenience of the readers, an overview of the SCTP data transfer operation is given at the beginning of the chapter. The rest of the chapter provides a great deal of detail on

- How the SCTP sender transforms user messages into DATA chunks

- How the chunks are put together to form SCTP packets

- How fragmentation is done

- How bundling is done

- How the retransmission timer operates

- How the receiver acknowledges received DATA chunks

- How lost data is handled

- How SCTP deals with multi-homed hosts, etc.

Chapter 6 talks about SCTP congestion control and congestion avoidance algorithms. For those who plan to implement SCTP, this chapter is very important to understand.

The ability to detect failures and recover from them is one of the important design objectives of SCTP. Chapter 7 discusses how this is accomplished. The reader will find detailed discussions on the types of failures SCTP is capable of detecting, the internals of the failure detection and recovery algorithms, how the multi-homing and route arrangements interplay with SCTP failure detection and recovery, and so on.

In Chapter 8 we discuss some auxiliary functions within SCTP, particularly the handling rules for the out-of-the-blue (OOTB) SCTP packets and the rules dealing with the verification tags. Readers can skip this chapter if they only want to understand SCTP basics. But those who implement SCTP must obtain a full understanding of all of these rules.

Chapter 9 gives a detailed account of how an SCTP association is closed or terminated. It covers both the graceful shutdown case and the ungraceful abort of an association. This chapter is important for all readers to understand.

Chapter 10 talks about the procedures for creating future extensions of SCTP and assigning well-known SCTP port numbers through IANA.

In Chapter 11 we describe the proposed application programming interface (sockets API) for SCTP. Some readers may not find this chapter immediately useful, but implementers and application programmers who work on SCTP will benefit from the material in this chapter.

Chapter 12 discusses in detail some important differences between SCTP and TCP.

Chapter 13 gives examples to illustrate how the SCTP stream feature can be used.

In Chapter 14 we discuss the open-source SCTP reference implementation. We explain the architecture and design of the implementation and describe each of the main SCTP internal functions and the functional flow within the implementation. Implementers may find this chapter helpful if they wish to delve a bit deeper and look into the implementation itself.

## 1.7 Summary

In this chapter we first reviewed some basic concepts and the background of IP networking. We then introduced the SCTP protocol and described its basic features and its role in the IP architecture. We also talked about the motivation behind the creation of SCTP and provided a detailed feature comparison for SCTP, TCP, and UDP. The history of the SCTP protocol development was recounted, and some important IETF debates over SCTP design were summarized.

## 1.8 Questions

1.  Why is SCTP considered a message-oriented transport protocol?

2.  Why is UDP alone inadequate for transporting telephony signaling messages over an IP network?

3.  List a few advantages and disadvantages of running SCTP directly on top of IP.

4.  What is the limitation of TCP that SCTP's multi-stream feature intends to solve?

**2**

# SCTP Endpoint and Association

$\mathbf{A}$s we already discussed in Section 1.1, before two data communication hosts can engage in reliable communication in an IP network, the two parties must first pass state information and thus establish a relationship between them.

In SCTP these communicating parties are called **endpoints**, and the communication relationship between them is called an **association**.

In this chapter we will discuss in detail how SCTP endpoints and associations are logically defined and we will discuss some of their characteristics. The procedures for establishing an SCTP association will be discussed in Chapter 4.

## 2.1   SCTP Transport Address

There are different transport protocols used in IP networks. Different transport protocols use different transport headers and normally have their own transport port number space.

UDP and TCP are two of the best-known transport protocols and are in wide use in IP networks. They each have their own port number space, commonly known as **UDP ports** and **TCP ports**, respectively.

As a new general-purpose transport protocol, SCTP also has its own port number space, known as **SCTP ports**, assigned by the Internet Assigned Numbers Authority (IANA).

We define an **SCTP transport address** as a combination of an IP address and an SCTP port on the machine that "owns" that IP address. Following the same discussion we had in Section 1.1.1, it is easy to see that an SCTP transport address can uniquely identify a message receiver in an IP network. The IP address part of the SCTP transport address identifies the machine (or, more precisely, a particular network interface on the machine) that the message receiver resides on, while the SCTP port further identifies the message receiver on the machine.

It is important to note that the IP address of an SCTP transport address must be a routable **unicast address**. In other words, IP **multicast addresses** and IP **broadcast addresses** cannot be used in an SCTP transport address.

## 2.2   SCTP Endpoint

From the network's perspective, an **SCTP endpoint** is the logical end of the SCTP transport protocol. It is convenient to represent an SCTP endpoint using the notion of SCTP transport address that we defined in the previous section.

Let's look at an example. Figure 2–1 shows two communicating applications using SCTP as transport. On machine A, the application is assigned SCTP port 100, and on machine B the application gets SCTP port 200. In this example we can denote the SCTP endpoint on machine A by its SCTP transport address, [160.15.82.20:100], and denote the SCTP endpoint on machine B by [128.33.6.12:200].

### 2.2.1   Multi-homed SCTP Endpoint

Unlike a TCP communication endpoint, which can only have a single IP address, an SCTP endpoint can effectively control and aggregate multiple IP addresses on a multi-homed machine for sending and receiving data. We call such an SCTP endpoint a **multi-homed SCTP endpoint**. Figure 2–2 shows such an SCTP endpoint.

A multi-homed SCTP endpoint can be represented as a list of SCTP transport addresses on the machine **that share a single SCTP port**. We can therefore denote the SCTP endpoint serving application 1 in Figure 2–2 by the following:

endpoint = [160.15.82.20, 161.10.8.221, 10.1.61.11:100]

It may be convenient on most operating systems to form a multi-homed SCTP endpoint by binding the SCTP port to all the present IP addresses on a multi-homed machine, but it is **not** required. In fact, an SCTP endpoint can be formed over just a subset of the IP addresses on the machine. Some applications may wish this separation of traffic to control network loading and to optimize the usage of the local machine's networks better. Figure 2–3 shows an example of two such SCTP endpoints.

In Figure 2–3 the SCTP endpoint serving application 1 on port 100 utilizes only network interfaces NI-1 and NI-2, and not NI-3, while the SCTP endpoint

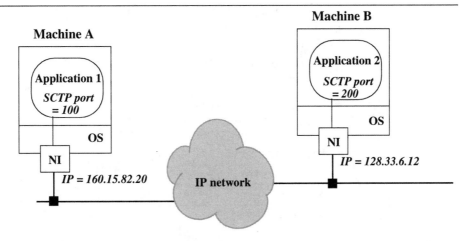

**Figure 2–1** *Two communicating applications using SCTP*

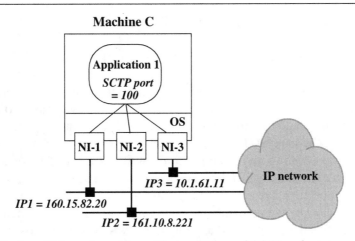

**Figure 2–2** *A multi-homed machine with a multi-homed SCTP endpoint*

serving application 2 on port 150 uses only NI-3. Using our convention, the two endpoints can be denoted by [160.15.82.20, 161.10.8.221:100] and [10.1.61.11:150], respectively.

It is very important to remember that under **no** circumstances can an SCTP transport address ever be present in more than one SCTP endpoint. For example, if you already have

endpoint A = [160.15.82.20, 161.10.8.221:100]

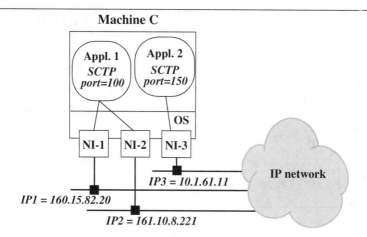

**Figure 2–3** *Multi-homed SCTP endpoints defined over a subset of the machine's IP addresses*

in existence, then you are **no longer** allowed to have

$$\text{endpoint B} = [161.10.8.221, 10.1.61.11{:}100]$$

as a valid endpoint definition, because SCTP transport address [161.10.8.221:100] has already been used by endpoint A. However, you can have both [160.15.82.20, 161.10.8.221:100] and [10.1.61.11:100] as valid endpoints at the same time, even though they use the same SCTP port.

In practice, forming an SCTP endpoint with a subset of the available IP addresses on a multi-homed machine, as shown above in Figure 2–3, may be difficult for some operating systems due to for instance, some programming interface (API) limitations. For example, in most Unix systems, the **bind()** system call currently only allows the user to bind a communications application to either **one** or **all** of the addresses visible to the operating system. The proposed SCTP extensions to the existing sockets API (which are discussed in Chapter 11) will give the user the flexibility of binding an SCTP endpoint to a subset of the available addresses.

## 2.3    SCTP Association

As you may recall from our previous discussion, SCTP is a **connection-oriented** transport protocol. This means that before any application data can be transported from one SCTP endpoint to another, the two SCTP endpoints must go through a

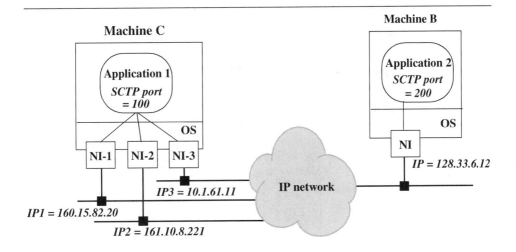

**Figure 2–4** *Example of an SCTP association*

setup procedure to establish a communication relationship by exchanging state information. This communication relationship is called an **SCTP association**.

An SCTP association can be conveniently denoted by a pair of two SCTP endpoints. An example of an SCTP association is shown in Figure 2–4.

Here we assume that the SCTP endpoint serving application 1 on machine C and the SCTP endpoint serving application 2 on machine B have already gone through the association setup procedure (which will be discussed in detail in the following chapters) and have established an association between them. We can then describe this SCTP association as follows:

association = {[160.15.82.20, 161.10.8.221, 10.1.61.11:100] : [128.33.6.12:200]}

| *Note* | Under any circumstances, there can be no more than one SCTP association between the same pair of SCTP endpoints. However, at any given time, an SCTP endpoint can have concurrent associations with different peer endpoints. |
|---|---|

Figure 2–5 shows an example of multiple concurrent SCTP associations established from a single endpoint, EP1, to its four peer endpoints (EP2, EP3, EP4, and EP5). In this example, EP1 may well be a server providing a simultaneous service to multiple clients on machines B, C, and D.

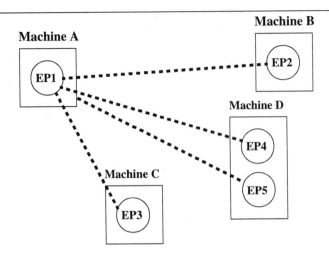

**Figure 2–5**  *Multiple associations from one SCTP endpoint*

## 2.4    Operation of an SCTP Association

### 2.4.1    Functional View of an Association

Figure 2–6 shows the functional view of an SCTP association between a pair of endpoints.

We use the term **host** as a logical representation of the communication process at either end of an association that includes the SCTP endpoint as well as the user message sender/receiver.

In Figure 2–6 the SCTP user application is shown sitting on the top of the SCTP host on both ends of the association. This user application is the originator and/or consumer of all user messages.

The SCTP transport service sitting in the middle layer on both ends is the focus of our book. It is the logical representation of the SCTP endpoint in the host, and it is responsible for providing SCTP transport services to the SCTP user application above it. This middle layer is also responsible for setting up and tearing down the SCTP association, as well as maintaining the operation of the association.

Among the various transport services, one is of particular importance to SCTP: providing the **multiple stream** function within an SCTP association. Within SCTP, the data reliability mechanism (responsible for tasks like data loss detection, retransmission timer control, etc.) has been separated from the message ordering mechanism. This makes it possible for the endpoints to transfer two or more separate sequences of ordered reliable messages at the same time, without

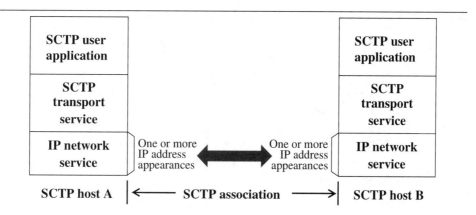

**Figure 2–6**  *A functional view of an SCTP association*

introducing interdependency among different message sequences. Each independently ordered message sequence is called a stream of the SCTP association.

Within a single SCTP association, up to 65,536 unidirectional streams can be created and used by either end for simultaneous data transfer. In order to indicate over which stream a specific message is to be transported, the sending user application is required to tag each of its outbound messages with a **stream identifier**.

Another service that is unique to SCTP and worthwhile to be noted is the **unordered** message transport service. In the normal case, each message is delivered to the receiver in its **order of transmission** within the stream; that is, the first message passed by the sending application to the SCTP endpoint on the sender side will be the first to be delivered to the receiving application on the receiver side.

But a message may also be specified by the sending application as unordered, meaning that it can be delivered to the receiving application regardless of its order of transmission. For details on SCTP stream and unordered message delivery, see Section 5.6.

The IP network service layer is responsible for running various IP network protocols, as well as controlling the network interfaces. Each of the STCP hosts will have one or more IP address appearances to the network, depending on whether the machine is multi-homed or not.

### 2.4.2    Functional Responsibilities of an SCTP Endpoint

In order to provide the services we described in Chapter 1, an SCTP endpoint usually needs to perform the following functions:

- *Stream queue management*—The endpoint needs to manage the operation as well as resources for each stream. For outbound streams, the endpoint will need to assign the stream sequence number to each outgoing message. For inbound streams, the endpoint will need to check the continuity of stream sequence numbers over the arrived messages and perform message reordering whenever necessary.

  The reordering service is important because of the fact that in an IP network, it is not unusual for IP datagrams to arrive at the destination host out of their transmission order. To perform the reordering, the endpoint needs to hold up a received message from delivery if another message with a smaller sequence number in that stream is still missing. This way the sequential delivery of the messages in that stream can be guaranteed.

- *User message fragmentation*—If the user application passes a message that is larger than the current path maximum transmission unit (PMTU) (Mogul and Deering 1990; McCann, Deering, and Mogul 1996), the endpoint will break the user message into small pieces, with each piece a size smaller than the current PMTU.[1]

- *Acknowledgment generation*—The endpoint needs to acknowledge the reception of user data from the other endpoint.

- *Congestion avoidance*—The endpoint needs to monitor whether there is a congestion problem in the network. If it detects that network congestion is occurring, the endpoint will need to make an adjustment in its sending operation in order to help lessen the network congestion.

- *Data bundling*—When small outbound messages are queued for transmission, the sending endpoint can bundle as many small messages together as the current PMTU allows[1] and then transmit them in a single IP datagram.

  Though this bundling service is not a mandatory feature to implement, it can allow more efficient utilization of the network bandwidth and hence improve the communication throughput. This improvement is especially noticeable when the user application is mostly sending a large number of small messages (as many telephony signaling transport applications do today).

---

1. In practice, each piece cannot have exactly the size of the PMTU because room must be left to accommodate the transport and IP headers, which will add to the total size of the final IP datagram.

- *Packet validation*—When a new SCTP packet arrives, the endpoint needs to examine whether or not the data is from the legitimate sender (that is, the peer endpoint of the association), and whether the data received has still maintained its integrity (that is, the data has not been corrupted or truncated during the transportation).

- *Path management*—The endpoint needs to examine the source and destination transport addresses of each arrived IP datagram in order to identify the sender. (Remember, there can be multiple concurrent associations existing between this endpoint and its different peers.) When the peer endpoint is multi-homed, it also needs to determine to which transport address (out of all available transport addresses of the multi-homed peer endpoint) the next outbound IP datagram should be sent.

These functional areas in an SCTP endpoint are shown conceptually in Figure 2–7 as different sublayers.

This sublayering view of an SCTP endpoint shows the functional areas and their positions relative to the user data flow. Association startup and shutdown functions do not involve user data processing and hence are shown aside the data path.

In practice, these functional areas may be merged with each other or further divided in the software of a particular SCTP implementation.

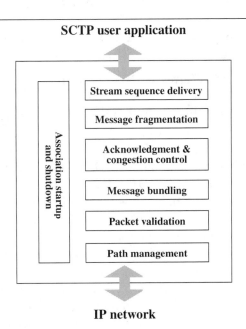

**Figure 2–7** *Functional decomposition of an SCTP endpoint*

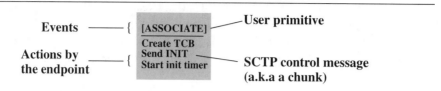

**Figure 2–8**  *Conventions used in the SCTP state notation*

### 2.4.3   Operation States of an Association

Once active, an SCTP association will transition through different operation states, driven mainly by the interactions between the endpoints and various events external to SCTP. In this section we will describe these operation states and the state transitions.

We will use the notations defined in Figure 2–8 to describe the triggering events and resultant actions associated with an SCTP state transition.

In this section we will only discuss the normal state transitions for SCTP association establishment and shutdown. Abnormal cases such as race conditions and duplicate messages will be discussed in detail in later chapters.

Figure 2–9 shows the state transitions for establishing an SCTP association. There are two different ways the establishment of an association can start:

1. When the endpoint receives the **ASSOCIATE** primitive from the user application

2. When the endpoint receives an INIT chunk from a peer endpoint

In the first case, the endpoint will send an INIT chunk to the peer endpoint indicated by the user application, start the *init* timer, and move into the COOKIE_WAIT state. When the peer answers with an INIT-ACK chunk, the endpoint will stop its *init* timer, send out a COOKIE-ECHO chunk, start its *cookie* timer, and move into the COOKIE_ECHOED state. From the COOKIE_ECHOED state, the endpoint will next move into the ESTABLISHED-state once the peer responds with the COOKIE-ACK chunk. The COOKIE-ACK will also cause the endpoint to stop its *cookie* timer. (SCTP cookie exchange is a security mechanism specially built in to guard against resource attacks. We will have more details on it in Chapter 4.)

In the second case of association establishment, the endpoint, upon receiving the INIT chunk from its peer, will respond immediately with an INIT-ACK but will not change state nor allocate resources for the new association. Instead, it will remain in the CLOSED state until it receives the COOKIE-ECHO chunk from the

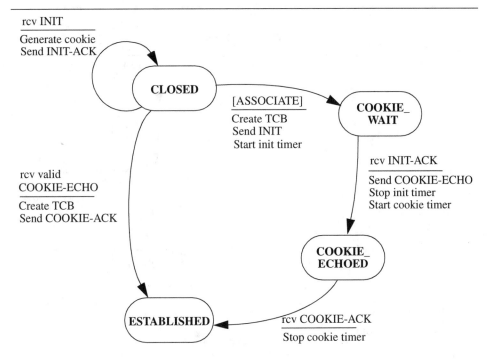

**Figure 2–9** *State transition I: establishment of an SCTP association*

peer endpoint. Once it receives and validates the COOKIE-ECHO chunk, the endpoint will create the association and move it directly into the ESTABLISHED state.

The state transitions involved in the termination of an existing association are depicted in Figure 2–10.

An association can be gracefully shut down, meaning that both sides of the association will be given a chance to finish sending any user data already queued for transmission.

A graceful shutdown can be initiated by either the reception of a SHUTDOWN chunk from the peer endpoint, or by the local user application invoking the **SHUTDOWN** primitive.

In the former case, when the SHUTDOWN chunk arrives, the endpoint will stop accepting new user messages from the local user application and move into the SHUTDOWN_RECEIVED state. The endpoint will continue transporting any queued user data and remain in the SHUTDOWN_RECEIVED state until all the queued outbound user data is sent out and received by the peer. Then the endpoint will send a SHUTDOWN-ACK chunk to its peer and move into the SHUTDOWN_ACK_SENT state, waiting for a SHUTDOWN-COMPLETE chunk from the peer. Once the SHUTDOWN-COMPLETE chunk arrives from the

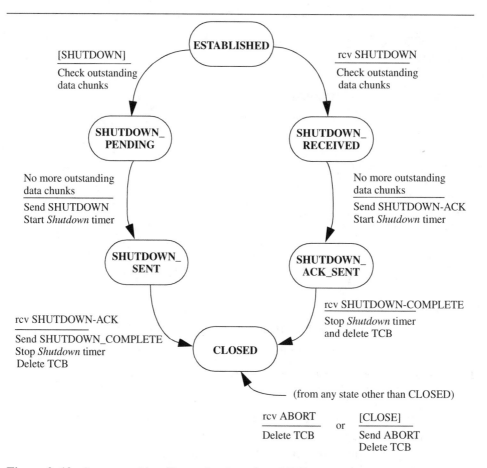

**Figure 2–10**   *State transition II: termination of an SCTP association*

peer, the graceful shutdown will be completed and the endpoint will move into the CLOSED state.

In the latter case (that is, when the shutdown process is triggered by a **SHUT-DOWN** primitive from the local user application), the endpoint will, as in the preceding procedure, first stop accepting new messages from the local user application. Then it will continue transporting any outbound messages queued locally until all of them are received by the peer endpoint. It will then send a SHUTDOWN chunk to its peer, enter the SHUTDOWN_SENT state, and wait for the response from the peer. Once the peer responds with a SHUTDOWN-ACK chunk, the endpoint will send a SHUTDOWN-COMPLETE chunk and move the association into the CLOSED state.

An association can also be torn down abruptly by either side under certain circumstances, such as the detection of some operation errors, resource shortages, etc. We use the term **abort** to describe such a unilateral breakup of an association.

As shown at the bottom of Figure 2–10, when the endpoint receives an ABORT chunk from the peer or when the local user application issues a **CLOSE** primitive, the endpoint will immediately close the association and release its resource. Any user data that is still queued locally for transmission will be abandoned.

## 2.5   IETF Debate and Issues

During the development of SCTP, the definition of an SCTP endpoint went through several evolutions. Before the IETF SIGTRAN working group changed SCTP to be directly over IP (based on a recommendation by the Transport Area Directors and some IESG members), we allowed each transport address in an endpoint to have its own UDP port. (At the time, UDP was chosen to be the transport protocol beneath SCTP.) Since the change, only one SCTP port is allowed per endpoint.

The change was proposed mainly because of the realization that SCTP had evolved gradually from a telephony signaling message transport protocol into a general-purpose transport protocol that could potentially benefit many other application areas in the IETF. Thus, to have SCTP positioned directly above the IP layer is more consistent with the IP protocol architecture. In practice, the change both simplifies the protocol definition and makes the implementation less complex.

As part of the change, it was agreed that IANA would define a separate port space for SCTP. Many of the traditional UDP and TCP ports are also reserved in SCTP, but it is important to realize that each protocol—TCP, UDP, and now SCTP—does have a separate port space.

## 2.6   Summary

In this chapter we discussed the definitions of SCTP endpoint and SCTP association. One fundamental difference between an SCTP endpoint and a TCP endpoint is that the SCTP endpoint can be multi-homed; that is, it is capable of encapsulating more than one IP address assigned to a host machine.

We defined an SCTP association as the communication relationship between two SCTP endpoints, similar to a TCP connection between two TCP endpoints. However, an SCTP association has several advantages over a TCP connection, such as the multi-stream capability, network-level fault-tolerance support, strong security, etc. These differences were compared and contrasted in this chapter as well.

Another important topic we discussed in this chapter is the operation states of an SCTP association and the normal state transitions. Discussions of race conditions and other state transitions can be found in later chapters.

## 2.7   Questions

1.   How is an SCTP association different from a TCP connection?

2.   How many IP addresses may be contained in an SCTP endpoint?

3.   Give some examples of SCTP endpoints in various configurations.

4.   How many SCTP associations are allowed between the **same** pair of endpoints?

5.   Can an SCTP endpoint establish more than one association with **different** peer endpoints simultaneously?

# 3

# Format of SCTP Messages

This chapter will discuss all the gory details of the bits that are transported between two SCTP endpoints. Much debate and thought went into the final layout. For instance, how could we make it extensible yet flexible? Should messages be byte-aligned or word-aligned? How should it all be structured and formatted?

The layout was completely restructured several times until the current SCTP format presented here was achieved.

## 3.1 Basic Layout—The Bits on the Wire

SCTP packets are made up of an SCTP common header and specific building blocks called **chunks**. The SCTP common header provides SCTP with specific validation and associative properties (which we will see as we look closer at these parts). Chunks provide SCTP with the basic structure needed to carry information. Chunks are divided into two classifications: control and data. A control chunk is by definition a chunk that carries information that is used to control and maintain the SCTP association. Data chunks are used to carry user messages across the association.

Figure 3–1 shows a high-level view of an SCTP packet. Notice that there is only one SCTP common header, followed by one or more "chunks." Each chunk is fully self-descriptive and represents a type of information being passed between one SCTP endpoint and its peer.

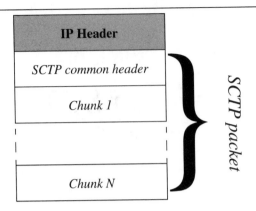

**Figure 3–1**  *A high-level view of an SCTP packet*

### 3.1.1   The SCTP Common Header

The SCTP common header provides three basic services to SCTP:

- The method to associate an SCTP packet with an association[1]

- Verification that the SCTP packet belongs to the current instance of this association

- Transport-level verification that the data is intact and unaltered by inadvertent network errors

Figure 3–2 diagrams the basic SCTP common header that is included on every SCTP packet. The fields and values of the common header are described as follows:

- *Source port number*—This field contains the sender endpoint's SCTP port number.

- *Destination port number*—This field contains the SCTP port number of the destination endpoint (that is, the intended receiver of the SCTP packet).

  The source and destination port numbers carried in the SCTP packet's common header, and the source and destination IP addresses carried in the IP header, can uniquely identify the SCTP association to which the IP datagram belongs.

  In practice, when an IP datagram arrives at a host, the first two tasks an

---

1.  This is usually done in conjunction with the source and destination addresses contained in the IP header.

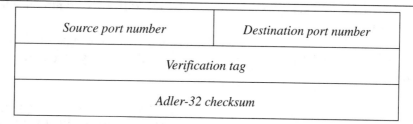

| Source port number | Destination port number |
| --- | --- |
| Verification tag | |
| Adler-32 checksum | |

**Figure 3–2** *The SCTP common header*

SCTP endpoint normally needs to perform are the following:

1. Verify that the data has not been inadvertently changed in transit by validating the checksum.

2. Find the Transmission Control Block or TCB of the corresponding association. This is done by simply matching the source and destination transport addresses.

- *Verification tag*—This value serves two purposes. First, it provides a discrimination method that prevents an SCTP packet from a previous incarnation of an association (between the same pair of endpoints) from being mistaken for an SCTP packet belonging to the current association. Secondly, it provides a protection against a blind attacker injecting data into an existing association.

- *Adler-32 checksum*—This value provides a data integrity check on the transport level to ensure the correct transportation of the SCTP packet.[2] The Adler-32 checksum covers the SCTP common header and all chunks in the SCTP packet. See Section 5.9 for details on how to generate the Adler-32 checksum.

### 3.1.2   Elements in a Chunk

Chunks were chosen as a basis for the protocol to establish a "building block"-style approach. The idea is that each "building block" would be fully self-descriptive and of a uniform format and size. In order to meet the uniform characteristics, all chunks must end on a 32-bit word boundary. Anytime a chunk does not end on the 32-bit word boundary, it is padded to the next word

---

2. However, it should be noted that the data integrity verification currently defined in the SCTP common header is not enough if an end-to-end data security is desired. For instance, the SCTP data integrity verification alone will not be able to detect if a malicious middle box in the path recalculates the header checksum and updates it after tampering with the data.

boundary. The self-descriptive nature is achieved from the chunk header itself, as illustrated in Figure 3–3.

The *Chunk type* field, an 8-bit value, represents the type of chunk that is present. The *Chunk flags* field, also 8 bits wide, defines any special flags that this type of chunk may wish to use.

> *Note*   Different types of chunks use *Chunk flags* bits differently; that is, the bits in the *Chunk flags* field will take on different meanings depending on what type of chunk the field is in. By default, any undefined *Chunk flags* bits are set to zero.

The *Chunk length* field (16 bits or 2 bytes wide) contains an unsigned integer indicating how long this chunk is in bytes. The value of *Chunk length* will include the 4 bytes used by *Chunk type*, *Chunk flags*, and *Chunk length*. This means that for a chunk that had no *Chunk data*, the *Chunk length* would still have a value of 4.

Moreover, as we mentioned above, a chunk will be padded to the next 32-bit word boundary if it does not end on a 32-bit word boundary by itself. In such a case, it is important to notice that the *Chunk length* will not count in the padded bytes.

Figure 3–4 illustrates a chunk with the word "hello" in it.[3] Notice that the last three bytes are paddings to align the chunk to a 32-bit word boundary and are therefore not counted in the *Chunk length*.

### 3.1.3   Defined Chunk Types and Extensibility

One of the main reasons that the preceding chunk-based format was chosen for SCTP was its extensibility. The format allows a total of 256 different chunk types to be defined. Currently 16 chunk types are defined in the base SCTP, leaving an additional 240 chunk types that may be defined in the future by the IETF. The currently defined chunk types can be found in Table 3–1. If for some reason the chunk space of SCTP is exhausted, the codes **0x3f**, **0x7f**, **0xbf**, and **0xff** have been reserved for extensions to the chunk type spaces.

---

3. This chunk is used for illustrative purposes only. An actual chunk that carries user data would have a different format from what is shown. See Section 3.2.5 for the actual data chunk format that would be used to send user data.

| Chunk type | Chunk flags | Chunk length |
|------------|-------------|--------------|
| Chunk data | | |

**Figure 3–3** *The layout of a chunk*

| Byte 1 | Byte 2 | Byte 3 | Byte 4 |
|--------|--------|--------|--------|
| *Chunk type = X* | *Chunk flags = 0* | *Chunk length = 9* | |
| 'h' | 'e' | 'l' | 'l' |
| 'o' | *pad = 0x00* | *pad = 0x00* | *pad = 0x00* |

**Figure 3–4** *A chunk that does not terminate on a 32-bit word boundary*

**Table 3–1** Chunk Types by Number

| Chunk Type | Chunk Name | Description |
|------------|------------|-------------|
| 0x00 | DATA | This chunk carries a user data payload. |
| 0x01 | INITIATION (INIT) | This chunk is used to begin an SCTP association. |
| 0x02 | INITIATION ACKNOWLEDGMENT (INIT-ACK) | This is used as the response to an INITIATION chunk. As we will see, this is the second leg of the four-way handshake procedure for setting up an association. |
| 0x03 | SELECTIVE DATA ACKNOWLEDGMENT (SACK) | This chunk is used to acknowledge the reception of user data by an SCTP receiver. |

**Table 3–1** Chunk Types by Number (cont'd)

| Chunk Type | Chunk Name | Description |
|---|---|---|
| 0x04 | HEARTBEAT | This chunk is used as a keep-alive message sent to idle destination addresses. |
| 0x05 | HEARTBEAT ACKNOWLEDGMENT (HEARTBEAT-ACK) | This is used as the response to a HEARTBEAT chunk. |
| 0x06 | ABORT | This is used to initiate an ungraceful termination of an association. |
| 0x07 | SHUTDOWN | Used to initiate a graceful termination of an association, this is the first message of the three-way graceful termination sequence. |
| 0x08 | SHUTDOWN ACKNOWLEDGMENT (SHUTDOWN-ACK) | A response to a SHUTDOWN, this is the second message of the three-way graceful termination sequence. |
| 0x09 | OPERATION ERROR (ERROR) | This chunk is used by an endpoint to report an operation error to its peer. |
| 0x0a | COOKIE ECHO (COOKIE-ECHO) | The third leg of the four-way association setup procedure, this is used to pass the state cookie. |
| 0x0b | COOKIE ACKNOWLEDGMENT (COOKIE-ACK) | Used as the response to a COOKIE ECHO, this is the final (fourth) leg of the association setup procedures. |
| 0x0c | EXPLICIT CONGESTION NOTIFICATION ECHO (ECNE) | Reserved for Explicit Congestion Notification (ECN). |
| 0x0d | CONGESTION WINDOW REDUCED (CWR) | Reserved for ECN. |

**Table 3–1** Chunk Types by Number (cont'd)

| Chunk Type | Chunk Name | Description |
|---|---|---|
| 0x0e | SHUTDOWN COMPLETE (SHUTDOWN-COMPLETE) | This is the final message of the three-way graceful termination procedure. |
| 0x0f-0x3e | (Reserved) | Reserved by the IETF for future use. |
| 0x3f | Special expansion code 1 | IETF defined chunk expansion code. |
| 0x40-0x7e | (Reserved) | Reserved by the IETF for future use. |
| 0x7f | Special expansion code 2 | IETF-defined chunk expansion code. |
| 0x80-0xbe | (Reserved) | Reserved by the IETF for future use. |
| 0xbf | Special expansion code 3 | IETF-defined chunk expansion code. |
| 0xc0-0xfe | (Reserved) | Reserved by the IETF for future use. |
| 0xff | Special expansion code 4 | IETF-defined chunk expansion code. |

### 3.1.4 General Rules When Dealing with Chunks

Chunks fall into two basic types: those that carry user information (that is, data chunks), and those that carry control information (that is, control chunks). The design philosophy makes no attempt to transfer the control chunks from one endpoint to the other with reliability. This is analogous to how TCP treats its RST segment (an internal control signal used by TCP). The startup and shutdown of an association therefore are special cases addressed by specific procedures. Data chunks (which carry user information) are subject to a reliable delivery mechanism, or notification to the user about a delivery failure and subsequent failure of the association.

Another consideration is that control chunks are always ahead of data chunks when both types of chunks appear in an SCTP packet. Thus all control chunk processing happens before any user data is processed. This puts some unique constraints and considerations on the bundling together of control chunks and data into one SCTP packet; these will be covered later in Section 5.8.4.

Late in the IETF process a modification was added to SCTP to facilitate the better handling of new chunk types by an older implementation. This concept was adopted from the IPv6 header handling procedures defined in Deering and Hinden (1998). These procedures were defined by considering the pattern of the upper two bits of the *Chunk type* as a descriptor for what to do if a receiver does not recognize a chunk. Table 3–2 illustrates this behavior.

The processing of the basic chunk types also conforms to these rules. An astute reader will note that all of the currently defined chunk types use the 00xxxxxx bit pattern. This means that the whole SCTP packet will be discarded. In the unlikely event that a base type is unrecognized, this will most likely result in the association failing.

When making an extension to SCTP in the future, two things must be considered in selecting the value of a new *Chunk type*:

- Do you want the SCTP packet and all it is carrying to be dropped if a receiver does not recognize the new chunk? If so, the value of the new *Chunk type* must be selected so that its first most-significant bit is a zero.

- Do you want feedback on the dropping of the chunk or the entire SCTP packet if a receiver does not recognize the new chunk? If so, the value of the new *Chunk type* must be selected so that its second most-significant bit is a 1.

Feedback is only useful if the sender of the offending chunk will take some action based on the feedback. Dropping the SCTP packet often leads to association failure.

The design choice aspect of selecting the upper bits in a chunk assignment is performed during the spirited debate that will accompany any new chunk proposal within the IETF. Any such proposal will be accompanied by an IETF Internet-Draft that, if support exists for it, may make its way to an RFC status.

### 3.1.5   Chunk Parameters

Besides the normal fields that are essentially a permanent part of the definition of every chunk, some chunks also have permanent variable-length fields and/or optional fields that are commonly referred to as **permanent chunk parameters** and **optional chunk parameters**, respectively.

The location of permanent chunk parameters is fixed in the chunk format, and the optional parameters, whenever they are used, are always placed **after** the permanent fields and permanent parameters.

**Table 3–2** Handling Rules for Unrecognized Chunks

| Chunk Type Bit Pattern | Handling Rule |
| --- | --- |
| 00xxxxxx | Stop processing the SCTP packet containing the chunk and silently discard the whole packet. |
| 01xxxxxx | Stop processing the SCTP packet containing the chunk and silently discard the whole packet, **and** send an OPERATIONAL ERROR chunk back to the peer, reporting that this chunk is unrecognizable. |
| 10xxxxxx | Skip this chunk but continue to process any other chunks within the SCTP packet. |
| 11xxxxxx | Skip this chunk but continue to process any other chunks within the SCTP packet. After the processing is done, send an OPERA-TIONAL ERROR chunk back to the peer, reporting that this chunk is unrecognizable. |

All permanent variable-length and optional chunk parameters use the Type-Length-Value (TLV) format shown in Figure 3–5. The TLV format's values and field are defined as follows:

- *Parameter type*—This value represents a 16-bit value that identifies the parameter type. The assignment policy that has been used is not to duplicate any parameter values across all SCTP chunks no matter what the chunk type is. This policy is safe considering the limited number of parameters currently defined in Stewart et al. (2000) and the total available type values (that is, 65,535).

- *Parameter length*—This 16-bit value is the length of the entire parameter. Note that like the *Chunk length*, this includes the size of the *Parameter type* and *Parameter length* themselves. Therefore, a chunk parameter that carried no parameter data would have a length of 4 octets.

- *Parameter Data*—This is a variable-length field that contains the information carried in the parameter. Like *Chunk data*, this field is padded to the next 32-bit word boundary. Figure 3–6 illustrates a fictitious parameter that is padded to a 32-bit boundary as required.

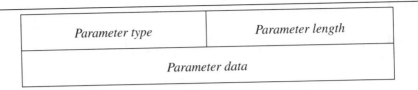

**Figure 3–5**  *The Type-Length-Value format of chunk parameters*

Also like *Chunk type*, the upper two bits of the *Parameter type* value will implicitly instruct a receiver that does not recognize the parameter type how to deal with it. Table 3–3 reflects the handling of the four possible bit combinations.

The processing of the permanent parameter types also conforms to these rules. All currently defined parameters, except the *ECN capable* optional parameter in INIT and INIT ACK chunks (which will be discussed in Section 3.2.1 and Section 3.2.2), use the 00xxxxxx-xxxxxxxx bit pattern. Notice that the *ECN capable* optional parameter uses the 10xxxxxx-xxxxxxxx bit pattern. This specifies that the parameter, if it is not understood, is ignored. ECN works based on both sides pledging that they understand and support ECN. If one of the sides fails to specify that it is ECN capable, then ECN is disabled. No reporting is necessary because both sides are required to make the ECN indication before it can become enabled.

### 3.1.6   Other Considerations

One thing to remember for all chunks and parameters is that any 16-bit or 32-bit integer is always carried in the **network byte order.** Network byte order is also known as "Big Endian"; that is, the most significant byte gets transmitted first.

## 3.2   Basic Chunk Descriptions

We will now take a closer look at all of the chunks that are currently defined by the SCTP specification (Stewart et al. 2000). In examining these, we will look in the order one would find them exchanged in a normal SCTP association's life cycle. After we cover this, we will then move on to additional chunks not covered by a normal association startup, data transfer, and shutdown sequence, such as the ABORT and OPERATIONAL ERROR chunks.

### 3.2.1   The INIT Chunk

The INITIATION chunk, often referred to as the INIT, is the very first chunk that one would see sent from one endpoint to its peer to attempt to establish the associ-

| Byte 1 | Byte 2 | Byte 3 | Byte 4 |
|---|---|---|---|
| Parameter type = X | | Parameter length = 6 | |
| 'h' | 'i' | Pad = 0x00 | Pad = 0x00 |

**Figure 3–6** *Padding of a chunk parameter that does not terminate on a 32-bit word boundary*

**Table 3–3** Handling Procedures for Unrecognized Parameters

| Bit Pattern of *Parameter type* | Handling Procedure |
|---|---|
| 00xxxxxx-xxxxxxxx | Stop processing the entire SCTP chunk that contains the offending parameter and discard the chunk silently. |
| 01xxxxxx-xxxxxxxx | Stop processing the entire SCTP chunk that contains the offending parameter and discard the chunk silently, **and** send back to the peer an OPERATIONAL ERROR reporting the unrecognized parameter. |
| 10xxxxxx-xxxxxxxx | Skip this parameter but continue to process any other parameters in the chunk and the rest of the chunks within the SCTP packet. |
| 11xxxxxx-xxxxxxxx | Skip this parameter but continue to process any other parameters in the chunk and the rest of the chunks within the SCTP packet. After the processing, send back to the peer an OPERATIONAL ERROR reporting the unrecognized parameter. |

ation. It is a request by the sender to set up an association, and it contains all the information a peer would need to know in order to maintain the new association.

The INIT has two parts: a "required" or mandatory part and an "optional" part. All of the INIT's optional parts are defined as optional parameters in TLV format. We will first look at a minimal INIT in Figure 3–7, and then we will look at each of the currently defined optional parameter types detailed in Table 3–4.

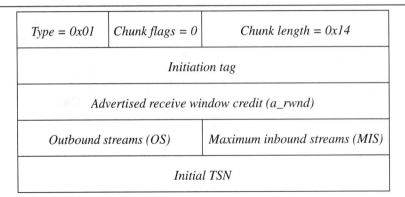

| Type = 0x01 | Chunk flags = 0 | Chunk length = 0x14 |
|---|---|---|
| Initiation tag | | |
| Advertised receive window credit (a_rwnd) | | |
| Outbound streams (OS) | Maximum inbound streams (MIS) | |
| Initial TSN | | |

**Figure 3–7**  *A minimal INIT*

The fields and values shown in the minimal INIT chunk are described as follows:

- *Chunk type*—The *Chunk type* for the INIT message is 0x01, as previously defined in Table 3–1.

- *Chunk flags*—No flags are used for the INIT message, and thus all bits are set to zero.

- *Chunk length*—Here we see the minimal INIT size of 20 octets. Optional parameters, if present, would increase this size. The *Chunk length* field will include the size of all mandatory and optional parameters.

- *Initiation tag*—This value is a random number between 0x1 and 0xffffffff that the sender will pick. The receiver of the INIT will store this value within its TCB and use it to fill in the *Verification tag* field of the SCTP common header. All SCTP packets sent by the receiver of the INIT must contain this value to tell the sender of the INIT that

  1. The SCTP packet is from the receiver of the INIT
  2. The SCTP packet is part of the current association (the one being established by this INIT)

  This may seem a bit confusing for now, but do not worry. Further clarification of *Initiation tag* and *Verification tag* will be given in Chapter 4.

- *Advertised receive window credit (a_rwnd)*—This value is used in flow control. In the INIT message, this value indicates the initial amount of user data that the sender of the INIT is allowing its peer to transmit. Section 5.2.1 will give a detailed view of how *a_rwnd* is used in the association.

- *Outbound streams (OS)*—This value represents the number of streams that the sender wishes to have open to the receiver. It may be reduced by the receiver of the INIT by sending a smaller value in the *MIS* of the INIT-ACK, but once agreed upon it cannot be changed unless the association is restarted.

*Note* Streams are relevant to SCTP in a one-way direction. There is no correlation made by SCTP between any two streams in the opposing direction. Details on stream usage will be given later in Section 5.6 as well as in Chapter 13.

- *Maximum inbound streams (MIS)*—This value represents the maximum number of streams that the sender of the INIT can support. It is the upper limit on the number of streams that the receiver may request in its INIT-ACK response.[4] If the receiver of the INIT wants more streams going to the sender than this value represents, its only recourse is to abort the association, because the sender of the INIT does not have the necessary resources to support the receiver's expectations.

- *Initial TSN*—This value represents the initial Transmission Sequence Number (TSN) that will be used by the sender of the INIT. This is normally a random number chosen from within the range of 0x0 to 0xffffffff. Further details on the use of the TSN values will be given in Section 5.1.1.

### 3.2.1.1 Optional Parameters for INIT

The INIT message may contain a number of optional parameters. Here we will detail all of those parameters. Specific usage of these parameters will be discussed in subsequent chapters. Table 3–4 lists all of the optional parameters that an INIT chunk can carry.

Now we will describe these optional parameters one by one.

The *IPv4 address* parameter pictured in Figure 3–8 has only one field beyond its parameter type and length, that is, the address itself. Because an IPv4 address is a 32-bit word, no padding is needed, and the length of the parameter is exactly 8 bytes (4 bytes for the chunk header and 4 bytes for the IP address).

Multiple *IPv4 address* parameters may be included in the INIT by the sender to indicate that it is a multi-homed endpoint and it wants to use more than one IP addresses in the association.

---

4. The receiver of the INIT will place its request for streams in the INIT-ACK chunk's *OS* field.

**Table 3–4** INIT Optional Parameters

| Parameter Name | Parameter Type | Description |
| --- | --- | --- |
| *IPv4 address* | 0x0005 | This parameter holds an IP version 4 address. |
| *IPv6 address* | 0x0006 | This parameter holds an IP version 6 address. |
| *Cookie preservative* | 0x0009 | When a state cookie goes stale, you need a cookie preservative to ask for more time. This parameter is used for that purpose. |
| *ECN capable* | 0x8000 | This parameter informs the peer that the sender is capable of using Explicit Congestion Notification. |
| *Hostname address* | 0x000b | This parameter holds a hostname in the form of a NULL-terminated ASCII string. Section 4.1.2 will give more details. |
| *Supported address type* | 0x000c | This parameter is included by the sending endpoint to tell the peer what types of addresses it will support for use in this association. |

For the purposes of SCTP, the *IPv6 address* parameter (see Figure 3–9) is much the same as the *IPv4 address* parameter, with the only major difference being the size of the address. An endpoint may send the INIT with any combination or number of both IPv4 and IPv6 address parameters.

The *Cookie preservative* parameter (see Figure 3–10) is used to request a longer cookie life. The parameter contains a 32-bit word that represents the number of milliseconds by which the sender is requesting that the standard cookie life be increased.

The *ECN capable* parameter (see Figure 3–11) contains no data. It simply notifies the peer that the sender is ECN capable. If each end makes this notification, then ECN procedures will be activated within the association. Section 6.6 will discuss ECN in more detail.

The *Hostname address* parameter (see Figure 3–12) gives to the peer a hostname for resolution. No syntax specification is defined for the hostname in Stewart et al. (2000), but normally the hostname will be a NULL-terminated ASCII string. How to resolve the hostname at the peer is up to the specific implementation. One possibility is that the peer will resolve the hostname by using a DNS query (Mockapetris 1987).

Parameter type = 0x0005
Parameter length = 0x0008
IPv4 address

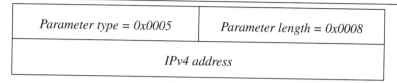

**Figure 3–8** *IPv4 address parameter*

Parameter type = 0x0006
Parameter length = 0x0014
IPv6 address

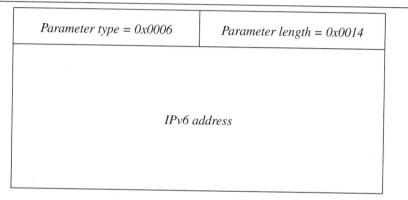

**Figure 3–9** *IPv6 address parameter*

Parameter type = 0x0009
Parameter length = 0x0008
Suggested life

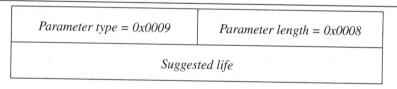

**Figure 3–10** *Cookie preservative parameter*

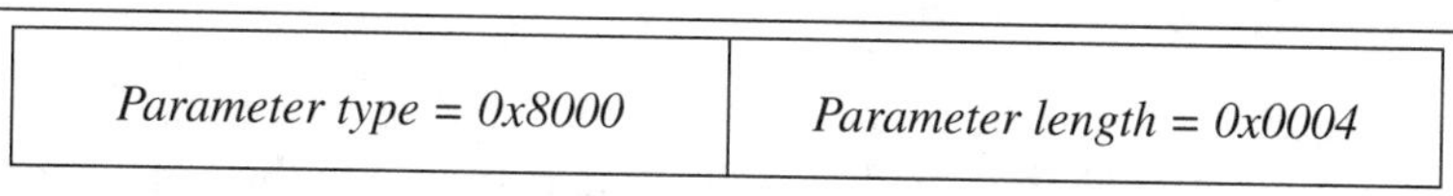

Parameter type = 0x8000
Parameter length = 0x0004

**Figure 3–11** *ECN capable parameter*

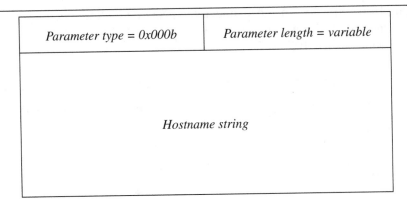

**Figure 3–12** *Hostname address parameter*

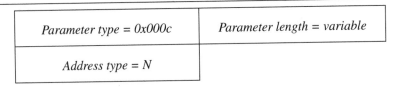

**Figure 3–13** *Supported address type parameter*

The *Supported address type* parameter (see Figure 3–13) indicates to the peer that the listed address types are supported. These address types match the parameter values of the three currently defined address types, that is, IPv4 address 0x0005, IPv6 address 0x0006, and hostname 0x000b. By default, if this parameter is not included by the sender of INIT, then all address types are supported. Otherwise, only the listed types will be supported.

Figure 3–14 shows three different examples of the *Supported address type* parameter. Note that if no *Supported address type* parameter is included in an INIT, the receiver will act as if example c) in Figure 3–14 had been included (that is, all address types are supported).

### 3.2.2   The INIT-ACK Chunk

The INIT-ACK is the second message exchanged during the setup of an association. The receiver of an INIT will send this chunk in response to the INIT message.

The minimal INIT-ACK chunk is shown in Figure 3–15. Notice that this looks much like the INIT chunk except that one variable-length TLV parameter is required to be included, the *State cookie*.

| Parameter type = 0x000c | Parameter length = 0x6 | |
|---|---|---|
| Address type = 0x0005 | Pad = 0x00 | Pad = 0x00 |

a) Support only IPv4 addresses

| Parameter type = 0x000c | Parameter length = 0x8 |
|---|---|
| Address type = 0x0005 | Address type = 0x0006 |

b) Support IPv4 and IPv6 addresses

| Parameter type = 0x000c | Parameter length = 0xc | |
|---|---|---|
| Address type = 0x0005 | Address type = 0x0006 | |
| Address type = 0x000b | Pad = 0x00 | Pad = 0x00 |

c) Support IPv4, IPv6, and hostname addresses

**Figure 3–14** *Three examples of the Supported address type parameter*

The fields and values shown in the minimal INIT-ACK chunk are described as follows:

- *Chunk type*—The *Chunk type* for the INIT-ACK chunk is 0x02, as previously defined in Table 3–1.

- *Chunk flags*—No flags are used for the INIT-ACK chunk, and thus all bits are set to zero.

- *Chunk length*—This is the size of the chunk.

- *Initiation tag*—This value is a random number between 0x1 and 0xffffffff that the sender will pick. The receiver of an INIT-ACK will store this value within its TCB and later use it to fill in the *Verification tag* field of the SCTP common header. All subsequent SCTP packets sent by the receiver of the INIT-ACK must contain this value to tell the sender of the INIT-ACK that

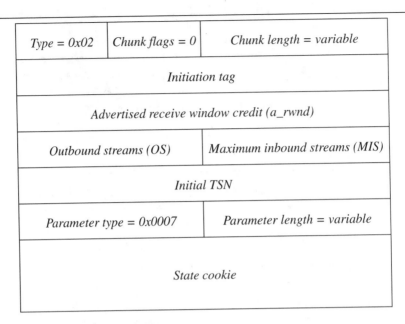

**Figure 3–15**  *A minimal INIT-ACK chunk*

1. The SCTP packet is from the receiver of the INIT-ACK

2. The SCTP packet is part of the current association (the one being established by this INIT-ACK)

Details about the use of the *Initiation tag* and *Verification tag* will be given in Chapter 4.

- *Advertised receive window credit* (*a_rwnd*), *Outbound streams* (*OS*), *Maximum inbound streams* (*MIS*), and *Initial TSN*—These fields have the same definitions as those used in the INIT chunk, as discussed in Section 3.2.1.

- *State cookie*—This chunk parameter will contain a state cookie. The format and content of the state cookie is entirely implementation-specific. Nonetheless, the state cookie is required to contain enough information to set up the TCB for the association. Normally, among other things, the state cookie will contain the information found in the various fields in the original INIT chunk and the information carried in the fields of the INIT-ACK chunk itself. It also normally will contains a set of tie-tags,[5] a value indicating the lifespan of the cookie, and a security signature.

---

5. Tie-tags are a special set of binding verification tags used to discriminate cases of association restart. We will discuss them in detail in Section 4.2.2.1.

The use of the state cookie gives the sender of the INIT-ACK a strong defense against potential resource attacks. We will discuss this in detail in Section 4.2.2.

### 3.2.2.1 Optional Parameters for INIT-ACK

INIT-ACK, like INIT, can also carry optional chunk parameters. Table 3–5 lists all
of the optional parameters allowed to be carried in an INIT-ACK. As you can see,
most of these parameters are identical to those used in the INIT chunk.

The definition, format, and usage of the *IPv4 address*, *IPv6 address*, *ECN
capable*, and *Hostname address* optional parameters for the INIT-ACK chunk are
exactly identical to those of the INIT, as described in Section 3.2.1.1.

The only new optional parameter in Table 3–5 is the *Unrecognized parameter*
parameter. Its format is shown in Figure 3–16.

When a receiver of an INIT processes the optional parameters carried in the
INIT, it may encounter a parameter type it does not understand. Depending on the
bit pattern of the *Parameter type* value of this unrecognizable parameter, the
receiver may need to report this error back to the sender of the INIT, following the
rules shown in Table 3–3.

**Table 3–5** INIT-ACK Optional Parameters

| Parameter Name | Parameter Type | Description |
|---|---|---|
| *IPv4 address* | 0x0005 | This parameter holds an IP version 4 address. |
| *IPv6 address* | 0x0006 | This parameter holds an IP version 6 address. |
| *Unrecognized parameter* | 0x0008 | The sender of the INIT-ACK uses this parameter to report the error back to the sender of the INIT, if an optional parameter in the just received INIT is not recognizable. |
| *ECN capable* | 0x8000 | This parameter informs the peer that the sender is capable of supporting ECN. |
| *Hostname address* | 0x000b | This parameter holds a hostname in the form of a NULL-terminated ASCII string. Section 4.1.2 will give more details. |

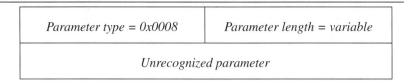

| *Parameter type = 0x0008* | *Parameter length = variable* |
|---|---|
| *Unrecognized parameter* | |

**Figure 3–16**  *Unrecognized parameter parameter*

In such a case, the receiver of the INIT will include an *Unrecognized parameter* optional parameter in its INIT-ACK to report this error event. The parameter body of the *Unrecognized parameter* parameter will carry the entire unrecognizable parameter, including its type and length fields.

### 3.2.3   The COOKIE-ECHO Chunk

Originally, much like TCP, SCTP began life with a three-way handshake setup sequence consisting of INIT, INIT-ACK, and finally a required SACK to start an association. The SACK was later replaced with a COOKIE-ECHO chunk when the four-way handshake was introduced to prevent resource attacks.

The COOKIE-ECHO can be bundled with user data to lessen the impact of having to do two round trips before data transfer can begin. The format of the COOKIE-ECHO chunk is shown in Figure 3–17.

The fields of the COOKIE-ECHO chunk are described as follows:

- *Chunk type*—The *Chunk type* for the COOKIE-ECHO chunk is 0x0a, as previously defined in Table 3–1.

- *Chunk flags*—No flags are used for the COOKIE-ECHO chunk, and thus all bits are set to zero.

- *Chunk length*—The size of the chunk is variable and depends upon the size of the *State cookie* field.

- *State cookie*—This is the exact same information copied byte by byte from the *State cookie* carried in INIT-ACK (see Section 3.2.2). As we mentioned before, the format and information contained within *State cookie* is private to the sender of INIT-ACK and is therefore not used by the receiver of INIT-ACK.

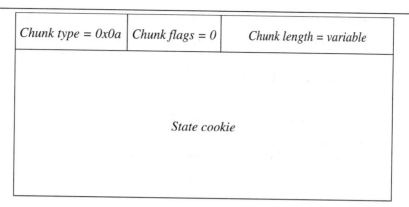

| Chunk type = 0x0a | Chunk flags = 0 | Chunk length = variable |
| --- | --- | --- |

State cookie

**Figure 3–17**  *The COOKIE-ECHO chunk*

### 3.2.4   The COOKIE-ACK Chunk

The COOKIE-ACK chunk is the last leg of the four-way handshake and thus completes the setup of an association. Similar to the COOKIE-ECHO chunk, user data is allowed to be bundled with the COOKIE-ACK chunk.

Figure 3–18 shows the format of the COOKIE-ACK chunk.

The fields of the COOKIE-ACK chunk are described as follows:

- *Chunk type*—The *Chunk type* for the COOKIE-ACK chunk is 0x0b, as previously defined in Table 3–1.

- *Chunk flags*—No flags are used for the COOKIE-ACK chunk, and thus all bits are set to zero.

- *Chunk length*—The size of the chunk is always 4 bytes.

### 3.2.5   The DATA Chunk

The DATA chunk is the container for all the user data transferred in SCTP. Its format is shown in Figure 3–19.

The fields of the DATA chunk are described as follows:

- *Chunk type*—The *Chunk type* for the DATA chunk is 0x00, as previously defined in Table 3–1.

- *Chunk flags*—The lower three bits of *Chunk flags* are used in the DATA chunk, while the upper five bits are reserved (unused) and are required to be

| Type = 0x0b | Chunk flags = 0 | Chunk length = 0x4 |
|---|---|---|

**Figure 3–18**  *The COOKIE-ACK chunk*

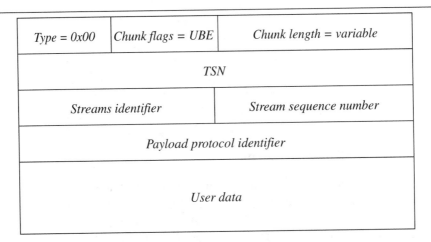

| Type = 0x00 | Chunk flags = UBE | Chunk length = variable |
|---|---|---|
| TSN | | |
| Streams identifier | Stream sequence number | |
| Payload protocol identifier | | |
| User data | | |

**Figure 3–19**  *The DATA chunk*

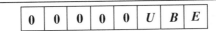

**Figure 3–20**  *The DATA Chunk flags bits*

set to zero. The lower three bits are named the *U*, *B*, and *E* bits, respectively, as shown in Figure 3–20.

The *U*, *B*, and *E* bits have the following definitions:

- *U*—This bit, if set to 1, indicates that the user data carried in this DATA chunk is unordered. This means that the receiver can deliver the data to its user application without performing the normal stream sequence reordering procedure on this data. Moreover, when this bit is set to 1, the meaning of the *Stream sequence number* field in the DATA chunk becomes undefined. When carrying ordered user data, this bit is always set to zero.

- *B*—This bit, when set to 1, indicates that the beginning part of a user message is present in this DATA chunk. For multipart (that is, fragmented) user messages, this indicates the first part in a sequence of DATA chunks that make up the entire user message.

- *E*—This bit, when set to 1, indicates that the ending part of a user message is contained in this DATA chunk. For multipart user messages, this indicates the last part in a sequence of DATA chunks that make up the entire user message.

When an entire user message is carried in a single DATA chunk, both the *B* and *E* bits of the DATA chunk will be set to 1, indicating that both the beginning and the ending parts of the message are present in the chunk. Otherwise, the DATA chunk will have either its *B*, *E*, or both bits set to zero, indicating that what is being carried in the chunk is just a part of a fragmented user message.

| *Note* | A single DATA chunk can never carry more than one user message. |
|--------|----------------------------------------------------------------|

DATA chunks carrying fragments of a user message will be put into a message reassembly queue in the receiver, where the receiver will use the TSN carried in each DATA chunk to order and reconstruct the user message.

Table 3–6 summarizes the meanings of the *B/E* bits.

- *Chunk length*—This field is variable because it is dependent on the length of the user data. It should have a value equal to or greater than 17, because a DATA chunk is required to have at least one byte of user data.

- *TSN*—This field contains the transmission sequence number. Each DATA chunk is assigned a TSN that is then used by both the sender and receiver to ensure that the chunk arrived at the destination. The *TSN* field is also used when a message is fragmented to order the multiple DATA chunks for reassembly, and to know if a DATA chunk is still missing.

- *Stream identifier*—This value indicates for which stream number the user data is destined. The stream is where message ordering within SCTP happens. Details on how streams are used will be discussed in Section 5.6.

- *Stream sequence number*—This value indicates what stream sequence number this user data contains. Messages within one stream are delivered in order with respect to each other. For fragmented user messages, *Stream sequence number* remains the same on all the DATA chunks containing the individual fragments.

- *Payload protocol identifier*—This value is a user-supplied value that is passed in every DATA chunk. SCTP itself ignores this field and carries it

**Table 3–6** Meanings of the *B/E* Bits in a DATA Chunk

| *B/E* Bits | Meaning |
|---|---|
| 1/0 | Indicates that this is the first DATA chunk that contains a fragmented message |
| 0/0 | Indicates the middle piece or one of the middle pieces comprising a fragmented user message |
| 0/1 | Indicates the last DATA chunk in a fragmented message |
| 1/1 | Indicates that the DATA chunk contains a complete (that is, non-fragmented) user message |

opaquely to the remote peer user. The remote peer user **may** wish to use this information in determining what type of data is present in the user message. This value is also available for network monitors and packet filters as a mechanism for screening and viewing data.

- *User data*—This is the payload data. It is variable in length but is limited by the PMTU of the network for that destination. When the user message is larger than the PMTU (minus header overhead), the sender may elect to fragment the message into multiple parts and send each part in a separate DATA chunk.

### 3.2.6    The SACK Chunk

This chunk is sent to the remote endpoint to acknowledge received DATA chunks. But it does more than that; it also fully describes the events that have transpired from the SACK sender's point of view since the last SACK was sent. If the sender receives DATA chunks out of order, it will illustrate these "gaps" in TSNs. It also will describe any duplicated DATA chunks received. This gives the receiver of the SACK a vision of the sender's view of the world (in respect to the DATA stream that the receiver of the SACK is trying to send).

Included in the SACK is an *a_rwnd* update, highlighting buffer space constraints that the receiver of the DATA chunks may be under. The handling of the SACK is described in detail in Section 5.3, and the receiver window calculation with the *a_rwnd* information is described in Section 5.3.5.3.

The SACK chunk is illustrated in Figure 3–21. The fields and values of the SACK chunk are described as follows:

| Type = 0x03 | Chunk flags = 0 | Chunk length = variable |
|---|---|---|
| Cumulative TSN acknowledgment | | |
| Advertised receiver window credit (a_rwnd) | | |
| Number of Gap ACK blocks = N | | Number of duplicates = X |
| Gap Ack block #1 start TSN offset | | Gap Ack block #1 end TSN offset |
| .... | | |
| Gap Ack block #N start TSN offset | | Gap Ack block #N end TSN offset |
| Duplicate TSN 1 | | |
| .... | | |
| Duplicate TSN X | | |

**Figure 3–21**  *The SACK chunk*

> *Note*    The initial *a_rwnd,* passed within the INIT and INIT-ACK chunks, is the dedicated amount of receive buffer space that the endpoint is allocating to this association. The *a_rwnd* in the SACK is different in that it illustrates how much of this allocation is left for the data sender to use.

- *Chunk type*—The *Chunk type* for the SACK chunk is 0x03, as previously defined in Table 3–1.

- *Chunk flags*—*Chunk flags* is not used for the SACK message and thus its bits are set to zero.

- *Chunk length*—This is the size of the chunk.

- *Cumulative TSN acknowledgment*—This is the highest TSN that is consecutive that the sender of the SACK has seen (sometimes also called the

**cumulative Ack point**). The receiver of this SACK may release any TSN data being held that is less than or equal to this number (using serial arithmetic). This value is also used to calculate any gap blocks as the base for addition.

- *Number of Gap Ack blocks*—This value contains the number of Gap Ack blocks that are included with this SACK. Each Gap Ack block tells the start and end of a range of TSNs that have been received relative to the *Cumulative TSN acknowledgment* value.

- *Number of duplicates*—This value contains the number of duplicate TSNs that are contained in this SACK. Duplicate TSNs represent TSNs that have been received more than once. Note that the same TSN may appear more than once on this list.

---

*Note*    Using serial arithmetic has some subtleties, so great care should be taken in programming the comparison of such values. The TSN space is finite, though very large. The space ranges from 0 to $2^{32} - 1$. All arithmetic dealing with TSNs must be performed modulo $2^{32}$.

Comparisons and arithmetic on TSNs normally use the Serial Number Arithmetic as defined in Elz and Bush (1996) with SERIAL_BITS = 32 for the **TSN space** and SERIAL_BITS = 16 for the **stream sequence number** space, respectively.

---

- *Gap Ack blocks start TSN offset* and *Gap Ack blocks end TSN offset*—For each *Number of Gap Ack blocks*, a set of beginning and end descriptors are contained within the SACK. This value contains the start of a range of TSNs that have been received. In order to calculate the actual TSN, this value is added to the *Cumulative TSN acknowledgment* contained in this SACK.

- *Duplicate TSN*—For each TSN received more than once, a duplicate TSN is attached. These values are not related to the *Cumulative TSN acknowledgment* because it is possible to receive a duplicate that is behind the cumulative Ack point.

### 3.2.7   The HEARTBEAT Chunk

After an association is established, it may become idle or, in the multi-homed case, the primary address will be used and the alternate destination addresses may never have data sent to them. In either case, the HEARTBEAT chunk is used to periodically probe reachability of the idle destination addresses.

The HEARTBEAT chunk (when responded to) will also be used to update the **round trip time** (RTT) of a destination address and detect various network events (for example, a failure or a return to service of a network). A complete description of how the heartbeat mechanism works will be presented in Section 7.2.1.

The HEARTBEAT chunk is illustrated in Figure 3–22.

The fields and values of the HEARTBEAT chunk are described as follows:

- *Chunk type*—The *Chunk type* for the HEARTBEAT chunk is 0x04, as defined in Table 3–1.

- *Chunk flags*—*Chunk flags* is not used for the HEARTBEAT chunk and thus its bits are set to zero.

- *Chunk length*—This is the size of the chunk, which varies based upon the size of the *HEARTBEAT sender-specific information.*

- *Heartbeat parameter type*—There is only one TLV parameter defined for the HEARTBEAT chunk, and its type is set to 1.

- *Heartbeat info length*—This will reflect the length of the TLV parameter.

- *HEARTBEAT sender-specific information*—Here is the actual data that will be returned intact to the sender of HEARTBEAT in the HEARTBEAT-ACK chunk (which is described in Section 3.2.8). This information generally includes the local system time and the address that the chunk was sent to, etc. This information is specific to the sender of HEARTBEAT and will be ignored by the receiver of HEARTBEAT.

### 3.2.8  The HEARTBEAT-ACK Chunk

Every time a HEARTBEAT chunk arrives, the receiver will always echo back a HEARTBEAT-ACK chunk. The HEARTBEAT-ACK chunk is illustrated in Figure 3–23.

The fields and values of the HEARTBEAT-ACK chunk are described as follows:

- *Chunk type*—The *Chunk type* for the HEARTBEAT-ACK chunk is 0x05, as previously defined in Table 3–1.

- *Chunk flags*—*Chunk flags* is not used for the HEARTBEAT-ACK chunk and thus its bits are set to zero.

- *Chunk length*—This is the size of the chunk, which varies based upon the size of the *HEARTBEAT sender-specific information.*

| Type = 0x04 | Chunk flags = 0 | Chunk length = variable |
|---|---|---|
| Heartbeat parameter type = 1 | | Heartbeat info length = variable |
| HEARTBEAT sender-specific information | | |

**Figure 3–22**  *The HEARTBEAT chunk*

| Type = 0x05 | Chunk flags = 0 | Chunk length = variable |
|---|---|---|
| Heartbeat parameter type = 1 | | Heartbeat info length = variable |
| HEARTBEAT sender-specific information | | |

**Figure 3–23**  *The HEARTBEAT-ACK chunk*

- *Heartbeat parameter type*—There is only one TLV parameter defined for the HEARTBEAT-ACK chunk, and its type is set to 1.

- *Heartbeat info length*—This will reflect the length of the TLV parameter.

- *HEARTBEAT sender-specific information*—Here is the actual data that was copied byte by byte from the HEARTBEAT chunk. This information is specific to the sender of the HEARTBEAT chunk and is always ignored by the receiver of the HEARTBEAT chunk.

### 3.2.9    The SHUTDOWN chunk

So far we have looked at all the messages involved in setting up, transferring data, and ensuring that all is well on the association. At some point one side or the other may wish to bring down the association in a graceful way. SCTP uses a three-way handshake[6] on graceful shutdown of an association. The SHUTDOWN chunk illustrated in Figure 3–24 is used to invoke the first leg of this three-way hand-

| Type = 0x07 | Chunk flags = 0 | Chunk length = 0x8 |
|---|---|---|
| Cumulative TSN acknowledgment | | |

**Figure 3–24** *The SHUTDOWN chunk*

shake. Detailed procedures on the use of the SHUTDOWN chunk may be found in Section 9.1.

The fields of the SHUTDOWN chunk are described as follows:

- *Chunk type*—The *Chunk type* for the SHUTDOWN chunk is 0x07, as defined in Table 3–1.

- *Chunk flags*—*Chunk flags* is not used for the SHUTDOWN chunk and thus its bits are set to zero.

- *Chunk length*—The size of the chunk is always set to 8.

- *Cumulative TSN acknowledgment*—This is the highest TSN that is consecutive that the sender of the SHUTDOWN has seen. The receiver of this SHUTDOWN chunk may release any TSN data being held that is less than or equal to this number (using serial arithmetic). The sender *may* bundle a SACK with the SHUTDOWN chunk to more completely describe the current view of what has been received.

### 3.2.10   The SHUTDOWN-ACK Chunk

After a SHUTDOWN chunk is received, no new data may be introduced to the association by either endpoint. In fact, the sender of the SHUTDOWN is required to ensure that *all* of its data has been received by its peer before initiating the shutdown procedure.

After reception of a SHUTDOWN, the receiver will first make sure that all of its outstanding data has been acknowledged. Once all data has been acknowledged and the receiver of the SHUTDOWN chunk has no data pending for transmission, the receiver will begin to send the SHUTDOWN-ACK chunk, as illustrated in Figure 3–25. It will send this chunk repeatedly until it receives a SHUTDOWN-COMPLETE chunk. In Section 9.1 we will discuss the detailed procedures.

---

6. There may be more than three SCTP packets exchanged if the peer endpoint still has data queued for the endpoint initiating the graceful shutdown. Unlike TCP, SCTP does not allow a half-closed state. See Section 9.1 for details.

| Type = 0x08 | Chunk flags = 0 | Chunk length = 0x4 |
| --- | --- | --- |

**Figure 3–25** *The SHUTDOWN-ACK chunk*

The fields of the SHUTDOWN-ACK chunk are described as follows:

- *Chunk type*—The *Chunk type* for the SHUTDOWN-ACK chunk is 0x08, as defined in Table 3–1.

- *Chunk flags*—*Chunk flags* is not used for the SHUTDOWN-ACK chunk and thus its bits are set to zero.

- *Chunk length*—The size of the chunk is always set to 4.

### 3.2.11   The SHUTDOWN-COMPLETE Chunk

The receiver of a SHUTDOWN-ACK chunk needs to always respond with a SHUTDOWN-COMPLETE, as illustrated in Figure 3-26. This chunk is sent whether the receiver has a TCB or not. The *T* bit described below is used to indicate this state.

Detailed procedures on the use of the SHUTDOWN-COMPLETE chunk will be discussed in Section 9.1.

The fields of the SHUTDOWN-COMPLETE chunk are described as follows:

- *Chunk type*—The *Chunk type* for the SHUTDOWN-COMPLETE chunk is 0x0E, as defined in Table 3–1.

- *Chunk flags*—The lowest bit of *Chunk flags* is used and termed the "*T* bit"; the upper seven bits are reserved, set to zero upon transmission, and ignored upon reception. The *T* bit is used to indicate whether or not the sender has a TCB. If the sender does not have a TCB, then the *Verification tag* in the SCTP common header is set to the *Verification tag* that arrived in the SCTP packet that carried the SHUTDOWN-ACK chunk, and the *T* bit is set to 1. If a TCB that was destroyed by the reception of the SHUDOWN-ACK exists, then the *T* bit is set to zero, and the *Verification tag* is set to the value found in the TCB (before its destruction).

- *Chunk length*—The size of the chunk is always set to 4.

| Type = 0x0E | Chunk flags = T | Chunk length = 0x4 |
|---|---|---|

**Figure 3–26**  *The SHUTDOWN-COMPLETE chunk*

### 3.2.12   The ERROR Chunk

This chunk is used by an endpoint to report problems or errors to its peer. In most cases, error reports are actually sent embedded in an ABORT chunk (see the ABORT chunk in Section 3.2.14). However, in some cases the problem to be reported is not fatal to the association (for example, receiving a DATA chunk carrying an invalid stream identifier), so the endpoint sends a standalone error report using an OPERATIONAL ERROR chunk. The basic OPERATIONAL ERROR chunk is illustrated in Figure 3–27.

The fields of the OPERATIONAL ERROR chunk are described as follows:

- *Chunk type*—The *Chunk type* for the ERROR chunk is 0x09, as previously defined in Table 3–1.

- *Chunk flags*—*Chunk flags* is not used for the ERROR chunk and thus its bits are set to zero.

- *Chunk length*—This is the size of the chunk, including all error causes.

- *One or more error causes in TLV format*—The rest of the ERROR chunk contains *Error causes* in TLV format. These error causes are common to both the ABORT chunk and the ERROR chunk and are thus listed on their own in the next section.

### 3.2.13   The Error Cause Parameters

Table 3–7 illustrates the *Error cause* parameters that can be included in either an ERROR or an ABORT chunk. Each *Error cause* parameter is discussed and illustrated in detail in the rest of this section.

#### 3.2.13.1   *Invalid Stream Identifier Error*

If an error occurs in an SCTP stack causing an invalid stream identifier to be sent to its peer in a DATA chunk, the receiver of the invalid DATA chunk will discard the data after updating its TSNs received. It may optionally send an OPERATIONAL ERROR to its peer to notify it that an error occurred. When such an error is generated, the *Cause code* and data format are generated as shown in Figure 3–28.

**Table 3–7** Error Cause Parameters

| Parameter Value | Error Cause Description |
|---|---|
| 0x0001 | Invalid stream identifier |
| 0x0002 | Missing mandatory parameter |
| 0x0003 | Stale cookie error |
| 0x0004 | Out of resource |
| 0x0005 | Unresolvable address |
| 0x0006 | Unrecognized chunk type |
| 0x0007 | Invalid mandatory parameter |
| 0x0008 | Unrecognized parameters |
| 0x0009 | No user data |
| 0x000a | Cookie received while shutting down |

| Type = 0x09 | Chunk flags = 0 | Chunk length = variable |
|---|---|---|
| One or more error causes in TLV format | | |

**Figure 3–27** *The OPERATIONAL ERROR chunk*

| Cause code = 0x1 | Cause length = 0x8 |
|---|---|
| Stream identifier | (Reserved) |

**Figure 3–28** *The Invalid stream identification error*

The values and fields of the *Invalid stream identifier* error are described as follows:

- *Cause code*—The *Cause code* of the *Invalid stream identifier* error is 1.

- *Cause length*—This is the length of the entire TLV, which is always set to 8.

- *Stream identifier*—This is the stream number that is invalid.

- *Reserved*—This field is reserved; it is filled with zero by the sender and ignored by the receiver.

### 3.2.13.2 *Missing Mandatory Parameter Error*

If a mandatory parameter is found missing in a received chunk, the receiver of the chunk will report the error to the sender of the chunk using this error code.

For example, if a sender of an INIT-ACK malforms the message and does not include a *State cookie*, the receiver of the INIT may send a *Missing mandatory parameter* error to its peer. It does this because a missing *State cookie* generally indicates that the peer set up the TCB for this association right away, thus violating the protocol. This ERROR is normally bundled with an ABORT chunk.

The *Missing mandatory parameter* error format is illustrated in Figure 3–29.

The values and fields of the *Missing mandatory parameter* error are described as follows:

- *Cause code*—The *Cause code* of the *Missing mandatory parameter* error is 2.

- *Cause length*—This is the length of the entire TLV, set to 8 plus twice the number of missing mandatory parameters.

- *Number of missing parameters*—This is the total number of missing mandatory parameters being reported in this error.

- *Missing param type*—Each field contains the *Parameter type* value of one missing mandatory parameter.

| Cause code = 0x2 | | Cause length = (8+ N×2) | |
|---|---|---|---|
| Number of missing parameters = N | | | |
| Missing param type #1 | | Missing param type #N | |

**Figure 3–29** *The Missing mandatory parameter error*

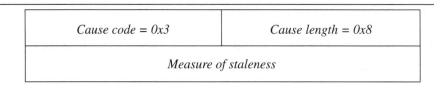

| Cause code = 0x3 | Cause length = 0x8 |
|---|---|
| Measure of staleness | |

**Figure 3–30**   *The Stale cookie error*

### 3.2.13.3   Stale Cookie Error

During association setup, it is possible, due to delays in the network, not to be able to get a COOKIE-ECHO chunk back to the endpoint that sent the cookie before it times out and is considered invalid. When this occurs, the receiver of the "stale" cookie will send a *Stale cookie* error, as seen in Figure 3–30. The sender can use this clue to **restart** the INIT sequence with a longer requested cookie life using the optional *Cookie preservative* parameter.

The values and fields of the *Stale cookie* error are described as follows:

- *Cause code*—The error *Cause code* for the *Stale cookie* error is 3.

- *Cause length*—This is the length of the entire TLV, set to 8.

- *Measure of staleness*—This field contains the difference, in microseconds, between when the cookie expired and when the cookie was processed. This gives the receiver of the error an idea of how much extra time it should request in the *Suggested cookie life* field. In general, if you use the suggested cookie life, the value found in this field should be doubled to give ample time to retransmit the new cookie and thus yield a higher probability of success on the reattempt.

### 3.2.13.4   Out of Resource Error

Sometimes an endpoint may not be able to form a new association or continue the operation of an existing association due to internal resource problems. In such a case it may send an **ABORT** with an error cause of *Out of resource,* as illustrated in Figure 3–31.

The values of the *Out of resource* error are described as follows:

- *Cause code*—The *Cause code* for the *Out of resource* error is 4.

- *Cause length*—This is the length of the entire TLV, which is always set to 4.

| Cause code = 0x4 | Cause length = 0x4 |
|---|---|

**Figure 3–31** *The Out of resource error*

### 3.2.13.5   *Unresolvable Address Error*

It is possible for an endpoint to receive a type of address that it cannot resolve.[7] For example, it may receive a hostname address parameter in an INIT and not have hostname address resolution capability. In this case, the endpoint would send back an ABORT chunk and include an *Unresolvable address* error, as illustrated in Figure 3–32.

The fields of the *Unresolvable address* error are described as follows:

- *Cause code*—The *Cause code* for the *Unresolvable address* error is 5.

- *Cause length*—This is the length of the entire TLV.

- *Unresolvable address*—This is a variable-length field that contains the full parameter that was sent containing the unresolvable address. Currently the possible values contained within this field could be an IPv4, IPv6, or host-name address parameter.

### 3.2.13.6   *Unrecognized Chunk Type Error*

An *Unrecognized chunk type* error (see Figure 3–33) should be generated when an SCTP endpoint does not recognize a received chunk and the *Chunk type* value indicates that the sender would like a report of the unrecognized type. (See Section 3.1.4 for a more detailed description on the mechanism used to request a report.)

The values and field of the *Unrecognized chunk type* error are described as follows:

- *Cause code*—The *Cause code* for the *Unrecognized chunk type* error is set to 6.

- *Cause length*—This is the length of the entire TLV.

- *Unrecognized chunk*—This is the entire chunk that was not recognized by the sender, including the complete chunk header and all of the chunk data.

---

7. This is because either it does not have the capability to resolve the address, or the address itself cannot be resolved (for example, *really.unlikelydotcomaddress.that.does.not.exist.com*).

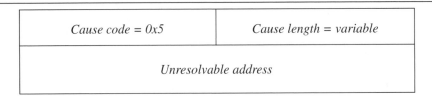

**Figure 3–32**  *The Unresolvable address error*

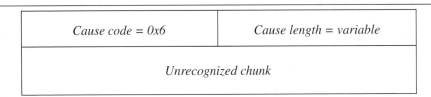

**Figure 3–33**  *The Unrecognized chunk type error*

**Figure 3–34**  *The Invalid mandatory parameter error*

### 3.2.13.7   *Invalid Mandatory Parameter Error*

It is possible that an INIT, INIT-ACK, or other chunk contains an **invalid** mandatory parameter. For example, a sender of an INIT may specify zero streams, which is not a legal value. The receiver of this illegal chunk parameter will normally send an ABORT including the error cause *Invalid mandatory parameter* (see Figure 3–34).

The fields of the *Invalid mandatory parameter* error are described as follows:

- *Cause code*—The *Cause code* for the *Invalid mandatory parameter* error is 7.

- *Cause length*—This is the TLV length, which is always set to 4.

### 3.2.13.8   *Unrecognized Parameter Error*

An *Unrecognized parameter* error (see Figure 3–35) will normally be generated when an SCTP endpoint does not recognize a parameter in an arrived chunk and the unrecognizable parameter has a type value that indicates that the sender would like a report of the event. (See Section 3.1.5 for details on parameter-type error processing.)

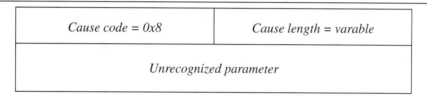

| Cause code = 0x8 | Cause length = varable |
|---|---|
| Unrecognized parameter | |

**Figure 3–35**  *The Unrecognized parameter error*

The values and field of the *Unrecognized parameter* error are described as follows:

- *Cause code*—The *Cause code* for the *Unrecognized parameter* error is 8.

- *Cause length*—This is the length of the entire TLV.

- *Unrecognized parameter*—This contains the entire unrecognized parameter, including its type, length, and all data fields.

### 3.2.13.9   No User Data Error

If an SCTP endpoint sends a DATA chunk carrying no user data (that is, the *Chunk length* of the DATA chunk is 16), the receiver is required to send an ABORT and destroy the association. When this occurs, a *No user data* error cause (see Figure 3–36) is included in the ABORT to report the TSN of the offending DATA chunk.

The fields of the *No user data* error are described as follows:

- *Cause code*—The *Cause code* for the *No user data* error is set to 9.

- *Cause length*—This is the length of the TLV, which is always set to 8.

- *TSN value*—This is the TSN of the DATA chunk that arrived with no user data.

### 3.2.13.10   Cookie Received While Shutting Down Error

When an association is going through a graceful shutdown, it is possible for the SHUTDOWN-COMPLETE chunk to be lost in the network. If this happens and the endpoint that sent the lost SHUTDOWN-COMPLETE chunk immediately attempts to restart the association, a race condition can occur. This will result in the sender of the lost SHUTDOWN-COMPLETE chunk sending a COOKIE-ECHO to the peer endpoint that may still be waiting for the SHUTDOWN-COM-PLETE from the previous association.

Upon receiving this unexpected COOKIE-ECHO, among other things, the endpoint that is still in the SHUTDOWN_ACK_SENT state is required to report

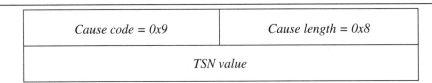

**Figure 3–36**  *The No user data error*

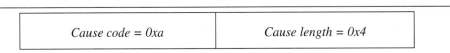

**Figure 3–37**  *The Cookie received while shutting down error*

the problem to the restarting endpoint by sending a *Cookie received while shutting down* error (see Figure 3–37).

The fields of the *Cookie received while shutting down* error are described as follows:

- *Cause code*—The *Cause code* for the *Cookie received while shutting down* error is set to 10.

- *Cause length*—This is the length, which is set to 4.

### 3.2.14    The ABORT Chunk

An ABORT chunk is a general-purpose method to terminate an association at any state. It is usually used when an endpoint encounters a severe error that makes the continued operation of the association improbable.

The general format of the ABORT chunk is illustrated in Figure 3–38.

The fields of the ABORT chunk are described as follows:

- *Chunk type*—This is the *Chunk type* for the ABORT, 0x06, as previously defined in Table 3–1.

- *Chunk flags*—The lowest bit of *Chunk flags* is used and termed the "*T* bit"; the upper seven bits are reserved, set to zero upon transmission, and ignored upon reception. The *T* bit is used to indicate whether the sender has a TCB. If the sender does *not* have a TCB, then the *Verification tag* in the SCTP common header is set to the *Verification tag* that arrived in the SCTP packet (which triggered the sending of the ABORT), and the *T* bit is set to 1. If a TCB that was destroyed by the reception of the ABORT exists, then the *T* bit

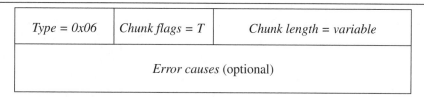

| Type = 0x06 | Chunk flags = T | Chunk length = variable |
|---|---|---|
| Error causes (optional) | | |

**Figure 3–38** *The ABORT message*

is set to zero, and the *Verification tag* is set to the value found in the TCB (before being destroyed).

- *Chunk length*—This is the total size of the chunk in bytes.

- *Error causes*—This field is optional. If present, it will contain one or more of the error causes defined in Section 3.2.13 to identify why the association is being aborted.

## 3.3   IETF Debate and Issue

Data format was one of the most hotly discussed and change-prone areas of the protocol as it was being developed. A lot of restructuring, rearrangement, and general rewriting went into SCTP's "bits on the wire" throughout its history. It started as a mainly bit-oriented, flag-type protocol in its early editions.

In one of the first design team meetings held in Orangeburg, New York, a major improvement to the design was made when the transport sequence number and stream sequence numbers were added. This effectively decoupled the reliability from the ordering, thus escaping the "head-of-line blocking" issues encountered with TCP.

In the fall of 1999 another design team meeting was held in Santa Clara, California. It was at this meeting that the current "chunk" structure was adopted, as well as most of the current basic protocol wire format. Once the chunk format was put forth (by Vern Paxson at the Santa Clara design team meeting), it became obvious that it was the right solution, providing good extensibility to the protocol.

With the "chunking" of the protocol, an idea put forward by Christian Huitema at the Oslo, Norway, IETF meeting (45th IETF) could also be easily re-incorporated[8] with no cost—bundling. With each chunk being self-descriptive, all one has to do is combine more than one chunk in an SCTP packet and thus bundle together multiple chunks. Along with bundling, fragmentation and reassembly also made their way back into the protocol (after having been deleted from earlier

---

8.  A form of bundling had been taken out of the protocol in earlier debate.

versions). They were added after some debate on signaling message sizes and, in particular, on the possible need to support non-binary signaling messages. A non-binary message format would result in much larger message sizes than those of the typical call control signaling messages found in *SS7* networks. This view formed a strong argument for the potential need for fragmentation.

The DATA chunk (sometime in late December 1999) had a new field, the *Payload protocol identifier*, added. The identifier invoked a lot of discussion on how it could be used by middle boxes and possibly by the upper-layer applications as well. The main body of discussion centered around how to use it. Would it replace the port numbers? How would an operating system gain any advantage from this new field? For now it appears that the port numbers will continue to be used for de-multiplexing to the application, but at some future date this may change or be augmented by the *Payload protocol identifier*.

Once the decision was made to move SCTP to run directly over IP, a set of port numbers was needed. It was desired to keep the same format as TCP and UDP, so the port numbers were added at the same byte position. When the port numbers were added, however, the *Verification tag* and the *Adler-32 checksum* were first put forward in the order opposite of that in which they currently appear in the protocol. After some discussion it was realized that the *Verification tag* had to precede the *Adler-32 checksum* due to SCTP's interaction with ICMP. ICMP, for IPv4, only ensures that the first 64 bits (not bytes) of the message that caused the error are returned to the sender. This meant that in order to ensure that the *Verification tag* was accessible to an SCTP stack receiving an ICMP message, it had to be in the first 8 bytes of the SCTP common header.

New chunk types were being added as late as after working group Last Call.[9] In particular the three-way handshake on shutdown added the third leg during this time period. Most of the general layout of the bits on the wire was quite stable by the seventh or eighth version of the SCTP specification.

One of the nicest things about SCTP is its extensibility. This extensibility provides a solid foundation for future enhancements to SCTP, unlike any existing IETF transport protocol. In the future, additional draft documents will be proposed that extend and enhance SCTP with things like the following:

---

9. Working group Last Call is a step of the IETF standardization process that is normally initiated when a document satisfies the working group chair as ready to be handed to the IESG. The chair reaches this decision based on the "rough consensus" of the mailing list of the working group. The Last Call period for the working group will last about two weeks. During this time comments are collected and issues are debated (sometimes fast and furious e-mails fly) and resolved. At the end of the last call, a new version of the document is normally put out, and the document is sent to the IESG to be considered for standardization. This then initiates yet another IESG last call, during which both IESG members and other IETF members are invited to comment on the document. These issues and comments may also be debated and result in one (or more) revisions of the document. After the IESG is completely satisfied with the document, it is sent to the RFC editor. Details of this process can be found in Bradner (1996).

- Partially reliable transport with congestion control (for example, for SCSI over IP, and for context transfer)

- The ability to add and delete transport addresses from an existing association without restarting the association

- Unique compression schemes that involve the transport layer

- Stream-based flow limiting

All of this is possible due to the extensibility of the basic protocol design.[10]

## 3.4 Summary

We have looked at the basic format and structure of SCTP. The bits on the wire have been presented in the preceding sections in the order in which one would see them in an association life cycle. We have also briefly discussed how SCTP ended up with its current format and design.

## 3.5 Questions

1. What are the SCTP control chunks? Please name a few.

2. When both SCTP control and data chunks are present in an SCTP packet, where should the control chunks be positioned?

3. What does the *checksum* in the SCTP common header cover?

4. If a chunk is padded with zeros at the end, does the *Chunk length* field in the chunk header count those padded zeros?

5. If an endpoint receives a chunk with an unknown *Chunk type*, and the highest two bits of the *Chunk type* value are "01," what should the endpoint do?

6. Describe the purpose of the *Stale cookie* error parameter.

---

10. The IETF requires any extension to an existing protocol to be put forward in an IETF Internet-Draft and to proceed through the normal IETF standardization process. This should hopefully limit rampant feature creep into the protocol.

**4**

# Setup of an Association

$\mathbf{W}$e will now turn our attention to the methodology behind the formation of associations. This is the process that will always take place before any data can be exchanged between two SCTP endpoints. It involves the exchange of at least four SCTP packets between the two endpoints. The exchange is designed to be hardened against the classic SYN flooding-type of denial-of-service attack (Ferguson and Senie 1998).

The overhead of passing four SCTP packets may seem like a lot, but the good news is that two of the SCTP packets can carry other types of information (such as user data). This minimizes the delay burden for the application without compromising the improved security.

This four-way handshake is fairly straightforward in the simplest scenario. However (you knew there had to be a catch), it gets quite complicated when one begins to consider application restarts[1] or two endpoints attempting to start an association with each other at about the same time. These incidents should be rare, but the protocol *must* be and *is* robust enough to handle each of these situations.

By the end of this chapter you should understand the following:

- The basic exchanges that take place in the setup of an association

- What timers are involved and how they are used

---

1. The SCTP designers decided to provide a mechanism in the protocol to detect and validate a remote peer restart event. When such an event is detected, the local endpoint can not only notify its upper-layer application about the event, but in most cases it can also restore the communication with the peer by updating the existing association without going through the setup process again. This may be especially beneficial to applications desiring additional system robustness.

- What a COOKIE-ECHO is, as well as its contents and its purpose

- How collision cases are handled (that is, restart cases or when association startups occur at about the same time)

Sections 4.1 through Section 4.4 will take a narrative approach and walk through each SCTP packet while following a budding association. Each section will describe the stimulus that occurred to cause the SCTP packet that it discusses to be formed, and any constraints that the SCTP endpoint is required to take into consideration before sending the SCTP packet.

Section 4.5 will discuss miscellaneous special considerations in the association setup.

By the time you finish these first five subsections, you will feel you understand completely how SCTP associations are set up. Then you will move on to sections 4.6 and 4.7 and realize all the strange cases that can occur. But do not fear, you will be walked through all of these cases and how SCTP handles each of them.

For those not interested in all the gory details, the basic overview of what happens when an association starts up can be seen in Figure 4–1. This drawing depicts the typical four-way handshake.

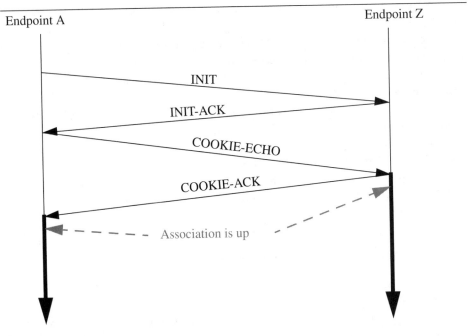

**Figure 4–1** *A simple view of an association startup*

In Figure 4–1 we see endpoint A deciding to create an association with end-point Z. Endpoint A sends out an INIT chunk, the first SCTP packet in the association setup procedure. Endpoint Z responds with the INIT-ACK. Inside the INIT-ACK is a state cookie that is echoed back to endpoint Z in the COOKIE-ECHO. Upon receiving the COOKIE-ECHO, endpoint Z returns an acknowledgment (the COOKIE-ACK), and the association is set up.

This gives us a general view of the four-way handshake. Readers who only need a casual overview of how SCTP initializes an association may wish to skip the rest of this chapter because from here out we will concentrate on the details and specifics of association initialization.

## 4.1   The INIT Chunk

After our SCTP endpoint is instantiated (for example, when a sockets API *open()* function is called or its equivalent is performed), one of the two following events will normally trigger our local SCTP endpoint to formulate and send an INIT chunk to a remote endpoint:

- Our application has data to send to the remote endpoint and there is no association existing between our local SCTP stack and the remote endpoint.

- Our application explicitly makes a request to the local SCTP stack to set up an association with the remote endpoint.

In either event, once our SCTP endpoint realizes it does not have an association with the remote endpoint, it will immediately build an INIT chunk and send it off in an SCTP packet to the remote endpoint.

### 4.1.1   Formulating the Chunk

There are several things an SCTP endpoint must do when it formulates an INIT chunk to send off to a potential new peer:

- It must build a local TCB in which to store information about the association.

- It must decide what value it wishes to place in the *a_rwnd* field in the outbound INIT. This choice is crucial in that this is a pledge to the remote endpoint on how much buffer space the local endpoint is dedicating to the association. As such, it represents a drain on the local systems resources.

- It must decide how many streams the local user is requesting to the remote peer. This may be a value passed into the SCTP stack, or it may be a set value that the application has set up as a default.

- It must decide what is the maximum number of inbound streams it is capable of supporting. Streams generally are fairly lightweight in terms of resources used, but they do have a small representation in the SCTP stack, and in the application they may represent a more significant investment. In such cases, the local application may have set a restriction on how many streams it is prepared to support (which is smaller than the number the actual SCTP implementation can support).

- The local SCTP endpoint is required to generate a random number for the *Initiation tag* value. This value will serve as a mechanism to verify that an SCTP packet truly belongs to this association and will appear in every inbound SCTP packet that the local SCTP endpoint reads on this association. The local endpoint will also select a second random value for the *Initial TSN*.[2] Note that the value "0" is *not allowed* for the *Initiation tag* but *is allowed* for the *Initial TSN*.

After deciding on all of the fixed values to be placed in the INIT chunk, the endpoint then will add the appropriate parameters, including both variable-length and optional parameters, to the INIT before sending it off.

### 4.1.2   INIT Parameters

There are a number of parameters that an SCTP endpoint may wish to place within an INIT chunk, although none of them are required. This subsection will detail why you should put parameters within the INIT and illustrate the few cases where you would not need to.

The allowable INIT parameters can be grouped into two general categories, those that deal with addresses and those that request additional services. The address parameters give SCTP three methods to communicate address information:

- *IPv4 address*—Initially this will be one of the most common address parameters included. When present, it indicates that the listed IP address is a pos-

---

2. Even though it is not a recommended practice, an implementation is nonetheless allowed to take a short-cut and set the *Initial TSN* to the same value as the *Initiation tag*. But using the same value weakens the security of the SCTP association by reducing the amount of information an attacker needs to guess. After all, it does not create that much overhead to call the random number generator function twice.

sible source of SCTP packets for this association, as well as a valid
destination to which the remote peer can send IP datagrams.

- *IPv6 address*—When present, this parameter indicates an IPv6 address from
  which the local endpoint may source IP datagrams, or to which the remote
  endpoint may send IP datagrams.

> *Note*   IPv6 and IPv4 parameters may appear together in the same INIT.
> This makes SCTP inherently dual stacked.

- *Hostname address*[3]—When present, this text string represents an entry to be
  looked up in an external database (such as the DNS). SCTP does not specify
  what database is being used, so it could be any namespace service. The end
  result is a translation of this name into some number of addresses. (This is
  the same as if the endpoint had placed IPv6 and/or IPv4 addresses, matching
  those returned from the hostname translation, within the INIT chunk.) When
  this parameter is present, any other address parameters (IPv6 or IPv4) are ignored by the receiver.

When the hostname feature is not needed or not supported, what should be
done? An endpoint will include in the INIT a list of its addresses, IPv6 or IPv4,
that are bound into the association.

Which address should be selected for a given association is a rather complicated issue, but, in general, when establishing a new association, an endpoint will
either choose to use all the IP addresses assigned to the host or choose to use only
a subset of the assigned addresses.

For example, if a host machine has four IP addresses, two IPv6 and two IPv4,
and the SCTP endpoint decides to bind all the addresses to the new association, the
endpoint will list in the INIT all four addresses in four separate address parameters.

Besides address parameters, there are a number of other optional parameters
that can be used to request services from the remote endpoint. They include the
following:

- *ECN capable*—This parameter is included to inform the remote endpoint
  that the local endpoint is aware of Explicit Congestion Notification (ECN)
  and would like to perform ECN with the remote peer. If the response chunk

---

3. The hostname address feature is optional; thus it may not always be supported by an endpoint. This feature is introduced to make SCTP more compatible with some network address translator (NAT) devices
   (Egevang and Francis 1994).

> *Note* | When sending the INIT, it is *crucial* for the SCTP endpoint to list all the addresses that may subsequently be used as a source address in outbound datagrams of the new association. Failure to do so may cause the association to fail to be set up, or worse, fail after the setup. More details on address selection will be discussed in Section 4.5.

(the INIT-ACK) contains an *ECN capable* parameter, then each endpoint will be expected to follow the ECN procedures detailed in Section 6.6.

- *Supported address type*—This parameter can be used to inform the remote peer of what address types the local SCTP endpoint can support.

- *Cookie preservative*—An endpoint may include this parameter to request extra life within the cookie if an earlier attempt at setting up an association with the same peer fails due to a delay within the network that causes a COOKIE-ECHO chunk to become stale.

All of these parameters may appear in an INIT chunk. For example, the *Supported address type* parameter can be used by an endpoint that does not support the hostname address type. In such a case, the endpoint would create a *Supported address type* parameter that specifies only the IPv4 and IPv6 address types as supported. This will inform the remote peer that it should *not attempt* to use the hostname address type in its INIT-ACK response.

ECN is a relatively new method aimed at detecting and avoiding congestion within the network before packet loss occurs. (You may wish to refer to Ramakrishnan and Floyd [1999] for details on how ECN works.) If both endpoints support ECN, then the endpoints should attempt to use ECN. Section 6.6 will discuss in detail how ECN can be supported in SCTP.[4]

The *Cookie preservative* parameter provides a method for error path recovery of a previously failed association setup. As we will see in Section 4.6, this can be used to set up an association that otherwise would not be able to be brought up. Normally this parameter is not included in an INIT.

Most INIT chunks contain, at a minimum, a list of addresses bound by the sending SCTP endpoint. But there is a case in which no parameters may be listed within the INIT. This occurs when the endpoint is not multi-homed (or it chooses

---

4. ECN was not added to the base SCTP specification (Stewart et al. 2000) because, at the time, ECN itself was an experimental RFC. The experimental classification prohibited SCTP from referring to ECN in any way except as non-normative. ECN has since become a standard track RFC. In the next step for SCTP, (promotion to draft standard) hopefully ECN will be not only referenced but also required.

to use only one IP address in this association) *and* it can fully support all addressing types.[5]

Under these circumstances, the endpoint does not need to include any additional parameters in the INIT chunk. Note that when no address parameters are listed, the source address is considered the only address usable by the endpoint.

### 4.1.3  Timer and Retransmission for INIT

At this point we have fully formed an INIT chunk, so all that is left to do is to send it off in an SCTP packet. After the chunk is sent, it is crucial that the sender start a timer (named the *T1-init* timer) so that if the IP datagram is lost within the IP network, it can be retransmitted. If the timer expires, a duplicate of the SCTP packet should be created (that is, another INIT chunk just like the one that went unanswered) and retransmitted. After the SCTP packet is retransmitted, the timer should be restarted as well, with its time value doubled from that used in the previous transmission. Doubling of the timer will give the remote peer extra time to respond and prevent additional network congestion.

At retransmission the sender should also increment a counter. If the counter exceeds the local endpoint's association setup threshold, the endpoint should not retransmit the INIT chunk. Instead, it should report to the upper layer that the remote peer is unreachable.

Given that we have in flight an SCTP packet that contains an INIT chunk and a retransmission timer *T1-init* running, the endpoint should enter the COOKIE_WAIT state once the INIT is sent. A pictorial view of this is shown in Figure 4–2.

## 4.2  The INIT-ACK Response

Assume that the destination of our INIT chunk eventually receives the SCTP packet. The reception of this SCTP packet (containing the INIT chunk) will cause the receiver to generate the next chunk, an INIT-ACK chunk, in the four-way handshake.

This INIT-ACK chunk is a direct response to the INIT chunk. It is very similar in content to the INIT chunk but has some interesting differences.

---

5. This is because if the endpoint does not support, for example, the hostname address type, it will have to include a *Support address type* parameter to inform the peer not to attempt the use of that address type. Otherwise, an INIT-ACK may arrive with a hostname address, and the endpoint may find it is not able to resolve it.

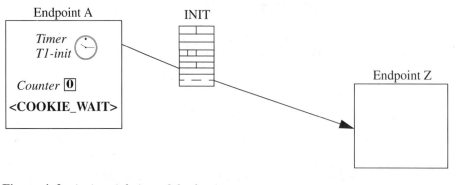

**Figure 4–2**  *A pictorial view of the first step*

### 4.2.1   Formulating the Response

There are several things an SCTP endpoint *is required to* do when formulating the INIT-ACK:

- It must *not* build a permanent local state information record (in other words, the TCB); instead it must decide what values would go in its TCB (if it were to build one). It places these into the INIT-ACK chunk. In particular, it will form a cookie that most likely will contain the entire INIT chunk and its entire INIT-ACK chunk. We will discuss the forming of the cookie in more detail in Section 4.2.2.1.

- Like the sender of the INIT, the sender of INIT-ACK needs to decide what value it wishes to place in the *a_rwnd* field of the INIT-ACK. This choice is crucial in that this is a pledge to the remote endpoint on how much buffer space the local endpoint is dedicating to the association. As such, it represents a drain on the local system's resources.

- It must decide how many streams the local user will require. This most likely will be a fixed value that the application specified when the endpoint was initialized, because INIT-ACK chunks are generated without consulting the application layer.

- It must decide the maximum number of inbound streams it is capable of supporting. Streams generally are fairly lightweight in terms of resources used, but they do have a small representation in the SCTP stack, and in the application they may represent a more significant investment. In such cases, the local application may have set a restriction on how many streams it is prepared to support (which is smaller than the number that the actual SCTP implementation can support).

- The local SCTP endpoint must generate a random number for the *Initiation tag* value. This value will serve as a mechanism to verify that an SCTP packet truly belongs to this association, and it will appear in every inbound SCTP packet that the local SCTP endpoint reads in this association. The local endpoint will also select a random value for the *Initial TSN*. Note that the value "0" *must not* be used for the *Initiation tag* but *may* be used for the *Initial TSN*.

- The local SCTP endpoint must place the *Initiation tag* value that is contained in the INIT chunk into the SCTP common header of the response SCTP packet. This will assure that the peer will recognize the INIT-ACK chunk as being part of the newly forming association.

After deciding on all the fixed values to be placed in the INIT-ACK chunk, the endpoint must add the appropriate parameters or variable-length fields to the INIT-ACK before sending it off.

## 4.2.2 INIT-ACK Parameters

There is a subset of parameters that overlap between the INIT and INIT-ACK chunks. In particular, the address parameters are the same. These parameters have the same considerations as discussed previously. Refer to Section 4.1.2 for details and considerations for the address parameters.

The other parameters that may be sent in the INIT-ACK are somewhat different than those in the INIT. They are described as follows:

- *State cookie*—This is a required parameter that is discussed in the next section.

- *Unrecognized parameter*—The sender of an INIT may request a report on any parameters that were unrecognized by the receiver of the INIT. This request is implicitly sought using the upper two bits of the *Parameter type* field, as we discussed in Section 3.1.5. Currently no defined parameter type uses this request, so it is unlikely that initial deployments of SCTP will include this parameter. However, future extensions to SCTP may require the reporting of unrecognized parameters. This parameter will be included in the outgoing INIT-ACK if the sender of the INIT-ACK encounters a parameter that it does not recognize.

- *ECN capable*—This parameter is the same as it was in the INIT; that is, it tells the remote endpoint that the ECN option is supported. This parameter can be included even if the sender of the INIT does not support ECN. However, it makes no sense to include this parameter unless the sender of the INIT also included it. This is because both endpoints *must* specify that they are ECN-capable before ECN can be performed. See Section 6.6 for more details.

### 4.2.2.1   Creating a State Cookie

One of the most critical pieces of information in the INIT-ACK chunk is destined not for the sender of the INIT but for the sender of the INIT-ACK.

The *State cookie* is a mandatory parameter included in the INIT-ACK, with the idea being that the receiver of the INIT-ACK will send this parameter in a chunk back to the sender of the INIT-ACK.

As we will see later in this chapter, because the ultimate consumer of the *State cookie* is the sender of the *State cookie* itself, the sender in theory can put **any** information in **any** form and shape into the cookie. In fact, the sender can even include no information in the cookie at all, that is, send an empty cookie. However, doing so will cause the security and usefulness of the state cookie mechanism to be severely compromised if not to vanish completely.

To really take advantage of the cookie mechanism, the sender will normally need to include the following information when building the cookie:

- *Information from the original INIT chunk*—A "lazy" implementation may well include just a complete copy of the received INIT chunk.

- *Information contained in this outbound INIT-ACK chunk itself*—This normally includes the addresses, stream numbers, *a_rwnd* value, etc. Again, a "lazy" implementation might include just a copy of the INIT-ACK (minus the cookie part of course). These will guide the sender of the INIT-ACK in setting up its state information (in other words, its TCB) when the cookie comes back, as we will see later.

- Some form of a timestamp recording in the local time when the cookie is created.

- *Some form of life span or time-to-live to indicate how long this cookie will remain valid*—This should be specified in local time too.

- *A signature*—The signature is an authentication mechanism that can be placed in the cookie so that when the cookie comes back, it can be verified as being authentic and not having been tampered with.

The choice of authentication measures is completely up to the sender of the *State cookie*. Those endpoints worried about memory/buffer resource attacks may use MD5 (Rivest 1992) or SHA-1 (Secure Hash Standard 1995) over the *State cookie,* and some random key to generate the signature. It is possible that some simpler authentication mechanism may also be used.

Usually such a mechanism is weaker against memory/buffer resource attacks, but it may well be more resistant to CPU resource attacks due to the fact that the authentication algorithm itself is less computation-intensive.

- *A set of tie-tags*—The tie-tags, two unsigned 32-bit integers, are protocol variables that are used to help solve some special association initialization cases, such as initialization collision and remote endpoint restart. We will discuss their usage in detail in Section 4.7.

An endpoint that decides to include all of this information in the cookie will normally take the following steps to generate the *State cookie* parameter:

- Initialize the MD5, SHA-1, or other hashing algorithm[6] that the implementation has decided to use.

- Create a temporary parameter that will hold all the outgoing information.

- In the order in which the data will appear in the outgoing SCTP packet, run the selected algorithm over each of the items (except the signature) and copy them into their respective memory location. Note that it is critical to run the algorithm and copy each item in the correct order so that a hashing of the response chunk—that is, the COOKIE-ECHO (minus the signature)—will result in the exact same signature.[7]

- Get the current secret key and run the algorithm on this as well; but *do not* copy the key into the outgoing parameter.

- Copy out the signature from the hashing algorithm into the fixed position of the temporary parameter.

Figure 4–3 is a pictorial representation of the cookie and its generation.

This example shows each piece being run through the hashing algorithm and copied into the reserved memory in the order in which each was run through the algorithm. After all pieces of the cookie have been hashed, the signature is copied

---

6. A hashing algorithm is normally designed so that when it is executed over a fixed set of data and a secret key, the execution will always generate exactly the same result. (The result is often a fixed-size integer number and is called the signature of the data.) However, if the data is changed in even the smallest way and run through the hash algorithm again, the execution result will be different and no longer match the signature of the original data. This characteristic of the hashing algorithm allows it be used as an efficient way of detecting modifications to the data without requiring a byte-by-byte comparison of the new version and the original.

7. Another approach is to initialize the complete parameter that does not include the signature and then run the hash function over this parameter. Either method will work, but for illustrative purposes we show the hash and copy method.

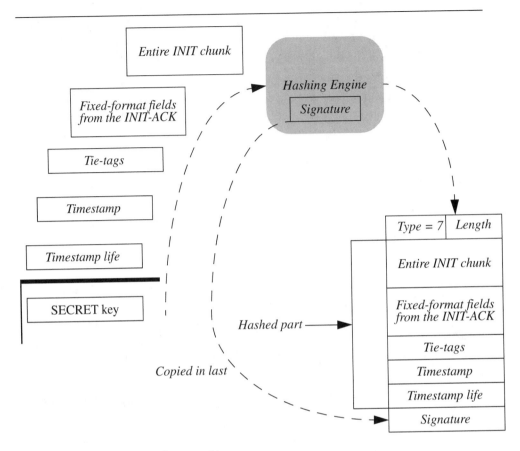

**Figure 4–3** *Generating a State cookie*

out of the hashing engine and placed in the cookie. Note also that the secret key is *not* copied into the cookie; instead it is a fixed part of the SCTP endpoint.[8]

As mentioned before, it is critical that the order in which the items are hashed is also the order in which they appear within the cookie. If this is not true, then when the entire cookie is hashed, the cookie will fail the signature test upon return. The order of appearance of the items in the cookie is solely an implementation issue, and the preceding example is just one of many possible layouts.

---

8. Generally more than one secret key is generated and kept by an SCTP endpoint. Periodically throughout the life of the SCTP endpoint, the oldest secret key (which has not been used in a while) is discarded and a new secret key is generated. Refer to Krawcyk, Bellare, and Canetti (1997) for details on generating and changing a hashing algorithm's secret key.

### 4.2.3   Preventing Resource Attacks

It is important that the SCTP endpoint that sends back the INIT-ACK does not keep any record or knowledge of the association. In other words, after sending off the INIT-ACK, the sender of the INIT-ACK does *not* keep a TCB, and it remains in the CLOSED state. This is because, by including all the information that is needed to build the TCB in the *State cookie*, the sender of the INIT-ACK does not need to keep a TCB.

This provides the local endpoint (that is, the sender of the INIT-ACK) with resistance to a common type of resource attack that is often referred to as the SYN flooding attack. There is nothing stopping an endpoint from building a TCB when the INIT arrives and sending no information in the *State cookie*. However, if an endpoint does this, it will be open to the SYN flooding attack.

The selection of the hashing algorithm is another important consideration for an implementation. Different algorithms used to "sign" the cookie have different computation complexities. Selecting an algorithm that requires extensive computation resources may well result in the opening up the endpoint to CPU resource attacks (in which the attacker sends countless invalid cookies, thus using up all available CPU cycles on a host). Which hashing algorithm to use is an implementation choice that should be based on the threat environment in which the association is being established.

In the normal case, no record of the forming association is maintained after sending off the INIT-ACK, so the forming association looks as depicted in Figure 4–4.

## 4.3   The COOKIE-ECHO Chunk

The INIT-ACK will arrive at the sender of the INIT as depicted in Figure 4–4. When the INIT-ACK arrives, the sender should do the following:

- Find the association. If it is not found, discard the INIT-ACK. If the association is found, the endpoint will first verify the *Verification tag* value contained in the SCTP common header, as described in Section 8.2.1.

- Stop the timer that was started when the INIT was sent.

- Clear any counter that may have been incremented due to retransmissions of the INIT.

- Update the address list by using all the listed address parameters that may be held within the INIT-ACK chunk.

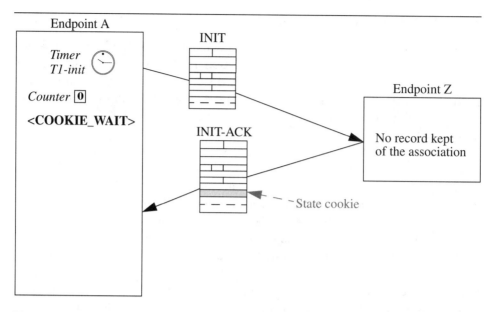

**Figure 4–4** *A pictorial view of the first and second steps*

*Note*  When attempting to find the association, the receiver of the INIT-ACK may need to look inside the INIT-ACK at any listed address parameters. This is because the TCB is normally referenced by the transport addresses (both source and destination), and it is very possible that the source address in the IP datagram carrying the inbound INIT-ACK is *not* the source address to which the INIT was sent. The original address *must* be listed within the INIT-ACK chunk, so further examination may be required of all the INIT-ACK parameters in order to find the TCB. Once the TCB is found, the *Verification tag* in the SCTP common header can be cross-checked against the *Initiation tag* sent and stored in the TCB. If these values do not match, the entire IP datagram must be discarded.

• Send a COOKIE-ECHO chunk to the remote peer.

• Start a new timer *T1-cookie* and enter the COOKIE_ECHOED state.

### 4.3.1 Formulating the Chunk

Formulating the COOKIE-ECHO chunk is quite easy. It is, in effect, a copy of the *State cookie* parameter modified to be a COOKIE-ECHO chunk. The easiest way to accomplish this is depicted in Figure 4–5.

Here we see a *State cookie* being changed into a COOKIE-ECHO chunk simply by changing the first two bytes of the *State cookie* parameter. The first byte is overwritten with the value *0x0a*, that is, the *Chunk type* for a COOKIE-ECHO. The second byte is overwritten with a value of "0" because the *Chunk flags* in the COOKIE-ECHO are always zero. The length field and the data that comprises the *State cookie* are not changed or examined, but rather just sent back untouched.

### 4.3.2 Bundling Data with the COOKIE-ECHO

At this point it may well be that there is a DATA chunk waiting to be sent to the remote endpoint, especially if the association was started implicitly by sending a user message to the destination endpoint.

If data is waiting, it can be bundled (by adding it to the end) to the outbound SCTP packet. SCTP chunks are fully self-descriptive and thus are just grouped together with an SCTP common header up to the PMTU size. More information about bundling will be discussed in Section 5.8.4.

Assuming that our application did use the implicit association startup and that we do have a user message waiting to be sent, our outbound SCTP packet now looks as shown in Figure 4–6.

### 4.3.3 Timer and Retransmission for COOKIE-ECHO

At this point, because we have fully formed a COOKIE-ECHO chunk, all that is left to do is to send it and any DATA chunk(s) bundled with it off in an SCTP packet. After the chunk(s) are sent, it is crucial that the sender start a timer so that if the IP datagram is lost within the IP network, it can be retransmitted.

If the timer expires, a duplicate of the SCTP packet (that is, another COOKIE-ECHO chunk just like the one that went unanswered)[9] should be created and retransmitted.

After retransmitting the SCTP packet, the timer should be restarted as well, after the previous timer value used is doubled. This doubling of the timer will give the remote peer extra time to respond and prevent additional network congestion.

---

9. Whether the sender should also retransmit any DATA chunks that may have been bundled with the COOKIE-ECHO is an implementation decision. It is allowed by the specification, but if the network is in a congested state (indicated by multiple SCTP packet losses of the COOKIE-ECHO), it may be beneficial **not** to bundle DATA with the retransmission, thus sending a smaller SCTP packet into the network.

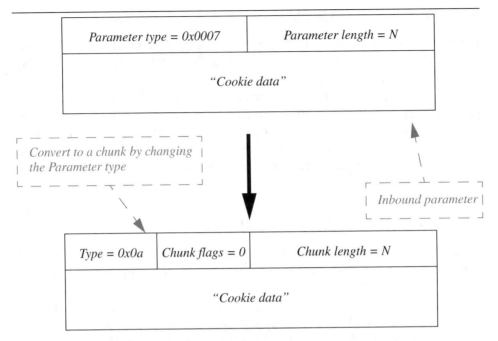

**Figure 4–5** *An example of the transmutation of a State cookie parameter into a COOKIE-ECHO chunk*

At retransmission the sender should also stroke a counter. If the counter exceeds the local endpoint's association setup threshold, the endpoint should give up attempts at contacting the remote endpoint and report to the upper layer that the remote peer is unreachable.

So we now have in flight an SCTP packet that contains a COOKIE-ECHO chunk and a retransmission timer (*T1-cookie* timer) running. The endpoint should enter the COOKIE_ECHOED state once the COOKIE-ECHO chunk is sent.

A pictorial view of all that has transpired is shown in Figure 4–7.

## 4.4 The COOKIE-ACK Chunk

At this point three legs of the handshake have transpired. However, endpoint Z has no record of the association. The arrival of the COOKIE-ECHO is the trigger for endpoint Z to do a number of things:

- Verify that the cookie is authentic.

- Unpack the cookie into an association TCB.

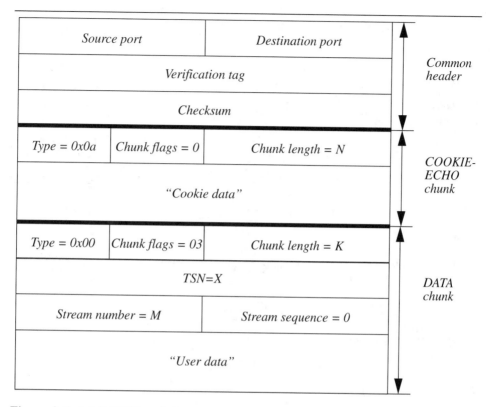

**Figure 4–6** *A full SCTP packet containing a COOKIE-ECHO and bundled user data*

- Read and process any other bundled chunks that arrived with the COOKIE-ECHO
- Send back the COOKIE-ACK
- Possibly bundle with the COOKIE-ACK any necessary SACK or pending data

### 4.4.1   Validating and Unpacking the Cookie

The first thing that *must* be done is to validate the cookie.

The validation is done by taking the entire data portion of the state cookie, minus the signature, and once again running the hashing algorithm over the entire block. We then take the secret key and hash this as well. We then pull out the signature from our hashing algorithm. This is compared to the signature included in the COOKIE-ECHO chunk. If this signature does not match, the entire SCTP packet is silently discarded.

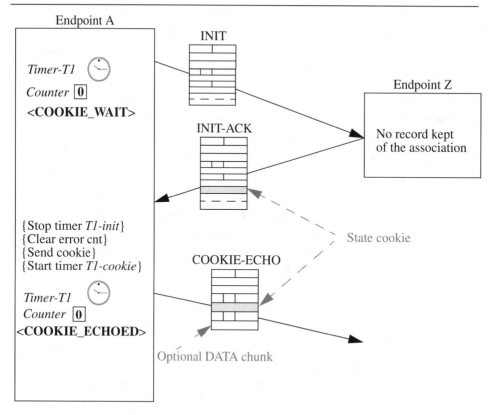

**Figure 4–7** *The third leg exposed*

If the signature is valid, the next step we take is to validate the timestamp within the cookie. We first take the time that the cookie was created (the timestamp value within the cookie) and add to it the cookie's life value (also contained in the cookie). This gives us the expiration time of the cookie. We then compare this expiration time to the current local time and verify that the cookie has not expired.

If the cookie has already expired, an ERROR chunk will be sent to the sender of the COOKIE-ECHO, and the entire SCTP packet will be discarded.

If the cookie proves to be valid and there is no existing association with the remote SCTP endpoint (that is, the sender of the COOKIE-ECHO), we unpack the cookie and build an association TCB. If there is an existing association, we may be in a race condition. The handling of race conditions is discussed in Section 4.7.

Figure 4–8 shows a pictorial view of this process.

After we have validated the cookie, we *must* send a COOKIE-ACK chunk back to the sender of the COOKIE-ECHO.

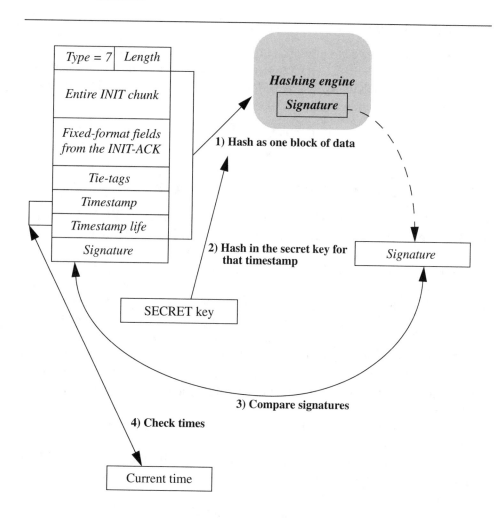

**Figure 4–8** *Consumption of a state cookie*

### 4.4.2   Formulating the COOKIE-ACK

The COOKIE-ACK is quite simple and contains no more than a *Chunk type* and a fixed length of 4 octets. Its purpose is to let the sender of the COOKIE-ECHO know the following:

- The cookie has been received and accepted.

- The peer is allowed to turn off its *T1-cookie* timer so it does not retransmit a duplicate COOKIE-ECHO. (Note that this duplication can still happen, because the COOKIE-ACK may be late or lost. Details on handling this situation are included in Section 4.7.)

- The peer can change its internal state of the new association to ESTAB-LISHED.

### 4.4.3   Bundling DATA and SACK with COOKIE-ACK

When sending a COOKIE-ACK, the sender (that is, the receiver of the COOKIE-ECHO) is considered in the ESTABLISHED state. This means that the sender may also send DATA chunks with the COOKIE-ACK.[10]

Moreover, the COOKIE-ECHO chunk may also come bundled with DATA chunks (as discussed in Section 4.3.2); if it does, the receiver of the COOKIE-ECHO may wish to bundle a SACK with the COOKIE-ACK. Both bundlings are allowed, and they are simply a matter of grouping an SCTP common header with the COOKIE-ACK and any subsequent items to be bundled.

Note that when bundled with other chunks, the COOKIE-ACK *must* always be placed as the first control chunk in the packet. This allows the peer to enter the ESTABLISHED state before processing any of the other chunks within the same SCTP packet.

Figure 4–9 depicts a typical response to a COOKIE-ECHO that arrived bundled with a SACK.

Note that even though bundling DATA chunks with the COOKIE-ACK is allowed, it is highly unlikely that the sender of the COOKIE-ACK will have any data ready for the peer. This is because the sender of the COOKIE-ACK *must* respond without waiting for the application level to respond. It may be that in some extreme cases (for example, when two endpoints are trying to set up an association at about the same time) this will occur, but in general it is unlikely.

The final picture of our four-way handshake looks as illustrated in Figure 4–10.

---

10. Unlike the COOKIE-ECHO and COOKIE-ACK, the INIT and INIT ACK chunks *must* be the only chunks in the SCTP packet.

| Source port | Destination port | Common header |
|---|---|---|
| Verification tag | | |
| Checksum | | |
| Type = 0x0b   Chunk flags = 00 | Chunk length = 4 | COOKIE-ACK |
| Type = 0x03   Chunk flags = 00 | Chunk length = 16 | SACK |
| Cumulative TSN Ack = X | | |
| Advertised receiver window credit = U | | |
| Number of Gap Ack blocks = 0 | Number of duplicate TSNs = 0 | |

**Figure 4–9** *A typical COOKIE-ACK bundled with a SACK*

## 4.5 Address Usage When Starting an Association

The selection of the address list to include in the INIT or INIT-ACK is a crucial part of the SCTP association setup. When filled out correctly, the list provides to the receiver detailed information that helps it identify to which association the SCTP packets belong. But if this list is filled out incorrectly, disastrous results may occur, either preventing the association from being set up, or worse, causing the association to fail later.

The two principles of address selection are as follows:

1. The sending endpoint of the INIT or INIT-ACK *must* include all the addresses that *may* potentially be used as the source address of an outbound SCTP packet during the lifetime of the association.

2. The sending endpoint of the INIT or INIT-ACK *must never* include any address that is invalid or out of scope on the receiver's side. *In other words, a locally defined address*[11] *should never be allowed to "leak" out of its intended valid scope.*

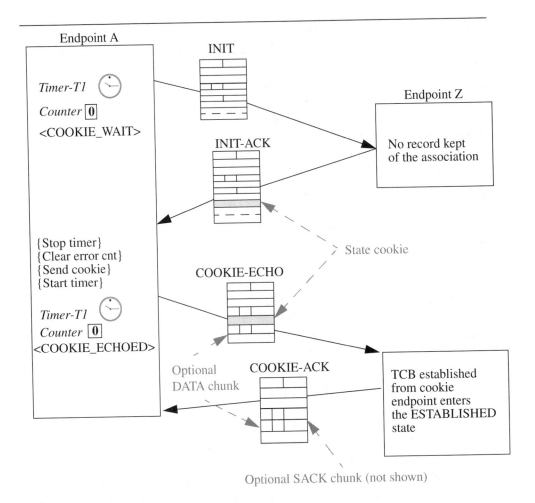

**Figure 4–10** *The completed four-way handshake*

The first principle is necessary because an SCTP endpoint relies on the source and destination transport address in each arrived SCTP packet to identify to which association the SCTP packet belongs. If an endpoint fails at setup time to inform a peer of any of the addresses that may later appear as the source address in an IP datagram sent to the peer, then when an SCTP packet carrying such an IP source address reaches the peer, it will not be able to identify the SCTP packet as being

---

11. A locally defined address is one that is routable only in its local scope. In IPv4 an example of such an ad-
    dress is a "private address." In IPv6 an example of such an address would be a "link-local" address,
    which is only valid on the physical link on which the interface card resides.

sent from the endpoint. In many cases, this can trigger the peer sending back an ABORT chunk and thus cause the association to fail.

Let us consider an example with the network shown in Figure 4–11.

Let us assume that endpoint E1 sends an INIT chunk to endpoint E2 but only includes local address IPA in the address list. We further assume that the SCTP packet containing the INIT is assigned source address IPA and routed through Router 1 and Router 2 before arriving at endpoint E2. In response to the INIT, endpoint E2 will now generate an INIT-ACK (listing both IPX and IPY in it) and send it back to address IPA (the only address known by endpoint E2 about endpoint E1), and the association between E1 and E2 is set up. Everything has worked fine so far.

Now, some time after the establishment of the association, endpoint E1 may send an SCTP packet to address IPY of endpoint E2, and this SCTP packet may unfortunately be assigned with source address IPB and be routed through Router 3 and Router 4 before reaching endpoint E2. Since the source address, IPB, carried in the IP header is unrecognizable, endpoint E2 will become confused and will not be able to associate the SCTP packet with the existing association. Depending on the type of chunk(s) carried in the SCTP packet, endpoint E2 may treat the SCTP packet as erroneous and ignore it.[12] But much more likely, E2 may consider the received SCTP packet an out-of-the-blue (OOTB) SCTP packet and respond with an ABORT chunk, as detailed in Section 8.1. When the ABORT arrives at endpoint E1, it will tear down the association. In the meantime, endpoint E2 is not aware of this action—because it did not realize that it was in effect aborting the association—and will not discover that the association is gone until it too receives an ABORT from endpoint E1 when it tries to send the next SCTP packet to endpoint E1. Thus, the association at this point has completely self-destructed.

The second address selection principle is very easy to understand but turns out to be complicated to enforce in practice. Part of the reason is that at the time of making the address selection decision, an endpoint may not have all the knowledge it needs about whether or not a particular address is valid or in scope at a remote peer's site.

An example of this is a multi-homed endpoint assigned both global addresses and local intranet addresses. When such an endpoint initiates an association with a peer outside the intranet, the endpoint must not include any of its intranet addresses when sending the INIT or INIT-ACK to the peer. This is because, first of all, any local intranet address will be totally unreachable and thus useless by the peer; and secondly, the consequence can be even worse if some other host on the peer's site is assigned the same local address. (Remember, by definition a local

---

12. This is particularly true if the SCTP packet contains an ABORT chunk.

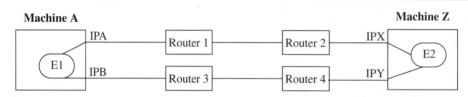

**Figure 4–11** *Two typical multi-homed hosts with endpoints*

intranet address is not guaranteed to be globally unique.) In the latter case, if the peer tries to send a packet (such as a heartbeat) to the bad address, what will happen is rather unpredictable. In most cases the association will simply fail.

However, if the same multi-homed endpoint is setting up an association with a peer inside its local intranet, the endpoint can freely select any of its intranet addresses or global addresses to list when sending its INIT or INIT-ACK.

When IPv6 addresses are involved, the second selection principle can become even more complicated to enforce due to the fact that IPv6 has a much more complicated address-scoping design than IPv4 and that most IPv6 hosts are technically multi-homed.[13]

However, in most practical situations, the protocol implementers and/or system administrators should be able to avoid the address leakage problem through either some thoughtful API design or network administrative arrangements, or a combination of both.

It is worthwhile to note that the prevention of address leakage is not a unique issue to SCTP; rather, it is a general issue concerning all multi-homed IP hosts with address scoping. The IETF has recognized the problem and is currently working on guidelines for dealing with this issue in various environments.

There is an implicit inclusion rule for the source address of the SCTP packet that carries the INIT or INIT-ACK. That is, whether or not it is explicitly listed as an address parameter in the INIT or INIT-ACK, the source address of the SCTP packet that carries the INIT or INIT-ACK is always considered a part of the association.

The sender of an INIT-ACK is always required to send its response SCTP packet to the source address of the IP datagram that held the INIT, but no restrictions are made on the source address of the IP datagram that holds the INIT-ACK itself. It is helpful for the sender of the INIT-ACK to use as the source address the same address that was the destination address of the IP datagram for the INIT chunk. This will expedite the initiator's location of the association.

---

13. This is because a network interface on an IPv6 host is often assigned a link-local address in addition to a site-local address and/or a global address.

The receiver of an INIT-ACK is also required to be prepared to handle the situation in which the INIT-ACK arrives with a different source address. The sender may do this for either of the following reasons:

- Routing table entries guide the sender to set this source address in the IP layer.

- The sender is indicating a different preferred primary address. (Note that the peer is *not* required to honor this hint.)

Now, in either case, the receiver of the INIT-ACK *must* use a couple of special procedures when looking up the association:

1. First it *must* do its ordinary lookup using the transport addresses and its local TCB table.

2. If the first step fails, it *must* parse the INIT-ACK chunk, finding each addressing parameter within it, and then repeat the lookup using the address specified in the parameter(s).

Only after going through these steps and *not* finding an association will a receiver of an INIT-ACK silently drop the SCTP packet.

## 4.6   Chunk Rejections During an Association Setup

You may have noted that there were a number of places in the previous sections where a receiver of an SCTP packet may not have liked something. This section will detail what occurred in all of those cases. The only exception to this is if you received a startup chunk and you already had an association; that long discussion has been saved for the next section (Section 4.7).

All of this discussion will revolve around the initiatee because we presume that the initiator has enough resources to start the association *and* is doing everything it can to get the association up. If the sender of the INIT (the initiator) does not have enough resources to begin an association, it should reject the upper layer's request before sending out the INIT.

Now, the receiver of the INIT, the initiatee, does not have this luxury. It may be that it does not have resources *or* that it just plain does not want to talk to the peer; that is, the application layer is either not available (no endpoint present) or it is not willing to accept associations. Other things may also occur that cause the initiatee not to want to start an association, for example, a stale cookie. Each of these reasons will be discussed and illustrated in this section.

### 4.6.1   When Is an INIT Not Acceptable?

When an INIT arrives, in general the proper response is to send back an INIT-ACK with a *State cookie*. This is a low-cost operation in that it does not tie up a TCB, and it is *not* a commitment to the sender that you have resources available for this new association. But there are a few instances when an INIT can be rejected without sending an INIT-ACK. In these cases, an ABORT is sent back to the sender of the INIT with the *Verification tag* set to the value found in the *Initiation tag* inside the INIT chunk. This will let the sender know that it is not an attacker sending an ABORT and that the receiver did not like the INIT. The following list identifies the cases where the endpoint would send back an ABORT, and the respective error code it would use (if applicable):

- The SCTP stack has no open endpoint set up on the specified port. In this case the stack should send an ABORT chunk to the peer.

- The *Initiation tag* is set to "0." If the *Initiation tag* is set to "0," the sender has violated the protocol. (It is an error to use a value of "0" for the *Initiation tag*.) In this instance the endpoint should send an ABORT with the error cause set to *Invalid mandatory parameter*.

- The INIT contains a *Hostname address* parameter and your stack *is not* capable of resolving hostname addresses. In this case the endpoint should send an ABORT chunk with the error cause set to *Unresolvable address*.

- The INIT or INIT-ACK contains an unacceptable number of streams to the application. In this case the SCTP implementation may wish to ABORT the association or settle for the minimum of the remote *MIS* and the local *OS* value. This decision is, of course, an implementation choice.

### 4.6.2   When Is a Cookie Not Worth Eating?

A COOKIE-ECHO is the next chunk that the **initiatee** will see in the four-way handshake. Great care must be taken to authenticate the cookie and verify that it is acceptable. The following list identifies cases where cookies are not acceptable and includes proper handling procedures for each case:

- The first and most fundamental problem that a cookie may have is an invalid signature. After an endpoint does a hash upon the inbound cookie and its secret key, it may find that the signature does not match. In this case the entire

SCTP packet should be silently discarded, and no association should be formed.

- If the cookie passes the signature test, the next thing that *must* be done is to verify that it is not stale. A stale cookie *could* indicate a replay attack. The receiver of the cookie must carefully validate the current time against the time the cookie was created and the valid cookie life. It may also wish to take into consideration any time extension that was asked for by the sender of the cookie (in the initial INIT and codified into the cookie itself). If the cookie proves to be stale, the endpoint should create an ERROR chunk with the type of error set to *Stale cookie*. It may also indicate the number of microseconds that the cookie is stale, so that the sender can request more time on the next attempt.

- Once the cookie is verified, the next thing that may cause a cookie receiver to reject a cookie is a no-resource condition. There are a number of resource shortages that may cause this, all of which are implementation dependent.

- Another thing that may occur is a problem with the address resolution. If the SCTP stack *does support* the hostname address, at this point the SCTP stack would attempt to resolve the hostname into a list of IP addresses. If the name resolution attempt fails, an ABORT chunk should be sent to the peer with the *Unresolvable address* error cause set.[14]

## 4.7  Handling Unexpected Initialization Chunks

We have now looked at how an association initializes and seen a couple of places where errors can occur in the setup procedures. One of the challenges with a four-way handshake is the possibility for overlapping of the initialization chunks (that is, INIT, INIT-ACK, COOKIE-ECHO, and COOKIE-ACK chunks). With four chunks being sent, we have sixteen distinct cases that in theory could occur. In reality the number of overlapping cases has been minimized and there are not quite so many, but all of these cases are required to be dealt with properly. In this section we will examine the overlapping scenarios and detail how they are treated and what they mean.

We define overlapping as when an SCTP endpoint holds a TCB for an association with a peer and receives another initialization chunk from the same peer.

Basically this overlapping can occur for a number of reasons:

---

14. Note that name resolution is **not** requested until the cookie arrives to prevent a resource attack.

- The two endpoints attempted to send INIT or COOKIE-ECHO chunks at about the same time (that is, an initialization collision).

- The remote peer endpoint has died and, before the local endpoint detects the failure, restarted itself and is now attempting to set up a new association with the local endpoint (that is, the restart case).

- An evil third endpoint (attacker) is attempting to spoof its way in and disrupt communication between the two legitimate endpoints (that is, the attacker case).

- After being delayed in the network, an old stale SCTP packet from either a previous association between the same pair or from this current association setup finally shows up at the local endpoint (that is, the stale chunk case).

- The network lost one of the initialization chunks of the current association setup (that is, the lost chunk case).

### 4.7.1    Association Tie-Tags and Their Values

To assist an endpoint in dealing with the initialization chunk overlapping cases, an additional pair of tags (called tie-tags), one for each of the two endpoints, is always included as part of a *State cookie*. Combined with the two verification tags, we get a total of four association variables that are the key to an endpoint distinguishing and correctly handling various overlapping cases:

- The local endpoint's *Verification tag* (*VT_local*)

- The peer's *Verification tag* (*VT_peer*)

- The local endpoint's *Tie-tag* (*TT_local*)

- The peer's *Tie-tag* (*TT_peer*)

Each tag is a 32-bit unsigned integer. The two verification tags are normally stored in the TCB at the endpoint, while, as mentioned earlier, the two tie-tags are always present in the *State cookie* when an endpoint sends out an INIT-ACK.

Now let us go through a **normal** association setup process to see how these tags are used and how their values change.

The values of *VT_local* and *VT_peer* are always initiated to zero when a new TCB is created at the initiator endpoint. Once the endpoint has formed and sent out the INIT to a peer, it will update the *VT_local* in the TCB with the value of the *Initiation tag* carried in the outbound INIT.

When responding to the INIT, the peer (with which the initiator endpoint has no association, as always should be in a **normal** situation) will first create a temporary TCB and then send back an INIT-ACK carrying a *State cookie*, as we discussed in Section 4.2. When forming the temporary TCB, among other things, the peer will fill the *VT_ peer* with the value of the *Initiation tag* found in the arrived INIT and fill the *VT_local* with the value of the *Initiation tag* to be used in the outbound INIT-ACK. Inside the *State cookie*, the value of the two tie-tags, namely *TT_local* and *TT_ peer*, will be set to zero.

When the INIT-ACK, with the *State cookie* inside, comes back to the initiator endpoint, it will copy the value of the *Initiation tag* out from the arrived INIT-ACK into the *VT_ peer* of the local TCB and move the association into the COOKIE_ECHOED state after answering back with the COOKIE-ECHO.

When this COOKIE_ECHO arrives, the peer will unpack the *State cookie*, create a permanent TCB out of it for the new association, and send the peer a COOKIE-ACK chunk, as we already learned in Section 4.4.

Finally, the COOKIE-ACK will arrive at the sender of the COOKIE-ECHO, and this will move it into the **ESTABLISHED** state.

It should now be clear that after a **normal** association initialization has been completed and both endpoints have moved into the ESTABLISHED state, the verification tags in their respective TCB will have the *VT_local* filled with the value of their own *Verification tag* and have the *VT_ peer* filled with their respective peer's *Verification tag* value. In addition, both the *TT_local* and *TT_ peer* used in the *State cookie* will have their values set to zero.

### 4.7.2   Handling Overlapping Initialization Chunks

We are now ready to discuss how to handle various overlapping cases correctly when an endpoint is in one of the three "front" states, which include the COOKIE_WAIT, COOKIE_ECHOED, and ESTABLISHED states. The handling of unexpected control chunks in the "back" states (that is, states entered in the association shutdown process) will be discussed in Chapter 9.

In the following subsections we describe the handling rules for various overlapping cases. Later on we will go through some overlapping examples to show how these rules are applied.

#### 4.7.2.1   *Handling Overlapping INIT Chunks*

The rules for handling an overlapping INIT chunk differ depending on the state in which the endpoint currently is.

In the COOKIE_WAIT state, the rules are as follows:

The endpoint will need to build a *State cookie* out of the information existing in its local TCB and then send the *State cookie* in an INIT-ACK to the peer endpoint. Moreover, the existing TCB, including all its current content, will remain unchanged during and after the processing.

The endpoint will follow the normal procedure of building a *State cookie* and sending out INIT-ACK, with just one important exception—instead of using a newly generated random number, the *Initiation tag* carried in the outbound INIT-ACK will take the value of the existing *VT_local* in the local TCB. In addition, the *Verification tag* in the SCTP common header of the outbound SCTP packet that carries the INIT-ACK will take the value of the *Initiation tag* found in the overlapping INIT. Other parameters such as *Initial TSN* and the number of streams requested should also be left the same as those found in the existing TCB.

Therefore, when the INIT-ACT is finally sent out, the tags inside the outbound SCTP packet will have the following values:

- *Verification tag* in SCTP common header = value of the *Initiation tag* copied out from the received overlapping INIT

- *Initiation tag* in INIT-ACK = value of the *VT_local* copied out from the existing TCB

- *VT_local* in the cookie = value of the *VT_local* copied out from the existing TCB

- *VT_peer* in the cookie = value of the *Initiation tag* copied out from the received overlapping INIT

- *TT_local* in the cookie = *VT_local*

- *TT_peer* in the cookie = 0

In the COOKIE_ECHOED state, the rules are as follows:

The handling procedure will be the same as that used in the COOKIE_WAIT state, with the only exception being that the tie-tags in the *State cookie* will be filled with the existing *Verification tag* values in the TCB. In other words, the tags in the outbound SCTP packet will take the following values:

- *Verification tag* in SCTP common header = value of the *Initiation tag* copied out from the received overlapping INIT

- *Initiation tag* in INIT-ACK = value of the *VT_local* copied out from the existing TCB

- *VT_local* in the cookie = value of the *VT_local* copied out from the existing TCB

- *VT_peer* in the cookie = value of the *Initiation tag* copied out from the received overlapping INIT

- *TT_local* in the cookie = value of the *VT_local* copied out from the existing TCB

- *TT_peer* in the cookie = value of the *VT_peer* copied out from the existing TCB

In the ESTABLISHED state, the rules are as follows:

The handling procedure will be the same as that used in the COOKIE_ECHOED state, with the only exception being that the *Initiation tag* in the outbound INIT-ACK will be a newly generated random number; that is, the existing *VT_local* is not reused in this case.

Therefore, the tags in the outbound SCTP packet will take the following values when the packet is sent out to the peer:

- *Verification tag* in SCTP common header = value of the *Initiation tag* copied out from the received overlapping INIT

- *Initiation tag* in INIT-ACK = a newly generated random tag

- *VT_local* in the cookie = value of the *Initiation tag* in INIT-ACK

- *VT_peer* in the cookie = value of the *Initiation tag* copied out from the received overlapping INIT

- *TT_local* in the cookie = value of the *VT_local* copied out from the existing TCB

- *TT_peer* in the cookie = value of the *VT_peer* copied out from the existing TCB

| | |
|---|---|
| *Note* | It is very important and worthwhile to repeat that in all these cases, *the local TCB, including all its content and the state of the local endpoint, will remain unchanged throughout the process, and the endpoint will take no other action after sending out the INIT-ACK.* |

### 4.7.2.2   Handling Overlapping INIT-ACK Chunks

The handling of an overlapping INIT-ACK is rather simple. If the chunk is received by an endpoint in any state other than the COOKIE_WAIT state, the endpoint will simply ignore the INIT-ACK chunk by silently discarding it. In the COOKIE_WAIT state, the INIT-ACK is expected and it is handled as part of the normal procedure described in Section 4.3.

### 4.7.2.3   Handling Overlapping COOKIE-ECHO Chunks

The handling of an overlapping COOKIE-ECHO is a little bit complex. In fact, the purpose of introducing and maintaining the tie-tags in the *State cookie* is solely for facilitating the handling of overlapping COOKIE-ECHO chunks. Fortunately, the handling procedure is the same in all three "front" states.

This handling procedure is centered on examining and comparing the two verification tags in the local TCB and the tags carried in the SCTP packet containing the overlapping COOKIE-ECHO chunk.

Table 4–1 encompasses all of those cases where the COOKIE-ECHO needs to be handled. In other cases (that is, those not covered by the table), the arrival of a COOKIE-ECHO indicates either an attacker case or an old stale COOKIE-ECHO chunk case, and the SCTP packet containing the COOKIE-ECHO will be ignored and silently dropped by the endpoint.

The rationale behind the case classification and handling procedures defined in Table 4–1 will become clearer when we go through the examples later in this section.

The procedures are defined as follows.

> *Procedure A*: In this case both *TT_local* and *TT_peer* get a match and thus confirm a "tie" to the old (previously existing) association, validating that the peer has restarted[15].

To handle this situation, the endpoint will normally first report the peer restart to its upper layer. It will then repopulate its local TCB with information unpacked from the received *State cookie*. This in effect replaces the old (previously existing) association with a new one built from the *State cookie*. When rebuilding the association, the endpoint may, at its option, requeue any data that was in transit in the old association.

> *Procedure B*: This case indicates an initialization collision; that is, the two endpoints are attempting to set up an association to each other at about the same time. In some instances, one side may have also lost an initialization SCTP packet in transit.

To handle this case, the endpoint receiving the *State cookie* should adopt the parameters carried in the cookie, updating any values such as the peer's *Verification tag*. The peer's *Verification tag* in the cookie may well be the most noteworthy item that the endpoint needs to adopt, as we will see in subsequent discussions.

> *Procedure C*: This indicates a rather unique initialization collision case, where the peer initiated its own setup sequence right after it responded to the INIT

---

15. A restart may be the result of an application restarting, recovery from a network outage, or a host computer restart.

**Table 4–1** Tag Comparison in Unexpected Cookie Processing

| TCB: VT_local vs. CK: VT_local | TCB: VT_peer vs. CK: VT_peer | TCB: VT_local vs. CK:TT_local | TCB: VT_peer vs. CK:TT_peer | Possible Cause of Event | Handling Procedure |
|---|---|---|---|---|---|
| X | X | M | M | Peer restarted | A |
| M | X | A | A | Setup collision | B |
| M | 0 | A | A | Setup collision | B |
| X | M | 0 | 0 | Setup collision | C |
| M | M | A | A | Lost chunk | D |

Legend:

X = The value in the *State cookie* does not match that in the TCB
M = The value in the *State cookie* matches that in the TCB
0 = The value of the *Tie-tag* is not filled into the *State cookie*
A = Any of the above (that is, X, M, or 0)

*Note* During a restart the peer is allowed to change its inbound and outbound stream parameters, such as *OS* and *MIS*. The local endpoint needs to take this possibility into account if it chooses to requeue any unsent data from the old association.

from the local endpoint. We will have a detailed description of this scenario later in this section.

To handle this case, the local endpoint must ignore (that is, silently discard) the received SCTP packet, including the *State cookie*.

*Procedure D*: This usually indicates a lost COOKIE-ACK in the network, as we will see later.

When handling this case, the local endpoint cannot use any value from the received *State cookie*. However, the local endpoint needs to immediately resend a COOKIE-ACK to the peer and move itself into the ESTABLISHED state if it hasn't done so.

#### 4.7.2.4    Handling Overlapping COOKIE-ACK Chunks

The handling of an overlapping COOKIE-ACK chunk entails simply ignoring the chunk if the endpoint is in any state other than COOKIE_ECHOED. In the COOKIE_ECHOED state, the arrival of a COOKIE-ACK is expected and is hence handled as part of the normal association setup.

### 4.7.3    Case Study 1: Initialization Collision

In this section we will walk through some variations of the initialization case and show how the rules and handling procedures we discussed earlier work.

#### 4.7.3.1    Colliding Initialization Scenario 1

The simplest scenario begins when two independent endpoints want to establish an association to one another at about the same time, with one end starting slightly ahead of the other. Figure 4–12 shows one of these INIT collision situations.

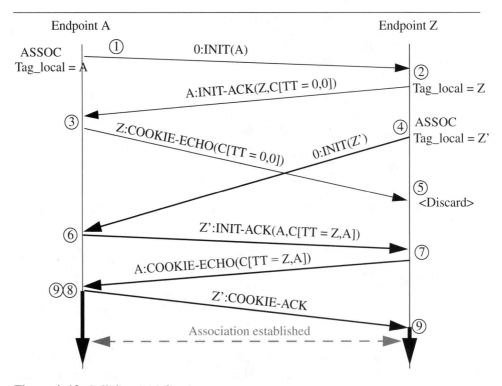

**Figure 4–12** *Colliding initialization*

Here are the "blow-by-blow" details:

1. Endpoint A starts the sequence by choosing $VT\_local$ = A and sending an INIT to endpoint Z. Endpoint A then enters the COOKIE_WAIT state.

2. Endpoint Z receives the INIT and responds with an INIT-ACK in the normal fashion, generating a random $VT\_local$ = Z, building a cookie, and sending the INIT-ACK with the cookie that contains $VT\_local$ = Z, $VT\_peer$ = A, and $TT\_local$ = $TT\_peer$ = 0. After sending off the INIT-ACK, endpoint Z destroys any record of the association request and temporary TCB.

3. Endpoint A receives the INIT-ACK. It first uploads all relevant association parameters carried in the INIT-ACK into the TCB, including coping out the *Initiation tag* (= Z) from the INIT-ACK into the $VT\_peer$ variable in the TCB. Then it responds to endpoint Z with a COOKIE-ECHO and enters the COOKIED_ECHOED state. So far, everything is normal.

4. Now, suddenly endpoint Z's application decides to create an association with endpoint A. Here the collision begins.

   Endpoint Z, not knowing about the INIT-ACK it previously sent, generates another random $VT\_local$ = Z' and sends off its own INIT to bring up an association with endpoint A. After sending off the INIT, endpoint Z enters into the COOKIE_WAIT state.

5. At this point, the COOKIE-ECHO from endpoint A arrives at endpoint Z unexpectedly. Using the procedure in Section 4.7.2.3 to examine the tag values, endpoint Z finds that both the $VT\_local$ (= Z) and $VT\_peer$ (= A) in the received *State cookie* do not match the $VT\_local$ (= Z') and $VT\_peer$ (= 0) in the TCB, and both tie-tags in the cookie are zero. This matches no case in the table, and therefore endpoint Z silently discards the COOKIE-ECHO chunk.

6. In the meantime, endpoint A receives the INIT from endpoint Z unexpectedly and recognizes that it is in the COOKIE_ECHOED state. So it takes the action described in Section 4.7.2.1 and replies with an INIT-ACK that contains a cookie with $VT\_local$ = A, $VT\_peer$ = Z', $TT\_local$ = A, and $TT\_peer$ = Z. Of course, the *Verification tag* and the *Initiation tag* in the outbound SCTP packet are also set to Z' and A, respectively.

7. When endpoint Z receives this INIT-ACK, following the normal procedure, it uploads all relevant information from the received INIT-ACK into its TCB, including filling up the $VT\_peer$ in its TCB with the *Initiation tag* value (= A) carried in the received INIT-ACK, and then sends back a COOKIE-ECHO.

8. Endpoint A, still in the COOKIE_ECHOED state, receives this COOKIE-ECHO unexpectedly. Taking the procedure of Section 4.7.2.3 to examine the tag values, endpoint A finds that the *VT_local* (= A) in the cookie matches that in the TCB, but the *VT_peer* (= Z') in the received cookie does not match the *VT_peer* (= Z) in the TCB. This falls under the second case described in Table 4–1; therefore endpoint A performs procedure B and adopts endpoint Z's new tag, Z', and any settings within the cookie. (Note that these may be different than the settings within the original INIT-ACK; in particular, the *Initial TSN* and number of streams may have varied.)

9. At this point endpoint A sends off the COOKIE-ACK and we reach the ESTABLISHED state. Note that endpoint Z will reach the ESTABLISHED state after endpoint A, on reception of the COOKIE-ACK.

### 4.7.3.2   *Colliding Initialization Scenario 2*

A variation of our previous scenario can occur if, due to a network reordering event, the INIT that endpoint Z sends crosses ahead of its previously sent INIT-ACK, as shown in Figure 4–13.

Here is the sequence of events:

1. Endpoint A starts the sequence by choosing a *VT_local* = A and sending an INIT to endpoint Z.

2. Endpoint Z receives the INIT and responds with an INIT-ACK in the normal fashion, generating a random *VT_local* = Z, building a cookie, and sending the INIT-ACK with the cookie that contains *VT_local* = Z, *VT_peer* = A, and *TT_local* = *TT_peer* = 0. After sending off the INIT-ACK, endpoint Z destroys any record of the association request and temporary TCB. But this time the INIT-ACK is to be delayed in the network.

3. Independently, endpoint Z's application suddenly requests an association with endpoint A, and a collision starts. Endpoint Z, not knowing about the INIT-ACK it previously sent, generates another random *VT_local* = Z' and sends off its own INIT to endpoint A. After sending off the INIT, endpoint Z enters into the COOKIE_WAIT state.

4. Still in the COOKIE_WAIT state, endpoint A receives the INIT unexpectedly. According to procedures in Section 4.7.2.1, it builds a *State cookie* containing *VT_local* = A, and *VT_peer* = Z', *TT_local* = A, *TT_peer* = 0, and sends off the INIT-ACK.

5. Then the INIT-ACK that endpoint Z had sent earlier arrives at endpoint A. Following the normal procedure, endpoint A uploads all relevant informa-

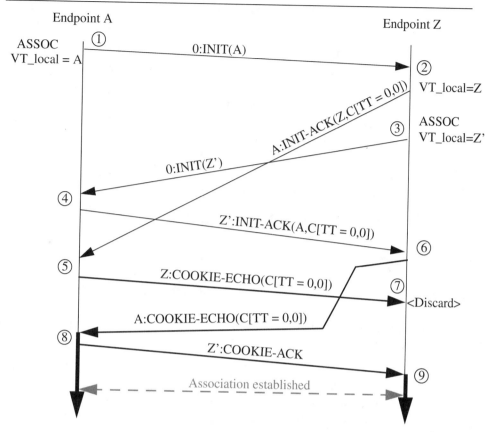

**Figure 4–13** *Colliding initialization with network reordering*

tion from the INIT-ACK into its TCB, including filling up the *VT_peer* in the TCB with the *Initiation tag* (= Z) from the INIT-ACK. Then it sends back a COOKIE-ECHO and enters the COOKIE_ECHOED state.

6. The INIT-ACK that endpoint A sent in step 4 arrives at endpoint Z. Because it is still in the COOKIE_WAIT state, endpoint Z handles this INIT-ACK normally, especially by filling up the *VT_peer* in the TCB with the *Initiation tag* (= A) from the INIT-ACK. Then it sends back a COOKIE-ECHO and enters the COOKIE_ECHOED state.

7. Now, unexpectedly endpoint Z receives the COOKIE-ECHO sent by endpoint A in step 5. Taking the actions described in Section 4.7.2.3, endpoint Z finds that the tags in the received cookie (*VT_local* = Z, and *VT_peer* = A, *TT_local* = 0, *TT_peer* = 0) match only one of the verification tags in its TCB

($VT\_local = Z'$, and $VT\_peer = A$). This case is covered in Table 4–1. End-point Z follows procedure C and discards the unexpected COOKIE-ECHO.[16]

8. The COOKIE-ECHO that endpoint Z sent in step 6 arrives at endpoint A. Because endpoint A is at this point in the COOKIE_ECHOED state, this becomes an overlapping case, and the procedure described in Section 4.7.2.3 is followed. After comparing the tags in the cookie ($VT\_local = A$, and $VT\_peer = TT\_local = TT\_peer = 0$) and the verification tags in its TCB ($VT\_local = A$, and $VT\_peer = Z$), endpoint A recognizes that this falls under the third case in Table 4–1 and hence follows procedure B. Finally, endpoint A sends a COOKIE-ACK to endpoint Z and enters the ESTABLISHED state slightly ahead of endpoint Z.

9. The arrival of COOKIE-ACK moves endpoint Z to the ESTABLISHED state.

### 4.7.3.3   *Colliding Initialization Scenario 3*

Another collision case illustrates what happens when the two INITs actually cross as illustrated in Figure 4–14. Here we see the following sequence of steps occur:

1. Both endpoints send off an INIT to each other, and the two INITs cross in the network.

2. Endpoint A, still in COOKIE_WAIT, unexpectedly receives endpoint Z's INIT message. According to procedures in Section 4.7.2.1, it builds a *State cookie* containing $VT\_local = A$, and $VT\_peer = Z$, $TT\_local = A$, and $TT\_peer = 0$, and sends off the INIT-ACK.

3. Endpoint Z, also in COOKIE_WAIT, unexpectedly receives endpoint A's INIT message. According to procedures in Section 4.7.2.1, it builds a *State cookie* containing $VT\_local = Z$, $VT\_peer = A$, $TT\_local = Z$, and $TT\_peer = 0$, and sends off the INIT-ACK.

4. Each side receives the INIT-ACK from its peer and, following the normal procedure, each endpoint uploads all relevant information from the INIT-ACK into its TCB. This includes filling up the $VT\_peer$ in the TCB with the *Initiation tag* from the INIT-ACK. Then, they each send back a COOKIE-ECHO and enter the COOKIE_ECHOED state.

5. The COOKIE-ECHO that endpoint Z sent in step 4 arrives at endpoint A. Because endpoint A is at this point in the COOKIE_ECHOED state, this becomes an overlapping case, and the procedure described in Section

---

16. Endpoint Z will reach a different decision if this unexpected COOKIE-ECHO arrives before step 6, but it will take the same action, that is, discard the COOKIE-ECHO.

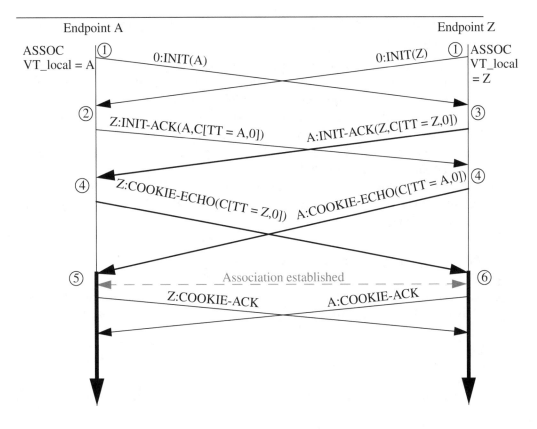

**Figure 4–14** *Crossing INITs*

4.7.2.3 is followed. After comparing the tags in the cookie (*VT_local* = A, and *VT_peer* = Z, *TT_local* = A, *TT_peer* = Z) and the verification tags in its TCB (*VT_local* = A, and *VT_peer* = Z), endpoint A recognizes that this falls under the fifth case in Table 4–1 and hence follows procedure D, moving into the ESTABLISHED state and sending a COOKIE-ACK to endpoint Z.

6. The COOKIE-ECHO that endpoint A sent in step 4 arrives at endpoint Z. Since endpoint Z is also at this point in the COOKIE_ECHOED state, this becomes an overlapping case as well, and the procedure described in Section 4.7.2.3 is followed. After comparing the tags in the cookie (*VT_local* = Z, and *VT_peer* = A, *TT_local* = Z, *TT_peer* = A) and the verification tags in its TCB (*VT_local* = Z, and *VT_peer* = A), endpoint Z recognizes that this falls under the fifth case in Table 4–1 and hence follows procedure D,

moving into the ESTABLISHED state and sending a COOKIE-ACK to endpoint Z.

Note that the two endpoints reached the same conclusion and went through the exact same procedures that they would have for a lost COOKIE-ACK. An end-point can discern the difference between a lost COOKIE-ACK and an INIT colli-sion by noting the tie-tags. In the collision case, the tie-tags will carry the endpoints' local tags, making a complete match as illustrated in steps 5 and 6 above. In the lost COOKIE-ACK case, the tie-tags will not carry the peer's tag.

It is interesting to note that in this case, even though both endpoints sent a COOKIE-ACK, neither one of them will require the COOKIE-ACK to enter the ESTABLISHED state. This means that both COOKIE-ACKs could be lost, and neither would be retransmitted.

### 4.7.3.4   Colliding Initialization Scenario 4

This scenario occurs when one of the two INITs in the previous discussion (sce-nario 3) is lost as illustrated in Figure 4–15. It looks much like the previous case, with a few differences. We see this case when the following steps occur:

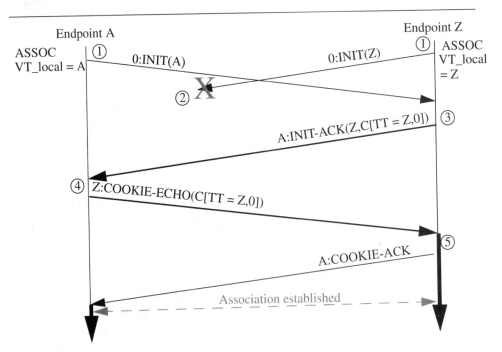

**Figure 4–15** *Colliding initialization with a lost INIT*

1. Each side again transmits an INIT and enters the COOKIE_WAIT state.

2. Endpoint Z's INIT is lost in the network.

3. Endpoint Z, in the COOKIE_WAIT state, unexpectedly receives endpoint A's INIT message. According to procedures in Section 4.7.2.1, it builds a *State cookie* containing $VT\_local = Z$, and $VT\_peer = A$, $TT\_local = Z$, and $TT\_peer = 0$, and sends off the INIT-ACK.

4. Endpoint A receives the INIT-ACK, unaware of the duplicate INIT scenario occurring. Following the normal procedure, endpoint A uploads all relevant information from the INIT-ACK into its TCB, including filling up the $VT\_peer$ in the TCB with the *Initiation tag* $(= Z)$ from the INIT-ACK. Then it sends back a COOKIE-ECHO and enters the COOKIE_ECHOED state.

5. The COOKIE-ECHO that endpoint A sent in step 4 arrives at endpoint Z. Because endpoint Z is also at this point in the COOKIE_WAIT state, this becomes an overlapping case as well, and the procedure described in Section 4.7.2.3 is followed. After comparing the tags in the cookie ($VT\_local = Z$, and $VT\_peer = A$, $TT\_local = Z$, $TT\_peer = 0$) and the verification tags in its TCB ($VT\_local = Z$, and $VT\_peer = 0$), endpoint Z recognizes that this falls under the third case in Table 4–1 and hence follows procedure B, moving into the ESTABLISHED state and sending a COOKIE-ACK to endpoint A.

Note that in this case the loss of the COOKIE-ACK in the network would cause a retransmission of the COOKIE-ECHO, and the lost COOKIE-ACK case would occur (as illustrated in Figure 4–18). Note also that if instead of the original INIT from endpoint Z being lost, the INIT-ACK from endpoint A was lost, the same scenario would occur.

### 4.7.3.5   Colliding Initialization Scenario 5

This case is similar to the previous one, except that in this case the network drops one of the COOKIE-ECHO chunks. This case is illustrated in Figure 4–16.

We see this case when the following steps occur:

1. Both endpoints send off an INIT to each other, and the two INITs cross in the network. Both endpoints enter the COOKIE_WAIT state.

2. Endpoint A, still in COOKIE_WAIT, unexpectedly receives endpoint Z's INIT message. According to procedures in Section 4.7.2.1, it builds a *State cookie* containing $VT\_local = A$, and $VT\_peer = Z$, $TT\_local = A$, and $TT\_peer = 0$, and sends off the INIT-ACK.

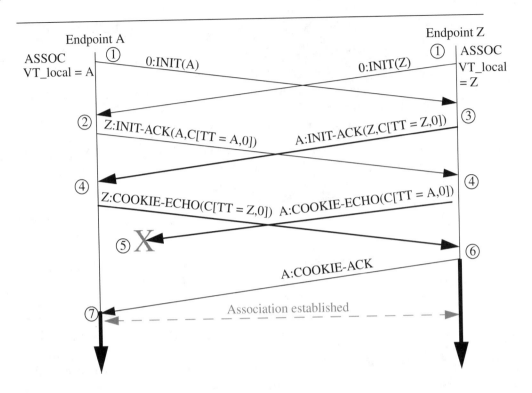

**Figure 4–16** *Colliding initialization with a lost COOKIE-ECHO*

3. Endpoint Z, also in the COOKIE_WAIT state, unexpectedly receives end-point A's INIT message. According to procedures in Section 4.7.2.1, it builds a *State cookie* containing $VT\_local$ = Z, and $VT\_peer$ = A, $TT\_local$ = Z, and $TT\_peer$ = 0, and sends off the INIT-ACK.

4. Each side receives the INIT-ACK from its peer and, following the normal procedure, the endpoints uploads all relevant information from the INIT-ACK into their TCBs. This includes filling up the $VT\_peer$ in the TCB with the *Initiation tag* from the INIT-ACK. Then they both send back a COOKIE-ECHO and enter the COOKIE_ECHOED state.

5. Endpoint Z's COOKIE-ECHO is lost in the network.

6. The COOKIE-ECHO that endpoint A sent in step 4 arrives at endpoint Z. Because endpoint Z is also at this point in the COOKIE_ECHOED state, this becomes an overlapping case as well, and the procedure described in Section 4.7.2.3 is followed. After comparing the tags in the cookie ($VT\_local$ = Z, and $VT\_peer$ = A, $TT\_local$ = Z, $TT\_peer$ = 0) and the ver-

ification tags in its TCB (*VT_local* = Z, and *VT_ peer* = 0), endpoint Z recognizes that this falls under the third case in Table 4–1 and hence follows procedure B, moving into the ESTABLISHED state and sending a COOKIE-ACK to endpoint A.

7. Finally, with the arrival of the COOKIE-ACK sent in step 6, endpoint *A* moves into the ESTABLISHED state.

Note again that the loss of the COOKIE-ACK sent by endpoint Z would result in the lost COOKIE-ACK scenario, because endpoint A is not aware of the lost COOKIE-ECHO of endpoint Z.

### 4.7.4   Case Study 2: Peer Restart

One of the more common cases that is likely to be seen is when one endpoint restarts before the other detects it. After restarting, the endpoint then sends an INIT to the old peer, which looks in its internal TCB table and finds an existing association. The scenario looks as depicted in Figure 4–17.

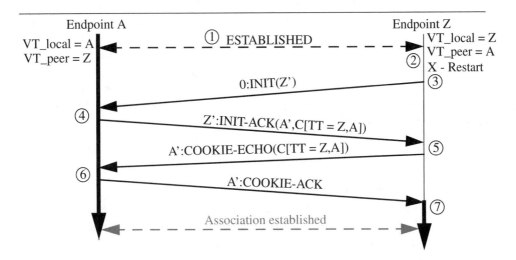

**Figure 4–17** *A restart*

Here we see that a typical restart has occurred. Endpoint A has an established association with endpoint Z. For some reason (not shown here) endpoint Z restarts and then sends an INIT to endpoint A to bring up an association. This all occurs before the normal heartbeats being sent by endpoint A can detect that endpoint Z has failed. What we see occur here is detailed as follows:

1. Endpoint A and endpoint Z are established with tags A and Z, respectively.

2. Endpoint Z restarts for some unspecified reason.

3. Endpoint Z chooses $VT\_local = Z'$ and sends an INIT to endpoint A.

4. In the ESTABLISHED state, endpoint A receives the INIT unexpectedly. According to procedures in Section 4.7.2.1, it builds a *State cookie*, choosing a new tag $VT\_local = A'$. It populates the *State cookie* with $VT\_local = A'$, and $VT\_peer = Z'$, $TT\_local = A$, and $TT\_peer = Z$, and sends off the INIT-ACK.

5. Endpoint Z receives the INIT-ACK, unaware of the previous association, and follows the normal procedure. Endpoint Z uploads all relevant information from the INIT-ACK into its TCB, including filling up the $VT\_peer$ in the TCB with the *Initiation tag* ($= A'$) from the INIT-ACK. Then it sends back a COOKIE-ECHO and enters the COOKIE_ECHOED state.

6. The COOKIE-ECHO that endpoint Z sent in step 5 arrives at endpoint A. Because endpoint A is also at this point in the ESTABLISHED state, this becomes an overlapping case, and the procedure described in Section 4.7.2.3 is followed. After comparing the tags in the cookie ($VT\_local = A'$, and $VT\_peer = Z'$, $TT\_local = A$, $TT\_peer = Z$) and the verification tags in its TCB ($VT\_local = A$, and $VT\_peer = Z$), endpoint A recognizes that this falls under the first case in Table 4–1 and hence follows procedure A, the restart case. This causes endpoint A to restart its association and send a COOKIE-ACK to endpoint Z. Note that throughout this procedure endpoint A remains in the ESTABLISHED state.

7. Finally, with the arrival of the COOKIE-ACK sent in step 6, endpoint Z moves into the ESTABLISHED state.

Notice the application of the new tags A' and Z' in this scenario. These protect the newly forming association from old stale data. In particular, if endpoint Z had queued into the network an ABORT that was delayed, the stale ABORT (if the old tag A were retained) would destroy the new association.

*Note*   One important issue in this scenario is that endpoint Z must not add new addresses to the association. If endpoint A detects new addresses, it is required to ignore the INIT-ACK when it arrives. This prevents a potential denial-of-service attack, in which an attacker sends in a false "new INIT" and adds its address to the list of valid addresses in the association.

### 4.7.5   A Lost COOKIE-ACK

Another possible scenario is a lost COOKIE-ACK during the startup sequence. These events are illustrated in Figure 4–18 and described as follows.

1.  Endpoint A starts the sequence by choosing $VT\_local$ = A and sending an INIT to endpoint Z. It then enters the COOKIE_WAIT state.

2.  Endpoint Z receives the INIT and responds with an INIT-ACK in the normal fashion, generating a random $VT\_local$ = Z, building a cookie, and sending the INIT-ACK with the cookie that contains $VT\_local$ = Z, $VT\_peer$ = A, and $TT\_local$ = $TT\_peer$ = 0. After sending off the INIT-ACK, endpoint Z destroys any record of the association request and temporary TCB.

3.  Endpoint A receives the INIT-ACK. Following the normal procedure, endpoint A uploads all relevant information from the INIT-ACK into its TCB, including filling up the $VT\_peer$ in the TCB with the *Initiation tag* (= Z) from the INIT-ACK. Then it sends back a COOKIE-ECHO and enters the COOKIE_ECHOED state.

4.  The COOKIE-ECHO that endpoint A sent in step 3 arrives at endpoint Z. Endpoint Z follows normal procedures and uploads all relevant information from the COOKIE-ECHO into a new TCB, including filling up the $VT\_peer$ in the TCB with the *Initiation tag* (= A) from the INIT-ACK. Then it sends back a COOKIE-ACK and enters the ESTABLISHED state.

5.  The COOKIE-ACK is lost in the network.

6.  A timeout occurs in endpoint A, still in the COOKIE_ECHOED state, and so endpoint A retransmits the COOKIE-ECHO to endpoint Z.

7.  The COOKIE-ECHO that endpoint A retransmitted in step 6 arrives at endpoint Z. Because endpoint Z is already at this point in the ESTABLISHED state, this becomes an overlapping case, and the procedure described in Section 4.7.2.3 is followed. After comparing the tags in the cookie ($VT\_local$ = A, and $VT\_peer$ = Z, $TT\_local$ = 0, $TT\_peer$ = 0) and the verification tags in its TCB ($VT\_local$ = A, and $VT\_peer$ = Z), endpoint A recognizes that this falls under the fifth case in Table 4–1 and hence follows procedure D. This causes endpoint Z to send a COOKIE-ACK to endpoint A.

8.  Finally, with the arrival of the COOKIE-ACK retransmitted in step 7, endpoint A moves into the ESTABLISHED state.

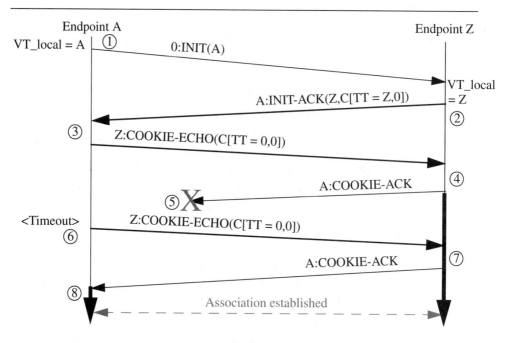

**Figure 4–18** *A lost COOKIE-ACK*

## 4.8   IETF Debate and Issues

At the conclusion of the IETF in Oslo, Scott Bradner (in a private conversation) strongly recommended that we look at the use of an encryption cookie. With the "chunking" of the protocol (in Santa Clara), it was simple to add a "cookie chunk" and insert the last leg of the handshake, the "cookie acknowledgment," as a separate chunk type. Following the interim meeting (in Santa Clara) much debate ensued on which type of signature to use: MD5, SHA-1, or something else. In the end, Krawcyk, Bellare, and Canetti (1997) was brought in as a reference for how to do the signing, and the choice of signature method was left open with only a recommendation but no strong requirement. In particular it was felt that the cookie itself could become an attack. If you were forced to use a particular cookie mechanism such as MD5 or SHA-1, without hardware support, an attacker could attack your CPU instead of your system's memory limits, making the SCTP stack spend all its time performing hashing algorithms on worthless cookies. Leaving the choice open allows a flexibility in the individual implementation to protect against the appropriate threat for the environment in which it is designed to operate.

One idea that did *not* survive to make it into the final specification was the dynamic stream open. The fundamental idea was to allow either endpoint to add new streams "on the fly" to the association. After much debate this was removed from the protocol. It was seen as unnecessary, because streams in themselves are *not* a costly concept to implement. Moreover it added a great deal of complexity to the protocol. By the Oslo IETF in 1999 the design team had reached a *stormy* consensus on the removal of dynamic streams.

Another idea that did *not* survive into the final protocol was the ability to proxy responses on an INIT or INIT-ACK. The concept was *not* to list the sender's address in one of these initial chunks, and thus *not* have the sender included in the new forming association. This may have been a useful feature, but the potential for abuses was a major concern; the mechanism was seen as adding an undesirable denial-of-service potential. In January 2000 the current requirement that the sender of an INIT or INIT-ACK be automatically considered part of the association, even if the sender's addresses were not listed within the INIT or INIT-ACK chunk, was added back into the protocol. (It had been taken out earlier to make way for this proxy concept.)

One crucial idea that made SCTP a better choice than some of the other protocol proposals was its ability to bundle DATA chunks on the third and fourth leg of the four-way handshake. This helps reduce the latency associated with the traditional three-way handshake, even when a fourth leg is added.

The *Hostname address type* parameter was another *hotly* debated issue. The idea behind this is to make the protocol easier for Network Address Translators (NATs). However, supporting this feature is quite difficult for an implementation of SCTP that resides within the operating system. The reason is that DNS (the system normally used for hostname resolution) is a user-level process. This means that in order to do a hostname resolution, the kernel (or operating system) must do an up-call to a user-level process, holding the initialization of the TCB for the completion of the resolution. After a *spirited* debate, a compromise was reached, allowing this feature to be disabled by either placing a *Supported Address Type* parameter in the INIT chunk or by sending an ABORT if the receiver of an INIT does not support the hostname address feature and the INIT includes a hostname address.

A final late development in the INIT sequence was with the tie-tags within the cookie. Originally, during a restart, the endpoint that did *not restart* retained its same tags and TSN sequence number. However this caused a problem in that an old SCTP packet could still infiltrate the restarted association. The current tie-tags were added to allow the *non-restarting* endpoint to choose new tags and sequence numbers yet still be able to recognize the restart condition.

## 4.9   Summary

We have looked at the association setup sequences and how the four initial SCTP packets are generated and used. Each of the chunks may arrive in various orders and collide as endpoints attempt to bring up associations with each other at the same time. The four-way handshake, though complex, provides a measure of security against a blind attacker. It has also been designed to be robust even in the case of SCTP packet loss.

## 4.10   Questions

1.   How does the *State cookie* mechanism protect two endpoints from a blind attacker?

2.   Can user data and the INIT-ACK chunk be sent in the same SCTP packet?

3.   Can user data and the COOKIE-ECHO chunk be sent in the same SCTP packet?

4.   When responding to an INIT, where should the endpoint send the INIT-ACK?

5.   What are the **initialization chunks**? What are the possible causes if one of these initialization chunks arrives *unexpectedly* at an endpoint?

6.   What are the **tie-tags** and where are they normally stored? Explain their purpose.

# 5

# User Data Transfer

$\mathbf{A}$fter the completion of the association initiation process described in the previous chapter, we have an established SCTP association between the two endpoints. Normal bidirectional data transfer can start once the association is in the ESTABLISHED state. (Note that there are a few exceptions in which transfer can happen outside the ESTABLISHED state. We will detail those special cases in later chapters.)

In the following section we give an overview on the process of sending and receiving user messages across an SCTP association. Detailed discussions on user message transfer is deferred to the later sections.

## 5.1   User Message Transfer Overview

### 5.1.1   How User Messages Are Sent

Figure 5–1 depicts the passage of the outbound messages through the SCTP sender.

#### 5.1.1.1   Converting User Messages into Data Chunks

As you can see in Figure 5–1, user messages passed to the SCTP layer for transmission will first be converted into SCTP DATA chunks. This conversion process can take two different courses, depending on the size of the user message.

When the user message is small enough, the conversion is simply to add a DATA chunk header to the message, forming a single DATA chunk.

When the user message is bigger than a certain threshold, the message will be first broken into several small parts, and then each of them will be converted into a

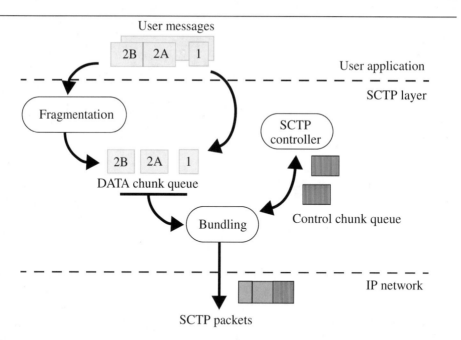

**Figure 5–1**  *Outbound message passage in SCTP*

separate DATA chunk. This process is termed **fragmentation** of the user message. The size threshold used to determine whether a user message is too big, and thus should be fragmented, is normally the current Path Maximum Transmission Unit (PMTU). We will discuss more details on user message fragmentation using the PMTU in Section 5.8.

To add the DATA chunk header to the user message (or to part of a fragmented user message), one must also fill in the stream identifier of the outbound stream to which the message belongs. If the message is an ordered message, the sender will also need to assign a stream sequence number (SSN) to the message and put the SSN into the DATA header *Stream sequence number* field, as shown in Figure 5–2.

If it is a large user message being converted into multiple DATA chunks because of fragmentation, the same stream sequence number will be shared among all the DATA chunks.

For unordered user message, the sender will not assign an SSN. Therefore, the *Stream sequence number* field in a DATA chunk that is carrying an unordered message will remain unspecific, meaning the receiver should ignore that field.

Regardless of whether it is carrying an ordered or unordered user data payload, each DATA chunk will be assigned a TSN before its transmission.

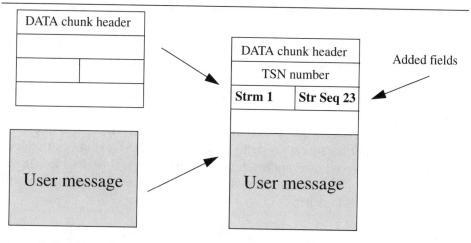

**Figure 5–2** *Adding the stream and sequence numbers*

When a large message is fragmented, it is important to note that consecutive TSNs *are required to* be assigned to the fragments in the order of the fragmentation. Otherwise, the message receiver may not be able to correctly regenerate the original user message even if it receives all the parts. More details on message fragmentation will be discussed in Section 5.8.

After the assignment of the SSN and TSN, the DATA chunk, regardless of the stream it belongs to, is normally put in a chunk queue. DATA chunks in this chunk queue are normally arranged according to their TSN order.

An empty user message is not allowed. In other words, the data sender is not allowed to transmit a DATA chunk with no user data under any circumstances. Transmission of such a chunk will cause the peer endpoint to abort the association.

### 5.1.1.2 Forming SCTP Packets from Chunks

The SCTP sender passes data to the IP layer in what we call **SCTP packets**, as shown in Figure 5–1.

As you may recall from our discussion in Section 3.1.1, an SCTP packet is composed of an SCTP common header and one or more SCTP chunks. The SCTP common header is composed of the source and destination SCTP ports, the receiver's *Verification tag*, and a checksum field. SCTP chunks are either composed of control or user data. Table 3–1 details all the currently defined SCTP chunks.

When the time comes to send data, the SCTP layer will form SCTP packets out of the queued SCTP chunks. These SCTP packets will include both the DATA chunks and SCTP control chunks (if there are any in the control chunk queue) as shown in Figure 5–1.

To achieve high data-transfer efficiency, the SCTP layer will always attempt to **bundle** as many control chunks and DATA chunks into the SCTP packet as possible.[1] The size of the resultant SCTP packet (plus the size of the IP header that will be added later after the SCTP packet is passed to the IP layer) should not exceed the current PMTU.

An application may request that no bundling be performed; if it does, the SCTP stack will not introduce any delay when sending DATA chunks to achieve bundling. This, however, does not mean that all **bundling** will be disabled. In the face of congestion or flow control from the remote peer, the SCTP stack may still bundle DATA chunks together.

> *Note*    When there are both control and DATA chunks waiting for transmission, the control chunks will always take precedence over the DATA chunks when the SCTP packet is being formed.

In other words, the DATA chunks are added to the SCTP packet only after all the pending control chunks are included and if there is still room left. When both types of chunks are bundled in one SCTP packet, the control chunk(s) will always be positioned before any DATA chunks. (Note that some control chunks are not allowed to be bundled with DATA chunks. See the corresponding sections for details on those restrictions.)

Figure 5–3 illustrates an SCTP packet bundled with both control and DATA chunks.

### 5.1.1.3   *Passing SCTP Packets to IP Layer*

When an SCTP packet is formed, it will be passed to the IP layer for its final transmission onto the network. An IP header will be prefixed to each SCTP packet by the IP layer. Each IP header will contain information such as the source and destination IP address of the resultant IP datagram, etcetra See Postel (1981a) and Deering and Hinden (1998) for details on IP datagram formats.

In Figure 5–4 we show an example of the anatomy of an IP datagram generated by an SCTP endpoint. In this example we assume that there are two control chunks and user messages, each of which occupies an SCTP DATA chunk carried in the SCTP packet.

---

1. Note that bundling is an optional feature and therefore may not be supported by all the implementations.

| |
|---|
| Common header |
| Control chunk 1 |
| Control chunk 2 |
| DATA chunk 1 |
| DATA chunk 2 |

**Figure 5–3** *An SCTP packet with both control and DATA chunks*

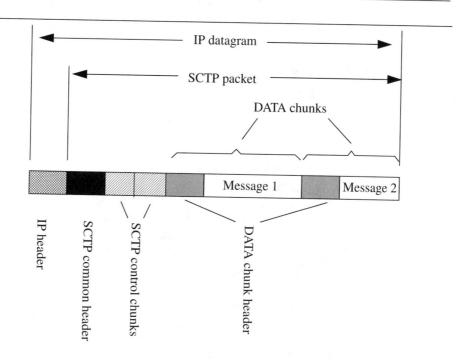

**Figure 5–4** *Typical components in an IP datagram sent by an SCTP endpoint*

## 5.1.2   How User Messages Are Received

In order to recover the original user messages from the received IP datagrams and to dispatch the messages to the user application in the correct order, the SCTP receiver will need to perform unbundling, reassembly, and reordering on the received data.

The SCTP receiver also needs to acknowledge the reception of each DATA chunk to the SCTP sender and to report any missing or duplicate DATA chunks.

### 5.1.2.1  Recovering User Messages from a Received Packet

When the IP datagram (containing an SCTP packet) arrives at the receiving endpoint, the IP layer at the endpoint will strip off[2] the IP header and then present the SCTP packet to the SCTP layer. The inbound data passage at the receiver is illustrated in Figure 5–5.

As shown in Figure 5–5, the SCTP layer will first unbundle the SCTP packages into control chunks and DATA chunks. The control chunks are forwarded to the protocol controller for further processing. The DATA chunks are stripped off their chunk header, and the recovered user messages are put into the corresponding stream's reordering queue for final dispatch to the user application.

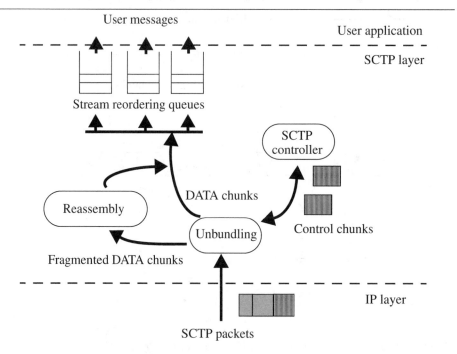

**Figure 5–5**  *Inbound message passage in the SCTP receiver*

---

2. The IP header will still be available for the SCTP layer to consult, even though the IP header is "conceptually" stripped from the IP datagram.

### 5.1.2.2   Reassembling Fragmented User Messages

For those arrived DATA chunks that do not carry a complete user message, that is, when the user data part of the DATA chunks contains only part of a user message due to the fragmentation process at the message sender side (see the previous section), the SCTP receiver will forward them to a reassembler.

After all the fragments of a user message are found, the reassembler will merge the data parts together to restore the original user message. The restored message will then be passed to the appropriate stream reordering queue for final dispatch.

### 5.1.2.3   Acknowledgment to the SCTP Sender

After sending out a DATA chunk, the SCTP sender will always expect an acknowledgment from the receiver to confirm the reception of this DATA chunk. If it does not receive this acknowledgment within a certain period of time, the SCTP sender will assume the previous transmission of the DATA chunk failed and will attempt another transmission of the same DATA chunk, that is, will **retransmit** the DATA chunk.

To acknowledge the reception of DATA chunks, the message receiver sends a Selective Acknowledgment (SACK) control chunk to the message sender. As you may recall from Section 3.2.5, the sender assigns to each of the outbound DATA chunks a TSN as its unique identifier. When the receiver receives a DATA chunk, it will indicate in the subsequent SACK the reception of the TSN of that DATA chunk. We will leave the details on how and when SACKs are sent to later sections in this chapter.

Once it receives a SACK acknowledging a specific TSN, the message sender will assume the DATA chunk with that particular TSN has been transferred successfully.

### 5.1.3   Summary of Data Transfer Overview

In this section we have given an overview of how user messages are transferred across an established SCTP association. We have discussed that the user messages will first be converted into SCTP DATA chunks, and then will possibly be bundled together with other DATA or control chunks to form SCTP packets. The resultant SCTP packets will then be passed to the IP layer for transmission to the network.

After arriving at the SCTP receiver, the SCTP packets will be unbundled into DATA chunks as well as control chunks, if they are present. The original user messages are then recovered from the DATA chunks and delivered to the application.

Finally, the receiver will acknowledge the reception of all the DATA chunks by sending back SACKs to the message sender.

In the remainder of this chapter we will discuss details of user message transfer. Those readers who are only interested in understanding the basic operation of SCTP can safely skip these details.

## 5.2   Obeying the Transmission Rules

A critically important part of a transport protocol like SCTP is controlling when to send data and how much data to send. This is because, first, the IP network is a packet switched network in which a limited bandwidth is shared by all the users. It would be unfair to the other users if one user were allowed to inject too much data into the network at once. Also, sending too much data in a short period of time will cause traffic congestion in the network and, as a consequence, force the routers in the network to drop IP datagrams. Secondly, the receiver's buffer space is always limited and the sender must avoid overwhelming the receiver by sending too much data at once.

It is also worthwhile to notice that the rules on data transmission only apply to user data, not to SCTP control chunks.

### 5.2.1   Congestion Window and Receiver Window

*Congestion window*, or *cwnd*, is a variable maintained and dynamically updated by the data sender. It is an indication of how much more data traffic, in number of bytes, the sender can inject into the path between the sender and the receiver before causing path congestion. In this section we will only discuss how to use *cwnd* to control our data transmission. The rules for maintaining and updating *cwnd* are part of the **congestion avoidance mechanism** and will be discussed in full detail in Chapter 6.

Besides *cwnd*, another important variable used by the data sender for controlling the data transmission is the *receiver window*, or *rwnd*, variable, which gives an indication of the size, in number of bytes, of the available buffer space at the data receiver. The *rwnd* variable is also maintained and calculated by the data sender, using the feedback information found in SACKs from the data receiver. Procedures on how to calculate *rwnd* will be described in Section 5.3.3.4.

### 5.2.2   Rules for Data Transmission

As we discussed in Section 5.1.1, the data sender transmits user data by getting DATA chunks from the outbound queue, bundling them into SCTP packets, and then passing the SCTP packets to the IP layer (see Figure 5–1).

> *Note*  When the data receiver is multi-homed, the data sender will need to maintain a separate *cwnd* for each transport addresses of the data receiver. The reasoning is that data sent to different transport addresses of the multi-homed receiver often take very different network paths before reaching the receiver, and the congestion status of different network paths is not related and hence needs to be tracked separately.

The following rules are used by the data sender to determine whether it is allowed to send out data:

**Rule 5–1**  The sender *must not* transmit any new data to a given transport address of the receiver if there are already *cwnd* or more bytes of user data to that transport address outstanding.

**Rule 5–2**  The data sender *must not* transmit new data to the receiver if the *rwnd* of the receiver indicates that there is no receive buffer space left (that is, the *rwnd* equals zero). However, regardless of the value of *rwnd* (including if it is zero), the data sender can always have one DATA chunk in flight to the receiver if it is allowed by *cwnd*.

**Rule 5–3**  When transmitting, the sender *must* first transmit any DATA chunks in the send queue that are marked for retransmission.

**Rule 5–4**  Regardless of the *rwnd* and *cwnd* values, the data sender *should* stop sending new DATA chunks if the next TSN to use is more than $2^{31}-1$ ahead of the current lowest outstanding TSN.

In Rule 5–1, **outstanding data** means the total amount of user data in all the DATA chunks that the sender has sent to a particular transport address of the receiver and for which the sender has not yet received acknowledgment. (When the receiver is single-homed, there will be only one transport address.)

This rule implies that for each transport address of the receiver, the data sender should keep a counter for how many bytes of data are outstanding. This counter is similar to the *flightsize* counter used in some TCP implementations, and we will use this same term to represent it.[3]

Figure 5–6 gives a conceptual view of controlling data transmission with a multi-homed data receiver. Notice that for each destination address, a sender

---

3. A *flightsize* counter variable is derived from fields in the protocol headers. An alternative approach is to count the total number of bytes outstanding whenever the value needs to be checked.

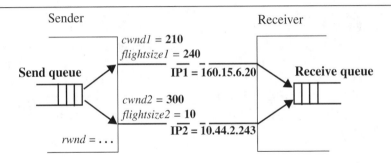

**Figure 5–6**  *Transmission control with a multi-homed data receiver*

maintains a *cwnd* and *flightsize* variable. However only *one rwnd* variable is maintained for the whole association.

In this particular example, according to Rule 5–1 the sender is not allowed to send new data to IP1 because the outstanding data (240 bytes) on that address already exceeds what is allowed by the current value of *cwnd1* of IP1, which is 210 bytes. However, the sender can still send up to 290 bytes more data to IP2 because there is still room left in the *cwnd2* of IP2.

It should be noted that multi-homing in SCTP is only specified for use for redundancy purposes. In this example only retransmissions would be sent to IP2. Multi-homing for use in load balancing is still being studied by researchers and is not part of the SCTP specification.

Rule 5–2 basically prohibits the sender from transmitting any new data if the *rwnd* of this receiver becomes zero. However, there is an important exception—the sender is still allowed to send one DATA chunk out if, at that time, there is no data outstanding on *all* the transport addresses. Figure 5–7 shows an example of such a case.

In this example, even though *rwnd* is zero, the sender is still allowed to transmit one DATA chunk, because both *flightsize1* and *flightsize2* are equal to zero. The transmission of this one DATA chunk, however, must still obey Rule 5–1; that is, a DATA chunk may only be sent if there is room in the *cwnd* of the destination address.

The purpose of this exception (in Rule 5–2) is to prevent the data transfer from being trapped in a potential deadlock. This deadlock can be triggered if a receiver engages the flow control (by setting its *a_rwnd* to zero) just as the last SACK is sent. Figure 5–8 shows this deadlock scenario.

In this scenario, after receiving some amount of data from the sender, the data receiver—for reasons such as resource schedule conflict, or under the command of its user application—wants to stop the sender temporarily from transmitting any new data. Therefore, at point 1 in Figure 5–8, the data receiver acknowledges

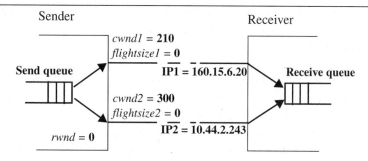

**Figure 5–7**  *An example of the exceptional case for Rule 5–2*

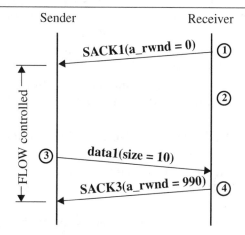

**Figure 5–8**  *Preventing deadlock in flow control*

all the data it has received and sets *a_rwnd* to zero in the outbound SACK1. The arrival of SACK1 will clear out all the outstanding data for the sender (that is, all *flightsize* counters will become zero) and cause the sender to set its *rwnd* to zero, which in effect prevents the sender from transmitting any data.

After a while, at point 2 in Figure 5–8, the data receiver's resource conflict clears, allowing it to raise its *rwnd* back up to 1,000 bytes. However, unfortunately there is no DATA outstanding, and thus the sender will never learn of the resource conflict change at the receiver. Without the exception to Rule 5–2, this association would enter a deadlock situation because the sender would not be able to send any new data, and the receiver would not transmit a new *a_rwnd* value unless it received new data that needed to be SACKed.

This problem is solved with the exception to the rule: the sender can always send out one DATA chunk regardless of the current *rwnd* value *if there is no data outstanding* (point 3 in Figure 5–8). This new data will trigger another SACK from the receiver, and the new *a_rwnd* value will get reported to the data sender (point 4 in Figure 5–8).

If the sender is allowed to transmit (in a single SCTP packet), the maximal number of bytes it can send to a particular transport address of the receiver will be the lesser of *rwnd* and [(*cwnd – flightsize*) + (PMTU – 1)] of the transport address.

In the example shown in Figure 5–9, the sender will be able to send up to 500 bytes of new data to IP1 and up to 300 bytes of new data to IP2.

Only complete DATA chunks are allowed to be bundled into an SCTP packet. When forming the outbound SCTP packet, the data sender must stop bundling more DATA chunks into the SCTP packet if the inclusion of the next DATA chunk will cause the data in the SCTP packet to exceed the receiver's *rwnd*. For this reason, the actual number of data bytes the sender can transmit is normally less than the maximum number of bytes allowed by Rule 5–2. The *cwnd* variable (unlike *rwnd*) does achieve full utilization, because the sender is always allowed to "slop over" the value of *cwnd* by (PMTU – 1). In other words, if the sender does have room to send in *rwnd*, and 1 byte of room in *cwnd,* a full PMTU's worth of data may be sent. Rule 5–1 allows this slop-over so that we can increase *cwnd*, as we will discuss in Chapter 6.

Once the outbound SCTP packet is formed and sent, the sender will deduct the actual number of bytes sent from *rwnd* and add that amount to *flightsize*. In the example in Figure 5–9, if the sender eventually sends out an SCTP packet containing 450 bytes of data to IP1, we will have *rwnd* = 50, *cwnd1* = 800, and *flightsize1* = 550 after the transmission.

A DATA chunk can be marked for retransmission by the sender if

- the DATA chunk has been sent to the receiver before, but no acknowledgment came back in time (that is, the retransmission timer has expired), or

- the receiver has explicitly reported the DATA chunk missing (through the fast retransmit algorithm)

For DATA chunks marked for retransmission, Rule 5–3 simply says that they must be sent out first, before any new DATA chunks can be transmitted. Note that Rule 5–1 and Rule 5–2 apply equally to both new and retransmitted DATA chunks.

Rule 5–4 exists to prevent an ambiguity that may occur at the data receiver when determining the position of a newly arrived DATA chunk, due to the fact that TSN is a circular value that "wraps" around to zero at $2^{32}$.

Such a situation only becomes a concern under an extremely high data-transfer rate in combination with a very large *cwnd*.

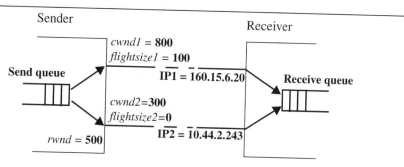

**Figure 5–9** *Determining how much data can be sent*

## 5.3    Acknowledgment Rules

As we described in Section 5.1.2, the message receiver is expected to notify the message sender of the reception of each DATA chunk. The message receiver does so by sending back a SACK indicating the TSN corresponding to the received DATA chunk. In this section we will discuss when to send the acknowledgment and what other information must be reported back to the data sender.

### 5.3.1    Where Should a SACK Be Sent?

SACKs are always sent back to the source IP address of the data sender, when it is not multi-homed. However, when the message sender is multi-homed—that is, when it can be reached by more than one transport address—the receiver must choose one of the transport addresses to which to send the SACK.

Whenever possible, the message receiver *should* always send the SACK back to the same transport address from which the DATA chunk being acknowledged was received.

Figure 5–10 shows an example in which the data sender is multi-homed with two transport addresses, IP1 and IP2. If the DATA chunk being acknowledged is received from IP1 (in other words, the IP datagram that carries the DATA chunk has IP1 as its source IP address), the receiver will send the SACK back to IP1.

This strategy may not always be able to be carried out this straightforwardly. This is because, as we will discuss later, a SACK is capable of acknowledging the reception of multiple DATA chunks. When a SACK does acknowledge multiple DATA chunks, those DATA chunks may not necessarily be received from a single transport address (if the data sender is multi-homed).

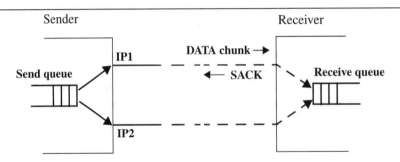

**Figure 5–10**   *Where to send the SACK in a multi-homed case*

In such a case, the implementation may pick any of the available addresses, with one easy choice being to use the locality principle and the address from the latest DATA chunk received.

### 5.3.2   When Should a SACK Be Sent?

Because SACK chunks consume network bandwidth when they are sent from one endpoint to the other, they become overhead to the user message traffic. In order to reduce this overhead, the SACK is designed to report the reception of multiple DATA chunks (see Section 3.2.6 and Section 5.3.3). The message receiver only needs to send a single SACK periodically to report all the DATA chunks received since it sent the last SACK. This scheme is called **delayed acknowledgment**.

The length of the delay, however, must be carefully controlled in order to prevent the following three problems:

1. *Unnecessary retransmissions*—If the message receiver receives a DATA chunk but delays the acknowledgment to the sender for too long, the message sender may mistake the DATA chunk as being lost and may start to retransmit the DATA chunk. This unnecessary retransmission can severely interfere with normal data transfer.

2. *Tie-up of sender's resource*—In order to be prepared in case retransmission becomes necessary (see Section 5.4.3), the message sender needs to keep the memory and other resources occupied by a DATA chunk. These resources are kept until the message receiver acknowledges the reception of the DATA chunk and the *cumulative acknowledgment* point moves past the DATA chunk's TSN. A prolonged delay in sending the SACK by the message receiver may cause a resource shortage at the message sender,

thus preventing the sender from accepting more user messages from its user application.

3. *Premature flow control*—To avoid overwhelming the message receiver with too much data, the message sender keeps an estimate of the amount of buffer space available at the message receiver. It does so by tracking the amount of data it has sent and the amount of data acknowledged by the receiver through SACKs. (This estimation is kept in the variable *rwnd*, as we discussed in Section 5.2.1.) The excessive delay on the SACK may cause the message sender to engage flow control prematurely and stop sending more data.

The following rules are therefore defined in SCTP for the message receiver to control the amount of delay when sending acknowledgments. (These rules are based on the guidelines for the delayed acknowledgment algorithm as specified in Section 4.2 of Allman, Paxson, and Stevens [1999].)

**Rule 5-5**    When an endpoint sends data to its peer, it should always bundle a SACK chunk to report any unacknowledged received DATA chunks.

When the association is carrying bidirectional traffic, Rule 5-5 is very effective in reducing the need to send separate SCTP packets to carry SACKs. Also, because the SACK is sent whenever the next SCTP packet is transmitted to the peer, the amount of delay can become insignificant if there are always SCTP packets traveling in the opposite direction.

**Rule 5–6**    After receiving an SCTP packet, if there is not an SCTP packet to be sent to the peer that can be used for bundling the acknowledgments, the message receiver then *must* acknowledge the reception of the new DATA chunks carried in the received SCTP packet within a certain time limit. The recommended delay limit in SCTP is 200 ms and should *never* be more than 500 ms. This rule is intended to prevent the message sender from unnecessarily retransmitting the data. These rules are defined in the SCTP specification itself, and failure to adhere to them may cause suboptimal performance.

**Rule 5–7**    The message receiver *must* send out at least one SACK for every other IP datagram it receives that contains data. In other words, if the endpoint receives two IP datagrams containing SCTP packets carrying DATA chunks[4] one after the other, even though the time since the arrival of the first SCTP

---

4. Note the use of the plural form, because multiple chunks may be in each of the two required IP datagrams.

packet is still within the delay limit set in Rule 5–6, the endpoint must acknowledge the reception of all the DATA chunks immediately when the second SCTP packet is received. This rule is intended to prevent the endpoint from accumulating too much data before sending out the SACK.

**Rule 5–8**   The receiver *must not* send more than one SACK for each SCTP packet it receives. This rule is intended to minimize the number of SACKs used to acknowledge the received data. Also, extra SACKs may confuse the congestion control and retransmission mechanism of the sender.

**Rule 5–9**   When an SCTP packet arrives with duplicate DATA chunk(s) and with no new DATA chunk(s), the endpoint *must* immediately send a SACK with no delay. Here, a **duplicate DATA chunk** is defined as a newly arrived DATA chunk that carries a TSN that is the same as that of a DATA chunk that arrived earlier.

Normally the reception of duplicate DATA chunk(s) indicates that a SACK previously sent by the data receiver was lost and that the data sender, without getting the acknowledgment in time, retransmitted the same DATA chunk(s).

Under such circumstances, it is necessary for the data receiver to immediately send the acknowledgment again in order to help the data sender clear the confusion.

**Rule 5–10**   After processing a newly received SCTP packet carrying DATA chunks, if the receiver finds that one or more TSNs becomes missing—that is, gaps exist in the TSN sequence (see Section 5.3.3)—the receiver should not delay but should immediately send out a SACK with Gap Ack blocks to report the potential missing DATA chunks. The data receiver will continue sending a SACK without delay at the arrival of each subsequent SCTP packet carrying DATA chunks if the SCTP packet fails to fill up the gap(s).

Figure 5–11 shows three examples using delayed acknowledgment rules between two communicating endpoints, endpoint A and endpoint B. Note that the SACKs are labeled to indicate the order, *not* which SCTP packets are being acknowledged.

In the first example, endpoint A first sends SCTP packet A1 to endpoint B, and endpoint B delays the sending of the acknowledgment. But while waiting for the delay time (200 ms) to expire, endpoint B realizes that it has an outbound SCTP packet to send to endpoint A. Using Rule 5-5 above, endpoint B does not wait for the delay time to pass; instead, endpoint B immediately sends out the SACK, bundling the SACK over the outbound SCTP packet B1.

This SACK bundling approach, however, can only be applied if there is still room left in the outbound SCTP packet to accommodate the SACK (see Section 5.8.4). Even though the SACK is always found in the SCTP packet ahead

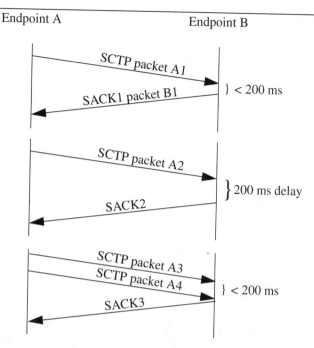

**Figure 5–11** *Examples of sending delayed SACKs*

of the data, the sender must assess if the SACK and the data will fit in one SCTP packet. If the SACK and data together consume too much space to fit in one PMTU-sized piece, the sender should let the receive timer expire, send the SACK, and *not* bundle the SACK with the outbound DATA chunk.

In the second example, endpoint A sends SCTP packet A2 containing some number of DATA chunks to endpoint B, and 200 ms later endpoint B sends SACK2 back to endpoint A to acknowledge the DATA chunks carried. This example shows Rule 5–6 at work.

In the third example, we see Rule 5–7 at work: when a second SCTP packet, SCTP packet A4, arrives at endpoint B after the arrival of SCTP packet A3, the endpoint stops waiting for the delay time to pass and immediately sends out a SACK to acknowledge the reception of all the DATA chunks in both SCTP packet A3 and SCTP packet A4.

In Figure 5–12, our first example shows how Rule 5–10 is applied. Here a second (duplicate) data packet SCTP Packet A5 arrives at endpoint B in under 200 ms. This causes endpoint B to immediately send SACK4.

In the second example in Figure 5–12, we see Rule 5–10 applied. Here SCTP packet A6 has been lost in the network. The arrival of SCTP packet A7 causes the

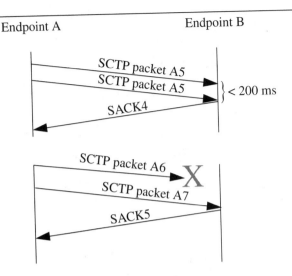

**Figure 5–12**  *Examples of sending non-delayed SACKs*

receiver (endpoint B) to reply without delay, sending SACK5 in response. Subsequent SCTP packets containing new DATA chunks from endpoint A will cause additional SACKs to be sent without delay until the missing DATA chunks (contained in SCTP packet A6) are repaired through retransmission.

### 5.3.3   What Should Be Reported in a SACK?

There are four kinds of information that needs to be reported back to the data sender in a SACK:

- Cumulative TSN
- Gaps found in a received TSN sequence, which can indicate possible data loss
- Reception of any duplicated DATA chunks
- Updated receive buffer availability

#### 5.3.3.1   *Cumulative TSN*

The data receiver needs to keep track of (in the variable *Cumulative TSN*) the last sequential TSN of all valid DATA chunks it has received. All the DATA chunks with a TSN earlier in sequence than the *Cumulative TSN*, as well as the DATA chunk carrying the *Cumulative TSN*, have already been received by the receiver correctly. However, the DATA chunk with a TSN exactly next to the *Cumulative TSN* (that is, *Cumulative TSN* + 1) has not yet arrived.

Every time an SCTP packet carrying DATA chunks arrives, the data receiver will try to advance its *Cumulative TSN*. Every time the data receiver sends out a SACK, it reports to the data sender its latest cumulative TSN using the SACK's *Cumulative TSN* field.

Figure 5–13 shows examples of the updating and reporting of *Cumulative TSN* by a data receiver. Here, when the SCTP packet carrying three DATA chunks (with TSNs 4, 5, and 6) arrives, the receiver advances its *Cumulative TSN* to 6.

However, the arrival of the second SCTP packet (containing two DATA chunks with TSNs 8 and 9) fails to advance the *Cumulative TSN* of the receiver, due to the absence of the DATA chunk with TSN 7. Therefore, when the receiver acknowledges the reception of the second SCTP packet, the *Cumulative TSN* reported in the SACK is still set to 6.

Finally, the third data SCTP packet arrives, carrying DATA chunks with TSNs 7 and 10.[5] This allows the receiver to advance its *Cumulative TSN* to 10 and to report the new *Cumulative TSN* in the subsequent SACK.

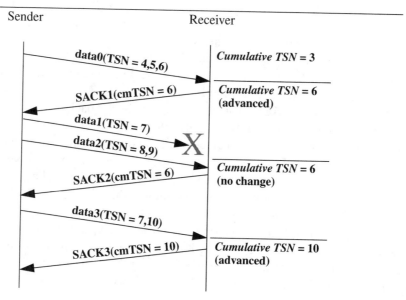

**Figure 5–13**  *Updating and reporting Cumulative TSN*

---

5. Note that this example is *not* intended to show proper fast retransmission behavior. Its sole purpose is to illustrate the *Cumulative TSN* advancement.

### 5.3.3.2 TSN Gap Ack Blocks

It is always possible for the receiver to receive a DATA chunk that carries a TSN greater than the latest *Cumulative TSN*. In this case the receiver cannot advance the *Cumulative TSN* because there is a discontinuity or gap between the newly received TSN and the latest *Cumulative TSN*. The arrival of the second data SCTP packet, *data2*, in the example given in Figure 5–13 shows such a case.

The receiver needs to report all such TSN gaps in the *Gap Ack block* fields of the outbound SACKs. The gap report can help the sender to detect data lost and to perform retransmission if necessary. The format of reporting TSN gaps is discussed in Section 3.2.6. In the example in Figure 5–13, among other values, SACK2 will report *Cumulative TSN = 6*, with one *Gap Ack block* starting from TSN 8 and ending with TSN 9.

> **Note**    The *Gap Ack block* fields report TSNs that were received, *not* missing TSNs.

In some special applications, such as when a very high-speed, loss-prone communication link is used between the data sender and the receiver, there is the possibility that a great number of gaps will be discovered and need to be reported. The data receiver may find it hard to fit all the Gap Ack blocks it is required to report into a single SACK. This is because the SCTP packet size is limited by the PMTU of the transport address to which the SACK is being sent.

In such a case, the data receiver will send out only one SACK within the size limit set by the PMTU, reporting the Gap Ack blocks from the lowest to highest TSNs, and leave the remaining DATA chunks with the highest TSN numbers unacknowledged. They will be acknowledged the next time a SACK is sent out (provided that the *Cumulative TSN* advances).

Note also that there is *no* requirement for Gap Ack blocks to be ordered from lowest to highest in the actual SACK itself. Even though it is hard to conceive of an algorithm that would create the Gap Ack block list out of order, *a SACK receiver should not depend on the Gap Ack blocks being ordered.*

### 5.3.3.3 Duplicate TSNs

If there are any duplicate DATA chunks received, the receiver needs to report their TSNs in the subsequent SACK, using the *Duplicate TSN* fields (see Section 3.2.6). Each duplicate TSN received is recorded in the outbound SACK for identification to the sender of the DATA chunk(s).

(The handling of a duplicate TSN report by the data sender is not yet defined in SCTP. It is for future study. In the future this valuable information may be used to detect SACK loss on the return path.)

### 5.3.3.4 Available Receive Buffer Space

Another important piece of information reported in the SACK is the "receive buffer space" currently available at the data receiver, which is carried in the *advertised rwnd* or *a_rwnd* field. This information will be used by the data sender to update its *rwnd* variable in order to perform flow control (see Section 5.3.5.3).

The data receiver is always responsible for managing and maintaining its receive buffers. How an implementation manages its receive buffers is dependent on many factors (such as the operating system in use, design of the memory management system, and the amount of memory available) and is out of the scope of SCTP.

The data receiver uses the following algorithm to calculate and report *a_rwnd*:

1. When the association is first initiated, the receiver sets its *a_rwnd* to the total receive buffer space it has allocated to the association. The receiver then tells the sender, through the INIT or INIT-ACK control chunk, this initial *a_rwnd* value. SCTP does specify that the minimum value of this initial *a_rwnd must be at least 1500 bytes.*[6]

2. As DATA chunks are received and buffered, the receiver decreases *a_rwnd* by the number of bytes received and buffered and reports the new *a_rwnd* value in subsequent SACKs. This, in effect, will cause the sender to lower its *rwnd*, restricting the amount of data the sender can transmit.

3. For traditional UNIX-style operating systems, after the DATA chunks are processed and the user data has been released to the user application, the receive buffer space occupied by the DATA chunks is released. In releasing the buffer space, the receiver increases *a_rwnd* by the number of bytes delivered to the user application. It then reports the new *a_rwnd* value in the subsequent SACK to the data sender. This, in effect, will cause the sender to raise its *rwnd*, allowing the sender to send more data.

Here we give an example to illustrate how the SACK is used to report the various information we just discussed.

Let us assume that the receiver is in the state shown in Figure 5–14.

Then a new SCTP packet arrives, carrying three DATA chunks, as shown in Figure 5–15.

---

6. This value is derived from the Ethernet MTU size.

1) *a_rwnd* = 1000

2) TSN receiving status:

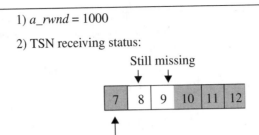

**Figure 5–14**  *TSN state in the receiver*

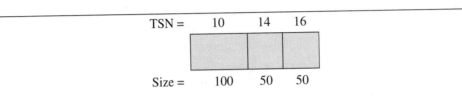

**Figure 5–15**  *Newly arrived SCTP packet at the receiver*

After processing this newly arrived SCTP packet, the receiver will have the updated state shown in Figure 5–16 (assuming that the receiver has not recouped the 100 bytes allocated to hold the newly received data chunks, and hence the available receiver buffer space at this point has dropped to 900 bytes).

Because a duplicate DATA chunk (TSN = 10) is discovered in the SCTP packet and there are gaps in the received DATA chunks, the receiver immediately responds with a SACK. According to the rules and guidelines we have talked about in this section, the outbound SACK would look as depicted in Figure 5–17. (Note that the Gap Ack block positions are coded as offsets from the *Cumulative TSN*.)

Note that this example also makes the assumption that none of the pending DATA chunks can be delivered to the upper layer. When data can be delivered to the upper layer (even if it is received out of order) *a_rwnd* would be raised based on what was delivered.

### 5.3.4   Revoking an Acknowledgment by the Receiver

Under certain rare circumstances, the data receiver is allowed to revoke the acknowledgment it made in a previous SACK. This will force the data sender to retransmit one or more DATA chunks.

But this procedure only applies to the TSN numbers covered by one of the Gap Ack blocks in the SACK. In other words, any acknowledged DATA chunk

1) $a\_rwnd = 900$

2) TSN receiving status:

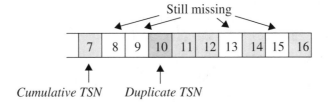

**Figure 5–16** *Receiver's updated state*

| Cumulative TSN = 7 | |
|---|---|
| $a\_rwnd = 900$ | |
| # of gap blocks = 3 | # of duplicates = 1 |
| Gap 1 start = 3 | Gap 1 end = 5 |
| Gap 2 start = 7 | Gap 2 end = 7 |
| Gap 3 start = 9 | Gap 3 end = 9 |
| Duplicate TSN 1=10 | |

**Figure 5–17** *SACK generated by receiver*

whose TSN is equal to or earlier in sequence than the current *Cumulative TSN cannot* be revoked.

An example of using this revoking procedure is when the receiver is in the middle of receiving a large message made up of a series of fragmented DATA chunks and finds that it is running out of receive buffer space. If the arrived fragments are out of order—that is, one or more earlier fragments of the series is still missing—the receiver will not even be able to assemble and deliver the first part of the message. (See Section 5.8.3.1 for details on partial message delivery.) To avoid a resource lockup, the receiver will have to drop some or all of the received fragmented DATA chunks that are out of order. This revokes from the data sender the acknowledgment made on those dropped DATA chunks.

To revoke those DATA chunks, the receiver, after dropping them locally, simply stops acknowledging them in any subsequent SACKs, until they are received again as a result of retransmission by the sender.

In addition, the receiver always updates its *a_rwnd* to account for the released buffer space after locally dropping the DATA chunks.

It is important to point out that this revoking procedure should be only used as a last resort by the data receiver to avoid a resource deadlock. This procedure can result in suboptimal retransmission strategies in the data sender, and thus in suboptimal performance, and it should be avoided if possible.

In the example shown in Figure 5–18, the receiver revoked its acknowledgment of the DATA chunk with TSN = 8 in order to make room for the newly arrived DATA chunk with TSN = 4.

### 5.3.5   Processing of Received SACK by Data Sender

First of all, the arrival of a SACK tells the data sender which of the DATA chunks that the sender transmitted has been received correctly. Those covered by the *cumulative acknowledgment* point therefore can be safely released, freeing the resources the sender allocated to hold those DATA chunks.

Secondly, the SACK gives the sender clues about the DATA chunks that may have been lost in the network during the transfer and may need to be retransmitted.

The arrived SACK also carries information on how much of the receiver's buffer space is still available for new data. This information is critical for the data sender to determine the amount of new data it can still send.

When processing the information carried in a SACK, one thing the data sender must take into account is that the information carried in the SACK is from the perspective of the data receiver and accurate only at the time the SACK was sent.

### 5.3.5.1   *Detecting Out-of-Order SACKs*

After a SACK arrives, if the data sender finds the *Cumulative TSN* value carried in the SACK is *earlier in sequence* than that of its own *Cumulative TSN* variable, the SACK is considered out of order (that is, an old SACK), and the data sender will discard the received SACK. This is due to the fact that *Cumulative TSN* only increases monotonically at both the data sender and the data receiver.

However, this method will not be able to detect the case in which two different SACKs carrying the same *Cumulative TSN* value arrive at the data sender out of order.

The failure of detecting out-of-order SACKs may cause the data sender to develop an incorrect view of the data receiver's receive buffer space. In most of the cases, this erroneous view can be corrected by later SACKs.

Because there is no explicit identifier that can be used to detect out-of-order SACKs more reliably, the data sender must use heuristics to determine if a SACK is out of order. Failure to use proper heuristics will result in suboptimal performance but will not hinder or disrupt the data transfer over an association.

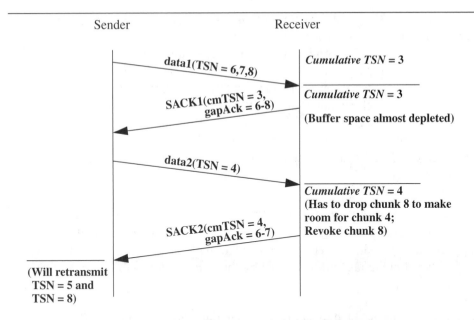

**Figure 5–18**   *An example of revoking an acknowledged DATA chunk*

To detect an out-of-order SACK, the receiver of the SACK must look at the *Cumulative TSN* contained within the SACK. Because this value is monotonically increasing, it should be equal to or greater than the last *Cumulative TSN* received. A *Cumulative TSN* that is smaller than the last *Cumulative TSN* is required to be dropped, because it is an out-of-order SACK. In some cases, where gaps in the sequence space exist, the *Cumulative TSN* will be the same as the previous one, but the value should never be less than the previous one. In such a case (where the *Cumulative TSN* in the SACK is the same as the currently recorded *Cumulative TSN*), the receiver should process the SACK, checking for both new Gap Ack blocks and any TSNs that may have been revoked.

### 5.3.5.2   *Updating the Send Queue*

When a SACK arrives and the *Cumulative TSN* value carried in the SACK is more advanced in sequence than that of the *Cumulative TSN* variable kept by the sender (in other words, the *Cumulative TSN* point has advanced), the data sender can safely assume that all the DATA chunks with a TSN earlier in sequence or equal to the new *Cumulative TSN* are received by the receiver. Any local resource allocated to those DATA chunks can be safely released.

The data sender marks as received the DATA chunks that are acknowledged in the Gap Ack blocks in the SACK. However, the data sender will not release the resource due to the possibility that some of the DATA chunks may be revoked by the receiver later and thus need to be retransmitted (see Section 5.3.4).

In either case, the sender will no longer count the acknowledged DATA chunks as outstanding and will subtract the data size of those DATA chunks from the *flightsize* counter of their corresponding transport addresses.

Those DATA chunks that fall into the gaps described by the Gap Ack blocks will be counted as being potentially missing. The handling of those potentially missing chunks will be described in Section 6.3.2.1.

Figure 5–19 gives an example of how the arrived SACK is used to update the send queue status.

### 5.3.5.3   *Maintaining and Updating rwnd*

As we mentioned before, the data sender is maintaining and updating its *rwnd* variable in order to predict correctly the amount of buffer space available at the receiver.

The following algorithm is used by the data sender to maintain and update its *rwnd*:

1. Upon the establishment of the association, the data sender initializes its *rwnd* to the value of the *Advertised receiver window credit* (*a_rwnd*) field found in the INIT or INIT-ACK message from the data receiver.

2. Anytime a DATA chunk is transmitted (or retransmitted) to the data receiver, the data sender subtracts the data size of the chunk from *rwnd*.

3. Whenever a DATA chunk is marked for retransmission[7] (due to, for example, a retransmission timer expiration as defined in Section 5.4.3, or the detection of a data loss as defined in Section 6.3.2.1), the data sender adds the data size of the chunk to *rwnd* and that size is subtracted again after the data is retransmitted.

4. Anytime a SACK arrives, the sender sets its *rwnd* equal to the newly received *a_rwnd* minus the total number of bytes still outstanding *after* processing the *Cumulative TSN* and the Gap Ack blocks and updating its send queue status as described in Section 5.3.5.2.

---

7. Here, *marked for retransmission* means that the DATA chunk will be retransmitted in the future when its time comes.

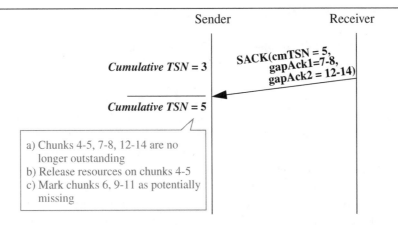

**Figure 5–19** · *An example of updating the send queue state using SACK information*

## 5.4 Management of Retransmission Timer

In order to be able to determine whether a DATA chunk is lost in the network in the absence of any feedback (that is, SACKs) from the data receiver, the data sender starts a retransmission timer, *T3-rtx*, each time a DATA chunk is sent out.

There are two strategies for implementing and managing this retransmission timer mechanism: one is to use a single retransmission timer for each destination transport address of the data receiver; the other is to use a separate retransmission timer for each DATA chunk outstanding. Both are equally effective for the purpose of detecting data loss.

In the ensuing discussion we will assume that the first timer management strategy is followed; that is, that there is a single retransmission timer, *T3-rtx,* for each of the transport addresses of the data receiver.

### 5.4.1 Determine Retransmission Timeout (RTO)

The duration of the timer is kept by the sender in a variable called *Retransmission timeout,* or *RTO*. This value has a fundamental impact on the communications efficiency and stability of an SCTP association. In this section we will detail how the *RTO* value is determined.

#### 5.4.1.1 What Is Round-Trip Time (RTT)?
*Round-trip time*, or *RTT*, is used by the data sender to calculate the *RTO*. It is defined as the difference between the time a DATA chunk is transmitted by the

data sender and the time that the SACK acknowledging that DATA chunk comes back to the sender.

*RTT* is specific to the route the DATA chunk took, and hence is specific to the particular transport address to which the DATA chunk was sent, in case the data receiver is multi-homed.

The data sender derives, or measures, the *RTT* of a particular transport address using the existing data traffic sent to that address and the corresponding SACKs sent back by the data receiver. Sometimes the data sender also uses certain control chunk exchanges to derive *RTT*. (See Section 7.2.3 for details on *RTT* measurement with this alternate mechanism.)

Moreover, *RTT* changes with time. This is because of the dynamic nature of the network, as well as the nondeterministic nature of the time the data receiver took to send back the SACK acknowledging the DATA chunk (see Section 5.3.2 for details).

### 5.4.1.2   Algorithm for Calculating RTO

The algorithm used in SCTP for computing and updating the *RTO* follows closely how TCP manages its retransmission timer (see Allman, Paxson, and Stevens [1999] and Jacobson [1988]).

To compute the *RTO*, the data sender needs to maintain two state variables: *SRTT* (smoothed round-trip time), and *RTTVAR* (round-trip time variation).

When the receiver is multi-homed, it is important to remember that there will be a separate set of variables (that is, *RTO*, *SRTT*, and *RTTVAR*) for each of the transport addresses.

The algorithm for computing and updating *SRTT*, *RTTVAR*, and *RTO* is as follows:

1. Initialization:

$$RTO \; = \; RTO_{Initial}$$

where $RTO_{initial}$ is a protocol parameter and normally has a value of 3 seconds.

2. When the first *RTT* measurement $R_{1st}$ is made, initialize the variables as follows:

$$SRTT \; = \; R_{1st};$$

$$RTTVAR \; = \; \frac{R_{1st}}{2};$$

Then update *RTO*:

$$RTO = SRTT + 4 \times RTTVAR$$

3. Whenever a new *RTT* measurement, $R_{new}$, becomes available, update

$$RTTVAR_{new} = (1 - \beta) \times RTTVAR_{old} + \beta \times \left| SRTT_{old} - R_{new} \right|$$
$$SRTT_{new} = (1 - \alpha) \times SRTT_{old} + \alpha \times R_{new}$$

where $\beta$ and $\alpha$ are protocol constants and are recommended to be equal to 1/4 and 1/8, respectively. If, as a result of the above computation, $RTTVAR_{new}$ becomes zero, it will then be set to $G$, which is the clock granularity used for *RTT* measurements.

After the above calculation, the new *RTO* value is computed as

$$RTO = SRTT_{new} + 4 \times RTTVAR_{new}$$

When the result from the above computation is smaller than the protocol parameter $RTO_{min}$ (normally 1 second), the new *RTO* will be rounded up to $RTO_{min}$. The reason for this is that *RTO* values that are too small are found to cause unnecessary retransmissions (Allman and Paxson 1999).

Similarly, an upper limit can also be imposed on the computed *RTO* value, using the protocol parameter $RTO_{max}$ (normally set to 60 seconds). This can help the data sender to detect communication loss faster.

There is no requirement in SCTP on the clock granularity used for computing *RTT*, *RTTVAR*, and *SRTT*. However, some experience (Allman and Paxson 1999) has shown that finer clock granularity ($\leq$ 100 msec) performs somewhat better than coarser granularity. Coarsely grained clocks are often used by implementations, even though more finely grained clocks may perform better.

### 5.4.1.3   When Should RTT Be Measured?

Due to the dynamical nature of the network, the frequency of *RTT* measurement can impact the behavior of the data sender and ultimately the performance of the data transfer.

The following guidelines are therefore important to obey:

**Rule 5-11**    When there is data to transmit to a particular transport address and when it is allowed by Rule 5–12 below, a new *RTT* measurement *must* be made by the data sender on that transport address for each round trip. Furthermore, new *RTT* measurements *should not* be made more than *once per round-trip time* for a given destination transport address.

There are two reasons for this recommendation. First, it appears that measuring more frequently does not in practice yield any significant benefit to the data transfer performance (Allman and Paxson 1999). Secondly, if *RTT* measurements are made more often than once per round-trip time, the values of β and α used for updating *RTTVAR* and *SRTT* in Section 5.4.1.2 will no longer be valid and will need to be adjusted. However, the exact nature of these adjustments remains a research issue.

**Rule 5–12**    Karn's algorithm (Karn and Partridge 1987) *must* be applied when making *RTT* measurements; that is, *RTT* measurements *must not* be made using DATA chunks that have been retransmitted. This is due to the ambiguity of matching an acknowledgment to a retransmitted DATA chunk; a mismatch can have bad effects on the current, as well as subsequent, *RTO* calculations.

### 5.4.2  Retransmission Timer Rules

The rules for managing retransmission timer *T3-rtx* are as follows:

**Rule 5–13**    Every time a DATA chunk is sent to a transport address (including both first-time transmission and retransmission cases), if the *T3-rtx* timer on that transport address is not currently running, start it running so that it will expire after the *RTO* of that address.

**Rule 5–14**    Whenever all the outstanding data sent to a transport address has been acknowledged, turn off the *T3-rtx* timer of that address.

Whenever a SACK arrives and acknowledges the DATA chunk that has the *earliest* outstanding TSN for that address, *restart* the *T3-rtx* timer for that address with the latest *RTO* of that address, if there is still data outstanding on the address.

Here, **restarting a timer** means to stop the currently running timer and then immediately start it again with the latest *RTO* value.

**Rule 5–15**    Whenever a SACK arrives and indicates a missing TSN that was previously acknowledged in a Gap Ack block of a previous SACK (in other words, the DATA chunk with the TSN is revoked by the receiver [see Section 5.3.4]), start *T3-rtx* on the transport address to which the DATA chunk was originally transmitted if the timer is not currently running.

> *Note*  The value of *RTO* used to start the *T3-rtx* timer in the preceding rules is always the latest updated *RTO* of the corresponding transport address, either obtained through the calculations in Section 5.4.1.2 or resulting from the exponential decay of the timer (as discussed in the algorithm for handling the *T3-rtx* timeout in Section 5.4.3).

Figure 5–20 shows the use of the *T3-rtx* timer in a typical bidirectional data transfer between two endpoints, A and B.

Assume both endpoints are single-homed. As shown in the example, after endpoint A sends out the first SCTP packet, *data1*, it starts the *T3-rtx* timer, waiting for an acknowledgment from endpoint B (per Rule 5–13).

Under the delayed acknowledgment strategy (see Section 5.3.2), endpoint B does not send a SACK right away after receiving *data1*. However, while waiting for the delay time to pass, a local SCTP packet becomes ready for transmission, and hence endpoint B decides to bundle back the SACK1 (to *data1*) over outbound SCTP packet *data2*. After sending out the bundled SCTP packet, endpoint B starts its own *T3-rtx* timer (per Rule 5–13).

Meanwhile, endpoint A, before the arrival of the bundled SCTP packet from endpoint B, sends out another SCTP packet, *data3*. Because the timer is already running, endpoint A needs to take no timer action after transmitting *data3* (per Rule 5–13).

The arrival of the bundled SACK1 and *data2* causes two actions at endpoint A:

1. SACK1 acknowledges *data1*, but because *data3* is still outstanding, endpoint A restarts *T3-rtx* per Rule 5–15.

2. Endpoint A, upon the reception of *data2*, applies the delayed acknowledgement rules (see Section 5.3.2) and schedules a delayed acknowledgement.

When the delay time passes, endpoint A sends SACK2 to acknowledge the reception of *data2*. After receiving SACK2, endpoint B stops its *T3-rtx* timer (per Rule 5–14).

Finally, the delay time also passes at endpoint B, and endpoint B sends out SACK3 to acknowledge *data3*. The arrival of SACK3 causes endpoint A to stop its *T3-rtx* timer.

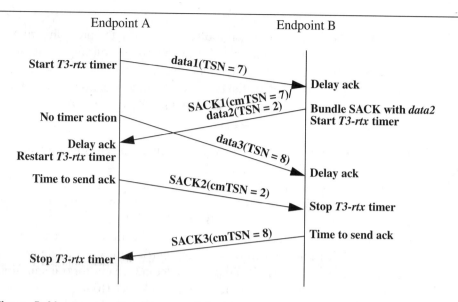

**Figure 5–20**  *An example of the use of the T3-rtx timer during data transfer*

### 5.4.3   Handling Retransmission Timer Expiration

The expiration of the *T3-rtx* timer (or ***T3-rtx*** timeout) on a transport address normally signals one of three events:

1. An SCTP packet carrying a DATA chunk was lost due to network congestion

2. A transport address is unreachable

3. The receiver is out of service

The handling procedure in this section focuses on dealing with events of type 1. The detection and handling of events of types 2 and 3 will be detailed in Section 7.2.2.

SCTP packet loss usually happens when the portion of network between the data sender and the data receiver is experiencing congestion. Therefore, the handling of *T3-rtx* timeout events is tightly coupled with the congestion avoidance mechanism that will be discussed in Chapter 6.

Under normal operation, network congestion is transient in nature. Therefore, when encountering data loss, the correct reaction for each data sender in the affected network is to throttle back its data transmission rate in the hope that reduced traffic to the network will eventually bring the network out of congestion. The procedure for handling *T3-rtx* timeouts is built around this principle.

The following is the algorithm that the SCTP data sender uses in dealing with a *T3-rtx* timeout event. Here we assume that the data receiver is multi-homed and that a *T3-rtx* timeout has occurred on one of the transport addresses of the receiver:

1. *Congestion control adjustment*—For the transport address on which the timer expires, adjust the congestion control variables as detailed in Section 6.3.2.

2. *RTO adjustment*—For the address on which the timer expires, set

$$RTO_{new} = RTO_{old} \times 2$$

   In other words, double the *RTO* value on that address. An upper bound $RTO_{max}$ may be used to limit this doubled operation, as we discussed in Section 5.4.1.2.

3. *Perform retransmission*—To perform retransmission, the data sender first needs to determine which DATA chunks should be retransmitted. If there is more than one address, which address should the retransmitted chunks be sent to? And how much data can be retransmitted right away? These are defined by the following guidelines:

   3a. Mark *all* the DATA chunks outstanding on the transport address where the timeout has just occurred for retransmission (being sure to add back the sizes to the *rwnd* value of the peer).

   3b. If the receiver is multi-homed, select one of the active alternate transport addresses for the following retransmission. Otherwise, the retransmission will take place on the same address (the one and only address) where the timeout occurred.

   3c. Determine how many of the earliest (that is, lowest in TSN sequence) DATA chunks marked in step 3a can fit into a single SCTP packet, subject to the current PMTU constraint of the transport address selected in step 3b.

   3d. Create an SCTP packet containing all the DATA chunks selected in step 3c and send the SCTP packet to the transport address chosen in step 3b.

   3e. Finally, start timer *T3-rtx*, if it is not currently running, on the transport address where the SCTP packet has been sent. Note that the *RTO* used for starting this timer is the one associated with the transport address selected in step 3b, which may not necessarily be the same one that was just doubled in step 2.

It is worthwhile to note that the DATA chunks that were marked for retransmission in step 3a but were *not* selected in step 3c, and hence were *not* retransmitted in step 3e, will remain marked for retransmission. They will be retransmitted later when the data sender gets another opportunity to send data as far as the transmission rules will allow it at that time. (This is normally when the SACK comes back in response to the SCTP packet we just sent.)

After the completion of the above procedures, the *RTO* of the transport address where the timeout occurred will remain doubled until a new *RTT* measurement is obtained on that address (normally through a new successful round of data or control chunks exchange on that address). Once a new *RTT* measurement becomes available for that address, the *RTO* will be calculated anew using the procedures in Section 5.4.1.2, resulting in the *RTO* "collapsing" back from its doubled value.

If a timeout happens again on the address before its *RTO* "collapses" back, the value of the *RTO* will be doubled again, and so on, until it hits the upper bound set by $RTO_{max}$. For a more detailed analysis, you may want to consult Jacobson (1988) and Allman, Paxson, and Stevens (1999).

| | |
|---|---|
| *Note* | For those implementations that maintain a *T3-rtx* timer for each outstanding DATA chunk, step 3a will be changed to mark only the DATA chunk whose timer expired for retransmission. |

## 5.5 Multi-homed Data Sender and Receiver

To support multi-homed data endpoints is one of the primary goals of SCTP. In this section we will discuss some specific considerations that should be made when transferring data in a multi-homed environment.

### 5.5.1 Selection of Primary Transport Address

When an endpoint is multi-homed, its peer will need to select one of the multiple transport addresses of the endpoint as the **primary transport address**. A primary transport address is needed so that the normal congestion control algorithms will function as designed. If no primary transport address was selected, and an application attempted to **load-balance** across multiple destinations, the IP network might become unstable, experiencing rotating blocks of congestion. By having a primary address, the sender will follow the well-tried congestion control mechanisms used by TCP and thus maintain network stability. The additional destination address(es) can then be used as alternates during retransmission and for general failure of the primary path. Let us consider an example.

In Figure 5–21 we have both endpoints A and B in a multi-homed association. Endpoint A has IPA1, IPA2, and IPA3 as its transport addresses, while endpoint B has IPB1 and IPB2 as its transport addresses. After the association is set up, endpoint A can select IPB2 as its primary transport address for reaching endpoint B and make IPB1 a backup address for reaching endpoint B.

It is worthwhile to note that this selection of primary address for reaching endpoint B is made by endpoint A unilaterally, and endpoint B in fact is not aware of which of its transport addresses is chosen by endpoint A as primary.

Similarly, in the example endpoint B chooses IPA1 as its primary transport address for reaching endpoint A, leaving IPA2 and IPA3 as backup addresses for reaching endpoint A.

The initial selection of the peer's primary is normally done when the association is established. However, the user application at either side of the association can later change the primary transport address if it so desires.

### 5.5.2   Transferring Data between Multi-homed Endpoints

When the receiver is multi-homed, the data sender *will* automatically transmit data to the primary transport address of the receiver. The sender's user application may explicitly override this behavior by specifying a different transport address to use for sending a particular message. The sending user application can always change the primary setting if it wants to have all subsequent messages automatically transmitted to a different primary address.

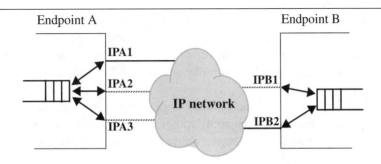

**Figure 5–21**   *Selection of primary address for peer endpoint*

When the data sender is multi-homed, the data receiver does *not* necessarily use the sender's primary transport address when sending back a SACK. Instead, the data receiver should follow the guidelines given in Section 5.3.1. Whenever possible, it should send the SACK back to the transport address from which the SCTP packet being acknowledged was received[8].

### 5.5.2.1   Failover from an Inactive Address

During the data transfer operation, the data sender continuously monitors whether any of the transport addresses of the data receiver are reachable. As part of the fault management mechanism (see Chapter 7), a transport address will be marked as **inactive** if the data sender finds itself no longer capable of reaching the receiver by that address. This is sometimes called a **path failure**. It is important to note that the SCTP specification does not require this **inactive** state to be shared among all associations that include a destination that is discovered to be out of service. It is therefore an implementation decision as to whether this **inactive** state is discovered once and then shared between all associations, or it is discovered individually by each association.

If the data sender is about to transmit an SCTP packet, and the primary transport address for reaching the receiver is **inactive**, the sender will try to send the SCTP packet to an alternate transport address (if one exists and is active).

The same procedure will be followed if the user application tries to explicitly send data to an **inactive** destination transport address. In other words, the SCTP stack will silently override the decision of its user application in this case.

### 5.5.2.2   Retransmitting to a Multi-homed Receiver

When the receiver is multi-homed and the data sender needs to retransmit one or more DATA chunks, special considerations should be taken. In order to benefit the most from the network redundancy built into the receiver, the sender should consider retransmission to an alternate address.

The need for retransmitting a DATA chunk generally indicates either that the address used on the last transmission of the DATA chunk is unreachable or that the network path to that address is enduring congestion. If the retransmission can be made using a different route between the sender and the receiver, there will be a better chance of success.

Therefore, part of the retransmission management of the data sender is to consider each source-destination transport address pair, between the sender and the receiver, and to attempt to pick the most divergent source-destination pair to use

---

8. Note that the address that the SACK was received from is not necessarily the primary address that the endpoint has selected.

for the retransmission. How to pick the most divergent source-destination pair is normally an implementation decision and is not specified in SCTP. Picking a source-destination pair that is divergent should not be confused with source address routing. The Internet of today does not use source-based routing, and only the destination IP address is considered in most routing decisions.

One simple method would be a round-robin approach. Each time a retransmission is to take place, choose a different "active" address than was used last time. For example, if the peer has addresses IPA, IPB, and IPC marked as "active," the first transmission would be sent to IPA (that is, IPA is the primary address), the first retransmission would be sent to IPB, and the second retransmission would be sent to IPC. If a third retransmission were necessary, the sender would cycle back to IPA. The sender may also want to vary its source address (if it is multi-homed). A detailed discussion of why and when to vary the source address can be found in Section 7.4.3.

One thing to notice is that in any case, if a DATA chunk is retransmitted to a different destination transport address than the one used in the last transmission, the outstanding data count on both addresses will need to be adjusted accordingly. In other words, the size of the DATA chunk will be subtracted from the *flightsize* counter of the previous address and added to that of the new address.

Furthermore, when the retransmission is switched to a different destination transport address, the data sender will leave the *T3-rtx* timer running on the original address if there are other DATA chunks still outstanding on that address (and a timeout has not yet occurred). At the same time, the rules in Section 5.4.2 will be used to determine whether a *T3-rtx* timer needs to be started on the new address once the retransmission is sent out. If the timer is required, the timer will be started using the current *RTO* value of the new destination address.

### 5.5.3 Sending a SACK on Duplicate Data

There is a special case in which a single asymmetric path failure in the network may cause the association to fail even when backup paths exist.

This case is illustrated in Figure 5–22, in which one of the addresses on the data sender's side, IPA2, becomes unreachable by the receiver.

Assume the data sender, unaware of the unreachability of IPA2, sends a SCTP packet **with source address** set to IPA2 to the receiver (IPB). According to the rules described in Section 5.5.2, the receiver will then send a SACK to IPA2, and because IPA2 has failed, the SACK will never reach the sender. Every time the retransmission timer fires, the sender selects the **source address** of IPA2. The sender, unable to receive any acknowledgment on the data it has sent out, will eventually consider (mistakenly) the receiver out of service. This will

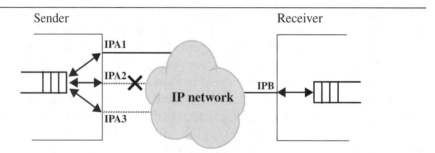

**Figure 5–22** *Asymmetric path failure in a multi-homed sender*

subsequently bring down the association, even when there are in fact still reachable addresses on both sides.

To avoid this problem, the data receiver should follow these guidelines:

- When receiving a duplicate DATA chunk, if the data sender is multi-homed, the data receiver should send a SACK to an alternate transport address.

- The alternate address should be *different* from the one found in the source address field of the received IP datagram that contains the DATA chunk.

The reasoning behind this is that when the SACK is lost, the data sender will eventually retransmit the DATA chunks, and the retransmitted DATA chunks will be received as **duplicates** by the receiver. Therefore, by sending the subsequent SACK to a different address of the sender in response to the **duplicate** data, the receiver will have a better chance of reaching the data sender, and hence the association may survive.

However, even if the association can survive, the data transfer efficiency for the sender will degenerate considerably if the data sender continues to use the failed address (IPA2) as the source address for its outbound IP datagrams. One possible solution is for the data sender to use the duplicate TSN reports carried in the SACKs as a **cue** to change the source address on its outbound IP datagrams to a different one.

## 5.6 Stream Identifier and Stream Sequence Number

In an SCTP association there can be multiple unidirectional streams from the data sender to the data receiver. Each stream provides a means of ordering messages to ensure a sequence of messages are not delivered out of order. Inside each stream, head-of-line blocking is purposely created. Note that this head-of-line blocking in one stream does *not* affect other streams. This allows a user application to send a sequence of messages and guarantee the order of their arrival, and at the same time, send other messages that are *not* effected by this ordering.

Figure 5–23 shows an SCTP association between endpoints A and B, with three streams (*A_s0*, *A_s1*, and *A_s2*) from **endpoint A to endpoint B** and one stream (*B_s0*) from **endpoint B to endpoint A**.

Note that between endpoint A and endpoint B, the streams shown in Figure 5–23 are all within one association and thus are carried over the same set of transport addresses (that is, each stream does not have its own set of transport addresses).

The valid range of stream identifiers is negotiated for both sides during the initialization of the association (see Chapter 4), and once the association is established, the data sender is obliged to use only the stream identifiers within the agreed-upon range. In the example shown in Figure 5–23, the valid stream range that endpoint A can send to is 0 to 2, while the only valid stream ID endpoint B can send to is 0.

| | |
|---|---|
| *Note* | Each of the user messages sent from the sender to the receiver ***must*** be placed in one of the streams. It is up to the user application to decide on and instruct the underneath SCTP data sender on which message should be sent through which stream. The DATA chunk carrying the user message will contain the stream ID in the DATA chunk header. |

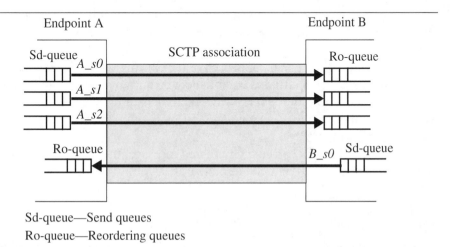

Sd-queue—Send queues
Ro-queue—Reordering queues

**Figure 5–23** *Logical view of a multiple-streamed association*

It is important to note that although streams do provide a way to escape the classic "TCP head-of-line blocking," they do not override or change any limits put on the overall association by *rwnd* or *cwnd*. Both *rwnd* and *cwnd* are association-level variables and are always used to dictate the sending of data onto the wire for the association, no matter the stream to which the data is sent.

### 5.6.1   Ordered and Unordered Message Delivery

When passing a new user message to the data sender for transmission, the user application needs to choose whether to deliver the message in **ordered** or **unordered** delivery mode.

For ordered delivery, the data receiver, after receiving each of the messages, will deliver them to the user application in the same order in which they were passed for transmission by the message sender, relative to other ordered messages sent over the same stream.

For unordered delivery, the data receiver will deliver each message to the user application whenever the message arrives, regardless of the status of other messages in any stream.

By default, messages are always delivered as ordered. The user application must explicitly instruct the SCTP data sender if it wants to send a message in the unordered mode.

#### 5.6.1.1   Handling Ordered Messages

All **ordered** messages sent over a given stream will be assigned a stream sequence number (SSN) by the SCTP data sender in the same sequence in which they are passed down from the user application. The SSN will enable the data receiver to discover out-of-order messages and reorder them before delivering them to the application.

The stream sequence number in each of the existing steams is *required* to start at zero when the association is established. After a user message is sent to a stream, the sequence counter is always incremented by one. When the stream sequence number reaches the value 65535 it will wrap around to zero; that is, it will be set back to zero again.

If a DATA chunk is carrying an ordered message, the data sender will leave the $U$ bit in the chunk's flag field unset; that is, $U = 0$.

#### 5.6.1.2   Handling Unordered Messages

When a message is passed from the user application for unordered delivery, the data sender will *not* assign a stream sequence number to it (that is, transmitting an unordered message will *not* cause an increment to the stream sequence number of a stream). Instead the sender will set the *U* flag of the DATA chunk(s) carrying the message to 1 to indicate to the receiver that this is an unordered message.

At the receiver side, an unordered message is indicated by the *U* flag set to 1 in the arrived DATA chunk (or DATA chunks in the case of a fragmented message). After reassembling the message, if needed, the receiver will bypass the reordering mechanism and can immediately deliver the message to the user application.

In DATA chunks with the *U* flag set, the *Stream sequence number* field has no significance (see Section 3.2.5). The sender may leave the field with any arbitrary value. Therefore, the receiver is required to ignore the field when receiving DATA chunks with the *U* flag set.

Since the unordered messages have no SSN and can be delivered independently to other messages in the stream, an implementation can in effect turn the unordered delivery into a way of transmitting "out-of-band" messages in a given stream. For example, when bundling outbound messages (see Section 5.8.4), the data sender implementation may put the DATA chunks carrying unordered messages in front of other DATA chunks in its transmission queue for faster transmission. Then, whenever an unordered message arrives in a stream, the receiver may insert the message into the head of the deliver queue so that it will be read first by the user application.

Moreover, an entire stream can be made into an "unordered stream" by simply sending each message in unordered mode over that stream.

## 5.7   Passing a Payload Protocol Identifier

When passing a message to the data sender for transmission, the user application can optionally[9] attach a *Payload protocol identifier* to the message. The *Payload protocol identifier* can be thought of as part of the user data and is not meant to be understood by the SCTP data sender or receiver. The data sender simply copies the value of this identifier into the *Payload protocol identifier* field of the DATA chunk that carries the message (see Section 3.2.5).

The *Payload protocol identifier* is assigned and managed by IANA much the same way that the UDP, TCP, and SCTP port number space is managed. See Section 10.5 for further details.

When the message arrives at the receiver, the user application (*not* the SCTP data receiver) may use the *Payload protocol identifier* to assist in the further distribution of the message.

---

9. If the user does not wish to specify a *Payload protocol identifier*, the value "0" will be used to indicate the sender did not specify a *Payload protocol identifier*.

It is also possible that routers or security gateways (for example, firewalls) in the network may use this *Payload protocol identifier* to perform intelligent message routing and filtering.

## 5.8   Fragmentation and Bundling of User Messages

As a general-purpose transport protocol, SCTP must be prepared to transfer user messages of various sizes across the association. However, as we already know, an IP network, like other routed packet networks, does not work very well when the IP datagrams crossing the network are too big or too small. Therefore, there is a need to "repackage" the user messages into optimal sizes for better data transport performance.

In this section we will first discuss when and how to fragment big user messages, then we will discuss how SCTP bundles small user messages to gain efficiency.

### 5.8.1   When Should User Messages Be Fragmented?

For each new outbound user message, the data sender needs to assess what would be the size of the SCTP packet if the user message were to be sent in a single DATA chunk. This assessment must take into account the following:

- Size of the IP header(s)

- SCTP common header

- DATA chunk header

- Size of the SACK chunk going in the opposite direction (if one is to be bundled in the SCTP packet)

If the assessed size of the final SCTP packet is bigger than the current **association PMTU**, the user message should then be fragmented. When the data receiver is multi-homed, the association PMTU is generally the smallest PMTU of all the available transport addresses of the receiver. (For details on the PMTU, see Section 6.5.)[10]

It is worth mentioning that an SCTP data sender is allowed *not* to support message fragmentation. In such a case, if a large user message of a size greater than the current association PMTU is passed from the user application to the data

---

10. This is not an SCTP specification requirement, but in most implementations it provides a good way to ensure that retransmission of a DATA chunk to an alternate network will not cause the retransmitted chunk to exceed the PMTU of the alternate destination address.

sender, the data sender will reject the message (for example, by reporting an error to its user application).

### 5.8.2 How Should a User Message Be Fragmented?

Fragmentation involves the following steps:

1. The data sender breaks the user message into a series of pieces such that each of them, together with all the overhead mentioned in Section 5.8.1, is small enough to be put into one SCTP packet no larger than the current association PMTU.

2. The data sender then puts each of the pieces into a DATA chunk and assigns *in sequence* a separate TSN to each of the DATA chunks in the series.

3. The data sender also must assign the same stream ID, the same stream sequence number, the same *Payload protocol identifier*, and the same *U* flag setting of the original message to *each* of the DATA chunks in the series.

4. Finally, the data sender will set the *B/E* bits of the first DATA chunk in the series to "10," the *B/E* bits of the last DATA chunk in the series to "01," and the *B/E* bits of all other DATA chunks in the series to "00."

Figure 5–24 shows an example of fragmenting a large user message into four pieces.

In the example, the user application instructs the SCTP stack to send the original large message over stream 3 using the ordered delivery mode, and it also sets the *Payload protocol identifier* of the message to 15. The data sender, after accepting the message from the user application, determines that the message needs to be fragmented into four pieces. After fragmentation, the DATA chunks will be transmitted in four separate SCTP packets. The four DATA chunks are assigned continuous TSN numbers in sequence (100 to 103).

#### 5.8.2.1 Dealing with Association PMTU Changes

The PMTU of an association may change due to, for example, a route convergence in the network (see Section 6.5.1).

If the association PMTU shrinks during the data transfer, there is a chance that one or more pieces of a fragmented message that is already in flight will be rejected by the network. This will occur because the size of the SCTP packet carrying the piece is no longer able to comply with the new association PMTU.

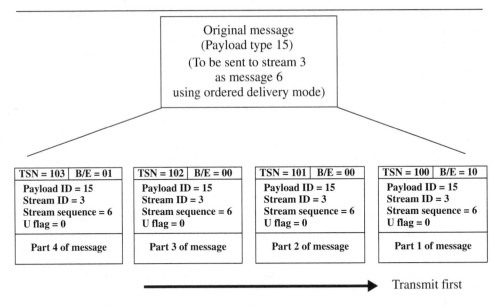

**Figure 5–24**  *An example of fragmenting a large message*

In such a case, an ICMP message will be sent back to the data sender indicating the PMTU violation. This is because all normal outbound SCTP packets will have the "Don't Fragment" (*DF*) bit set (for IPv4).

In response, the data sender will *not* refragment the user message. Instead, it will resend the same IP datagram carrying the piece with the *DF* flag in its IP header set to zero, instructing the IP network to perform the necessary fragmentation on the IP datagram.

For IPv6 networks, the originating IPv6 endpoint will be required to place the necessary fragment headers on each IPv6 datagram.

### 5.8.3   Reassembling a Fragmented Message at the Data Receiver

An SCTP data receiver is always expected to be able to reassemble a user message from the fragments. In other words, support for reassembly is not optional for the data receiver.

By examining the values of the *B/E* flags carried in a received DATA chunk, the data receiver will be able to determine whether or not the chunk belongs to a fragmented user message, and furthermore, will be able to determine whether it is the first piece, the last piece, or one of the middle pieces of the fragmented message.

Once the data receiver confirms that the DATA chunk carries a fragment of a message, the data receiver will put the chunk on a reassembly queue. Once all the pieces are received, the receiver will reconstruct the user message from the pieces and deliver the message to the user application following the normal message delivery procedures outlined in Section 5.6.

### 5.8.3.1  Partial Message Delivery by the Data Receiver

If the data receiver runs out of buffer space while waiting for more fragments to complete the reassembly of a large message, it will dispatch the first part of the message to the user application if it can. This will allow the receiver to free up buffer space so that it has the necessary resources to receive the rest of the message. The implication of this is that the SCTP user is required to handle this partial delivery case in some form.

This partial delivery can only take place if the pieces already arrived contain enough data to reconstruct the first part of the message. In cases in which the first part of the message cannot be reconstructed (because, for example, the first fragment is still missing), the receiver will have to drop some of the received pieces to avoid an association lockup (unless other resources can be applied to the association). See Section 5.3.4 for more details.

## 5.8.4  User Message Bundling

An SCTP packet is designed to carry multiple chunks, including both control and user data. In this section we will discuss the benefits of and rules for bundling multiple user messages into a single SCTP packet.

The main benefit of bundling small user messages into one SCTP packet is a gain in network bandwidth efficiency. It not only can reduce the overhead of the resulting additional SCTP and IP headers, it can also substantially reduce the number of SACKs needed by the data receiver.

### 5.8.4.1  When Should User Messages Be Bundled?

The data sender will attempt user message bundling when *either* of the following occur:

1. Multiple DATA chunks are ready for transmission in the send queue

2. The user application explicitly requests bundling of small user messages

Message bundling in the first situation is part of the designed operation procedures of the SCTP sender and hence is *not* under the control of the user application. This is because message bundling in this situation does not incur any delay penalty and is therefore always beneficial to perform.

The second situation is essentially equivalent to the Nagle algorithm (Nagle 1984) normally applied to a TCP sender, in which the data sender will hold a small user message and await the returning acknowledgment, hoping that more small messages will be passed from the user application for transmission before the acknowledgment arrives. This way the accumulated messages can all be bundled together and transmitted in a single SCTP packet.

This algorithm can very effectively boost the network bandwidth efficiency when there are a lot of small user messages to be transported. However, this efficiency gain normally comes with a transmission delay penalty.

In cases in which this delay penalty is undesirable by the user application, such as in many time-critical telephony signaling transport applications, this behavior can be turned off by the user application through an operation primitive.

### 5.8.4.2   How Should User Messages Be Bundled?

When bundling is seen as appropriate under either of the situations described in the previous section, the data sender will first construct the outbound SCTP packet by following the guidelines discussed in Section 5.1.1.2.

If the user application has explicitly disallowed bundling delay, the resultant SCTP packet will be transmitted immediately. Otherwise, the data sender may hold the SCTP packet for a short period of time (defined by the duration of a bundling timer or the wait for a SACK from a previously sent SCTP packet). When the delay ends, SCTP will bundle any messages passed down during that period of time into an outbound SCTP packet (as long as the size of the final IP datagram will not exceed the PMTU).

During bundling, the data sender will place DATA chunks within an SCTP packet in increasing order of TSN. Partial chunks *must not* be placed in an SCTP packet. This implies that if the inclusion of a new DATA chunk into the SCTP packet would result in the final IP datagram becoming larger than the PMTU, the data sender will transmit the current SCTP packet and start a new SCTP packet to accommodate the new DATA chunk.

### 5.8.4.3   Unbundling User Messages at the Data Receiver

An SCTP data receiver must be capable of processing SCTP packets containing multiple bundled user messages. It processes the received DATA chunks in the order in which they were placed in the SCTP packet.

The receiver uses the length field of a chunk to determine the end of the data in the chunk. It then sets the beginning of the next chunk at the next 4-byte word boundary after the end of the data of the current chunk.

If the receiver detects a partial chunk at the end of the SCTP packet (normally shown as inconsistency between the length of the chunk and the total size of the IP datagram), it is required to drop the partial chunk.

### 5.8.4.4 *What Chunk Types Cannot Be Bundled?*

Some SCTP control chunk types are not allowed to be bundled with any other chunks. In particular, the following chunks will be sent alone:

- INIT

- INIT-ACK

- SHUTDOWN-COMPLETE

Note that some chunks, such as the SHUTDOWN-ACK chunk, are allowed to be bundled with other chunks, even though doing so may have little usefulness.

## 5.9 Adler-32 Checksum

In order to protect the user data as well as the SCTP control information from being corrupted during the transportation, SCTP includes an *Adler-32 checksum* field in the SCTP common header of each SCTP packet (see Chapter 3).

Adler-32 checksum was chosen because it is known to provide a stronger protection against data corruption than the traditional checksum used in TCP and UDP (Postel 1980, 1981b).

### 5.9.1 Generation of the Adler-32 Checksum by the Data Sender

Before sending an SCTP packet, the data sender will calculate an Adler-32 checksum over the *entire* outbound SCTP packet. It will place the result in the checksum field in the SCTP common header of the SCTP packet.

The checksum calculation is performed only after the outbound SCTP packet is fully constructed (containing the SCTP common header bundled with one or more control and/or DATA chunks, as described in Section 5.8.4), and all the fields in the SCTP packet and chunk headers, except the checksum field itself, are filled with their proper values.

The data sender will use the following steps to compute and fill in the *Adler-32 checksum* of the SCTP packet:

1. Initialize the checksum field in the SCTP common header to all zeros.

2. Calculate the Adler-32 checksum of the whole SCTP packet, including the SCTP common header and all the chunks, using the algorithm defined in Stewart et al. (2000).

3. Put the resultant checksum value into the checksum field in the SCTP common header and leave the rest of the bits of the SCTP packet unchanged.

### 5.9.2   Validation of the Adler-32 Checksum by the Data Receiver

When an SCTP packet is received, the data receiver *must* first perform a checksum validation on the SCTP packet in order to detect any data corruption in the received SCTP packet.

The receiver performs the following steps:

1. Store the received *Adler-32 checksum* value found in the SCTP common header of the SCTP packet.

2. Fill the checksum field with all zeros.

3. Calculate an *Adler-32 checksum* value over the modified SCTP packet.

4. Verify that the newly calculated *Adler-32 checksum* value is the same as the *Adler-32 checksum* value found in the received SCTP packet.

If the comparison in step 4 fails, the receiver will treat the received SCTP packet as an invalid SCTP packet and silently discard it.

## 5.10   Error Handling

### 5.10.1   Handling a Data Chunk with an Invalid Stream Identifier

During data transfer, if the data receiver receives a DATA chunk with an out-of-range stream identifier (that is, the chunk was sent to a nonexistent stream by the sender), the receiver will still send a SACK to acknowledge the reception of the TSN of the DATA chunk, following the normal procedures as described in Section 5.3. However, the receiver will discard the DATA chunk and immediately send an ERROR chunk with the cause code *Invalid stream identifier* (see Chapter

3) to report the error. The receiver may optionally bundle the ERROR chunk in the same SCTP packet as the SACK.

### 5.10.2   Handling an Empty Data Chunk

Empty user messages are not allowed in SCTP. If the data receiver finds a received DATA chunk that contains no user data, it will treat the situation as a protocol error and abort the association by sending an ABORT chunk, with the error cause set to *No user data*.

### 5.10.3   Handling Out-of-State Data

The majority of data transferring normally happens only when both endpoints are in the ESTABLISHED state. However, in some exceptional cases, DATA chunks can legally be accepted even when the endpoint is in the COOKIE_ECHOED, SHUTDOWN_PENDING, and SHUTDOWN_SENT states as well.

Section 4.3.2 and Section 9.1 provide more details on those exceptional cases.

If a DATA chunk is received in the CLOSED state (that is, the chunk is sent to a nonexistent association), the receiver will treat the chunk as an **out-of-the-blue** chunk according to the rules defined in Chapter 8.

DATA chunks received in any other state will be silently discarded by the data receiver.

Similarly, there are exceptional circumstances that may cause a SACK to be received by the data sender in the COOKIE_ECHOED, SHUTDOWN_PENDING. or SHUTDOWN_RECEIVED state. Detailed discussions of those cases can be found in Chapter 4 and Chapter 9, respectively.

If a SACK arrives in the CLOSED state (that is, the association is nonexistent) it will be treated as **out-of-the-blue** chunk following the rules in Section 8.1.

SACK chunks received in any state other than those mentioned will be silently discarded by the endpoint.

## 5.11   IETF Debate and Issues

As noted earlier, fragmentation came in and out of the protocol. Its first form did not use bits, but instead used two 16-bit values: the fragment descriptor numbers and offset. In the early debate these were discarded from the protocol in the quest to simplify things, especially because SCTP was first envisioned for signaling only. In July 1999 it was noted that this limited you to 512-byte messages in the worst case. After a lot of discussion it was added back as a sender-side option. Of course, a receiver must understand how to defragment a message, but a sender is *never* required to fragment messages. Instead it can set a sending size limit of the PMTU and reject messages sent by the upper layer that exceed this limit.

One idea that *was* in the protocol until the very end was the "cancel chunk." Two different versions were used with this concept, but both were an attempt to solve the same problem. The idea was to improve support of the application in giving up on retransmission. When an implementation decided it no longer was worth retransmitting a chunk (usually via a time limit set by the application), it could send a special chunk to indicate that this TSN and sequence number would be skipped. In its first incarnation this special chunk type was dropped quite quickly. It was decided that the gain was little with the addition of a new "cancel chunk." Then this evolved into the concept of sending an empty DATA chunk.

This would still allow the protocol to meet the requirements of keeping the TSN and stream sequence numbers in synchronization but without the excess of sending data that would be discarded for its lateness by the receiving application. In the end, an attempt to use a "zero-length" DATA chunk had an undesirable complication in that a "zero-length" data read has always had special meanings in most socket APIs. Because applications may well depend on seeing every stream sequence number, there was no way to hide the "zero length" data read. The only safe way was to drop the concept completely from the base protocol. It was decided that an implementation is always allowed to set a life timer on transmission of a chunk, but once a chunk has been committed to transmission (that is, sent on the wire at least once), it could not be revoked and had to be sent.

Another hotly debated item was the partial-delivery API. The problem is that without the partial delivery API, a user may well send a million-byte message or larger when the *rwnd* (or buffer space the receiver has) may be smaller. When this occurred, the SCTP stack on the receiver side could never hold all the data, and had no hope of reassembling the incoming message. In the end, after heated discussion, the consensus was that the partial-delivery API is the only method that could be added to avoid a potential deadlock situation.

Another late addition to the protocol was a shift in what a SACK meant. The original design called for data acknowledged past the cumulative TSN (via Gap Ack blocks) to be considered final and not advisory. This meant the sender could release the resources upon the first SACK that acknowledged a TSN. After quite some discussion, it was decided that in order to ensure a receiver had a way to get out of an extreme resource shortage, the SACK was changed to advisory. This led to the current wording in the specification, which allows the receiver to renege on data previously acknowledged by Gap Ack blocks.

As this book reached its final preparation stage, another serious issue arose with SCTP. The Adler-32 checksum was deemed weak for small messages. The reasoning behind this is that summing 8-bit quantities into a 16-bit integer does not cause the upper bits in the sums to get that much activity in small messages.

Because SCTP was primarily planned for small signaling messages, this is a serious flaw that will need to be addressed by a subsequent companion RFC. At this writing no replacement has been agreed upon by the working group. The leading candidate seems to be the ITU-T CRC-32 algorithm (ITU 1989), but there are still some that would rather see the use of Fletcher-16 (Zweig and Partridge 1990) or even a modified TCP-like checksum using 32-bit quantities. Even more so, some in the working group believe Adler-32 *is* adequate and should *not be* changed. The authors fully believe a checksum change will occur, but at this stage it is too early to tell which of the candidates will replace Adler-32.

## 5.12   Summary

In this chapter we have discussed the most fundamental function of SCTP—transportation of user messages. We first described how user messages are packaged into DATA chunks and how the DATA chunks and SCTP control chunks are put together to form SCTP packets for transmission by the sending endpoint.

We then explained how the receiving endpoint processes the arrived SCTP packets, including how SACKs are generated and used to acknowledge the reception of the user data, and how the ordered and unordered messages are handled.

We also discussed how the data reliability of SCTP is achieved when the sender retransmits lost DATA chunks. This retransmission process is controlled through the use of the retransmission timer. We listed and explained in great detail the rules the data sender should use for managing the retransmission timer.

Another important issue discussed in this chapter is the data transmission rules, which determine when the sender can send data and how much user data the sender is allowed to send out for a given moment. These data transmission rules are derived from the congestion control mechanism we will discuss in detail in Chapter 6.

Finally, we discussed some special data transfer features of SCTP, including message fragmentation, message bundling, reneging acknowledged data by the receiver, etcetra.

## 5.13   Questions

1.   How many user messages can be put into a single DATA chunk? How large can a DATA chunk be?

2.   What is a **delayed SACK**? What advantage can it bring? How much delay is allowed?

3.   What are the advantages and disadvantages of bundling small user messages?

4.   When retransmitting a DATA chunk, if the data sender finds that the DATA chunk is larger than the current PMTU, what should the data sender do? Can it resize the DATA chunk before the retransmission?

5.   If a data receiver runs out of buffer space while receiving a large fragmented message, what actions can it take to recover?

# 6

# Congestion Control and Avoidance

The congestion control function is a crucial part of any transport protocol. Without it, the Internet of today would be unusable. This is because the IP network itself does not have a built-in mechanism to police the amount of traffic a host can inject into the network. As the amount of data any given IP network can carry is always limited, when too much data is injected into the network at once, the network, or part of it, can become overwhelmed and, as a result, become incapable of transporting data with its normal efficiency. The situation is very similar to a traffic jam occurring during the rush hours on a major metropolitan highway; when it happens, all the cars are slowed down.

## 6.1   The Cause of Network Congestion Collapse

Severe network congestion can lead to so-called **congestion collapse** (Nagle 1984). This happens when a large number of hosts, all sharing some set of the same path through an IP network, send so much data into the network at about the same time that no useful data transportation or "goodput" is accomplished.

Congestion collapse can also be caused by a drastic and sudden increase in the *RTT* of a segment of the network.

In the late 1980s, congestion control was *not* part of TCP, although TCP did provide the basic flow control. But the flow control alone would not mitigate a TCP sender in the event of network congestion. In fact, TCP at the time was not even capable of recognizing network congestion. As a result, a series of Internet-wide congestion collapses was witnessed in the late eighties.

Let us use an example to illustrate how congestion collapse can be triggered in an IP network connecting some *imaginary* TCP data senders with no congestion control.[1]

Consider Figure 6–1. Here we see several hosts interconnected by some number of routers, and each router is interconnected by a set of fixed-sized communication links with two different bandwidths (large and small).

The routers with the different-sized links are most subject to a sudden spike in the *RTT*. As the offered load to the two indicated routers begins to increase, the *RTT* for the divergent sets of hosts (hosts 1 to 3 on one side and hosts 4 to 6 on the other) may take a drastic change for the worse. This drastic change will cause timeouts over the various TCP connections. The connections will retransmit the outstanding TCP segments in the queue, further filling the router queues with data already on its way and/or in queue to its eventual destination. At some point, few useful IP datagrams will be transmitted, because the majority of the IP datagrams in flight are unneeded retransmissions.

The routers in the congested state may become forced to drop IP datagrams (due to their limited buffer capacity), but because the requested load does not decrease, this will not alleviate the congestion collapse. Even if all the routers in the network are equipped with enough buffer capacity and thus do not need to drop a single IP datagram, the situation may still not improve, because the IP datagrams are always so late that they continually exceed the retransmission timer of the data senders. (See Nagle [1984] for a detailed analysis.)

As can be seen in the preceding example, without the involvement of the actual data sending endpoints, it is not possible to avoid congestion collapse in an IP network. Some method of reducing the offered load put into the network from the endpoints must be used in order to avoid this congestion collapse. This is where TCP's and SCTP's congestion control mechanism originates.

## 6.2   Basic Concept of Congestion Control

For the data sender to help prevent network congestion, it first needs to be able to realize or detect when the network is becoming congested. Then, after recognizing congestion, the data sender needs to slow down or stop its data injection into the network. This way, by effectively reducing the amount of data flowing into the network, the overloaded routers will have a better chance to recover. This simple concept forms the foundation for both TCP and SCTP congestion control algorithms.

---

1.  All TCP implementations now have congestion control built into them.

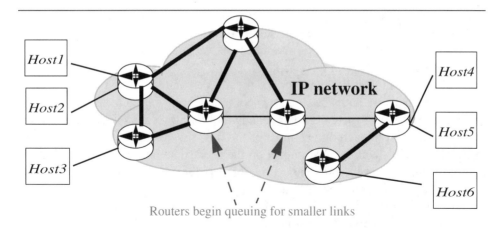

Routers begin queuing for smaller links

**Figure 6–1** *An example of congestion collapse*

This actual TCP congestion control and avoidance algorithm, which was originated by Jacobson (1988) and later documented in Allman, Paxson, and Stevens (1999), has become a part of the TCP standards.

The basic strategy of the congestion control algorithm can be described as follows:

1. When first sending data through a new connection (or through an old one that has not been utilized for some time), the data sender always starts at a very slow data rate. This is because the sustainable data throughput over this connection is unknown at this point, and the data sender wants to be conservative. Here, the sustainable data throughput is the amount of data that can be carried over this connection without causing network congestion.

2. Then the data sender gradually increases its data sending rate, as long as all data sent so far has successfully reached the destination (that is, no data has been lost). In a sense, the data sender is cautiously probing the ceiling of the sustainable data throughput of the connection.

3. However, once a data loss is detected (normally by the expiration of a retransmission timer at the data sender, as you may recall from Section 5.4), the data sender will take this as a sign of an emerging network congestion and therefore quickly cut down its data sending rate.

4. Once data loss stops, the data sender will go back to step 2 and gradually increase the data sending rate once again.

The congestion algorithm defined in Jacobson (1988) and Allman, Paxson, and Stevens (1999) requires the data sender to use an **additive increase multiplicative decrease** (AIMD) function to adjust its data sending rate, as we will discuss in more details later in this chapter.

One of the interesting behaviors of the above congestion control strategy is that if all the network paths between two communicating endpoints are adequately provisioned (that is, if there is enough bandwidth for all the data that the endpoints ever want to send to each other), most of the time the congestion control mechanism will have little noticeable impact on the users. The only time an application may notice the effects of the congestion control algorithm is on initial startup of an association or after a long period of being idle. During these times, if an application sends a burst of traffic, the congestion control algorithm mentioned may engage to slow the initial data output, slowly probing for available bandwidth.

In the remainder of this chapter we will walk through the internals of the congestion control algorithm and describe how it is realized in SCTP.

We will first discuss the congestion control variables that an SCTP endpoint needs to keep in order to track and control its data-sending rate into the network on any given path. These variables include *ssthresh*, *flightsize*, *cwnd*, and *partial bytes acknowledged*. After a discussion of these variables and how they are managed, we will turn our attention to some of the finer details of the algorithm.

Another variable that also keeps the sender from sending more data, is the receiver window, or *rwnd*. A detailed discussion of *rwnd* can be found in Section 5.3.5.3.

## 6.3    SCTP Congestion Control Algorithm

To perform proper congestion control on any SCTP association, the sender will need to track four independent pieces of information on *each* destination address. This means that each destination address that a peer indicates as part of the association (in its INIT or INIT-ACK chunk) will have a structure to track these four pieces of information. The four pieces of information are described as follows:

- The *ssthresh* variable represents the **slow start threshold**. This is the point where the congestion control algorithm moves from the slow start mode to the congestion avoidance mode (both of which are discussed later in this section).

- The *cwnd* variable represents the congestion window. This is the current estimate of how much a sender can inject into the network.

- The *partial bytes acknowledged* variable is unique to SCTP and is used in calculating *cwnd* growth during the congestion avoidance phase.

- The *flightsize* variable represents how much data has been sent but not acknowledged on a particular destination address. This indicates to the sender how much data is "in the network" making its way to its destination. The *flightsize* variable is an optimization. An implementation is not required to keep this information and, instead, *may* recount the sizes of all of the data inqueued to a particular destination each time it wishes to reference this variable.[2] In fact, this is how the SCTP reference implementation works. For ease of description, we will assume a *flightsize* variable in the following discussion.

The following rules are applied to an SCTP association at initial startup on *each* destination address:

- The *cwnd* variable is initialized to two MTUs (the MTU for a typical Ethernet link is normally 1,500 bytes).

- The *ssthresh* variable is initialized to an arbitrarily high value (but usually the peer's receiver window, that is, *rwnd*).

- The *flightsize* variable is initialized to zero (because no data has yet been sent).

- The *partial bytes acknowledge* variable is set to zero. (This variable is only used when the destination address enters the congestion avoidance phase.)

After initializing each of the variables for *each* destination, we end up with a pictorial representation of our association, as shown in Figure 6–2 (assuming an Ethernet-sized MTU and an initial association, with no piggyback data set up between endpoint A and endpoint Z). Note that the *ssthresh* variable is still an arbitrarily large value, that is, infinity (but in more practical terms it would normally be set to the value of the peer's *rwnd*).

Now, the basic rules for transmitting data are quite simple. (See Section 5.2.2 for a more complete description of the data transmission rules). Whenever you need to transmit user data (that is, DATA chunks) for the specific destination you are sending to, the following rules apply:

---

2. Remember that these variables are kept on a per-destination basis, so when performing an in-flight count, you must only count data that has been sent to the specific destination address that is being considered for transmission.

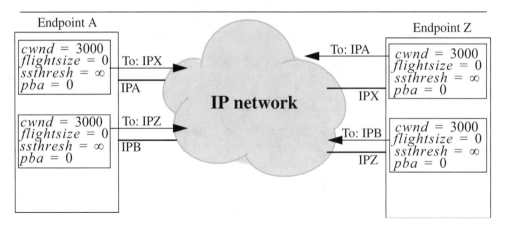

**Figure 6–2**  *The initial state of the association*

- If the *flightsize* value is smaller than *cwnd*, you are allowed to transmit data.[3]

- If the *flightsize* value is equal to or greater than *cwnd*, you are required to delay transmission until a SACK or retransmission timeout changes the condition.

- If you are allowed to transmit the data, you must add the **user data size** (in bytes) of each DATA chunk being transmitted to the *flightsize* variable.

So, using our same example, if endpoint A transmits two DATA chunks of 1,500 bytes each to IPX, the internal picture of the association will change to the one shown in Figure 6–3.

If our application sends a third data chunk, the transmission will be delayed, awaiting the arrival of a SACK from the previous transmissions. This is due to the fact that we are now using the full *cwnd* (3000 bytes) in our *flightsize* variable. Once the SACK arrives from the previous transmission, reducing our *flightsize*, the new DATA chunk(s) will be sent.

---

3. This means that in this transmission you may exceed the *cwnd* value by up to about PMTU bytes. For example, if *cwnd* is currently at 1,500 and *flightsize* is at 1,499, you are allowed to send and could send one DATA chunk of a size close to the PMTU. (The headers and control chunks will prevent you from having a full PMTU-sized chunk of data.) After this transmission you would have a *flightsize* that exceeded *cwnd* by almost PMTU bytes.

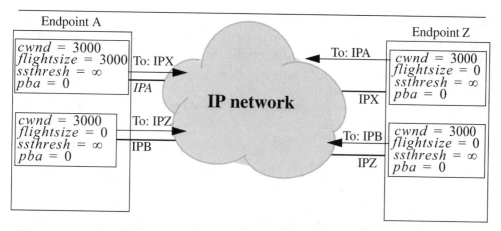

**Figure 6–3** *Changes after transmitting some data to destination IPX*

### 6.3.1 How Does Your *cwnd* Grow?

Notice that in Figure 6–3 the *cwnd* did not change. The only thing that varied was our *flightsize* because we transmitted data into the network. This begs the question, "How do you increase *cwnd*?"

The *cwnd* variable will grow in one of two methods: slow start or congestion avoidance. Slow start is used to carefully ramp the *cwnd* up during the initial startup of transmission to a destination, and after a dramatic collapse as well. Congestion avoidance is used to slowly probe for more bandwidth when the destination is approaching its saturation point.

The key to determining if you are in congestion avoidance or slow start is the *ssthresh* variable. When a destination's *cwnd* is less than or equal to the value in the destination's *ssthresh,* the slow start algorithm is used. If *cwnd* is larger than *ssthresh,* the congestion avoidance algorithm is used. In either case, *cwnd* is never increased if the current *cwnd* is not fully used.

When an endpoint receives a SACK chunk, it does two things:

**Rule 6–1**  It reduces the *flightsize* of any data being acknowledged. (Remember, this reduction must be apportioned to the appropriate destination address.)

**Rule 6–2**  It performs the appropriate *cwnd* increase algorithm if, and only if, two conditions are true: the *cumulative TSN* must have been advanced by the SACK, and the full *cwnd* must have been used on the destination address(es). To tell if the full congestion window was used, an implementation will compare *flightsize* (before processing the SACK) to *cwnd*.

### 6.3.1.1   *The Slow Start Algorithm*

The slow start algorithm is used (as previously mentioned) when *cwnd* is smaller than or equal to the *ssthresh* value. To perform the slow start algorithm, the implementation will add the total byte counts of all acknowledged data to *cwnd* as long as the total byte count of acknowledged data is *less than* the destination PMTU. If the total number of acknowledged bytes is *greater than* the PMTU value of the destination, then PMTU bytes are added to *cwnd*.

> *Note*   One important thing to remember when augmenting the *cwnd* variable is that the SACK being processed *may* acknowledge DATA chunks sent to more than one destination. If this is true, the increase to the *cwnd* variable must be apportioned to the appropriate destination address.

So, for example, if a SACK arrives acknowledging 500 bytes that were sent to IPA and 300 bytes that were sent to IPB, then IPA's *cwnd* could only be increased by 500 bytes, while IPB's *cwnd* could only be increased by 300 bytes. We use the word *could* here because the increase is subject to the conditions of Rule 6–2. This could result in one destination, both destinations, or neither destination receiving an advancement to its *cwnd*.

### 6.3.1.2   *The Congestion Avoidance Algorithm*

The congestion avoidance algorithm is used when *cwnd* is larger than the *ssthresh* value. In congestion avoidance, a much smaller increase is achieved by the use of our *partial bytes acknowledged (pba)* variable. The goal is to increase *cwnd* by one PMTU every RTT.

In order to approximate this behavior, the *pba* variable is incremented by the number of bytes acknowledged, each time a SACK arrives (subject to the same conditions of Rule 6–2 above). Remember that each destination address has its own *pba*, so any SACK that acknowledges data sent to multiple destinations must be apportioned, all subject to Rule 6–2 per destination.

Whenever the *pba* variable exceeds the value of *cwnd*, the *cwnd* variable is incremented by one destination PMTU and the *pba* variable is decreased by one PMTU. Whenever all data sent to a destination is acknowledged, the *pba* variable is reset to zero.

### 6.3.2   How Does Your *cwnd* Shrink?

Having discussed how *cwnd* increases, we now turn to the downside of things; that is, how does it decrease?

The *cwnd* value decreases on three separate events: idle time (see Section 7.2.1), timeout (see Section 5.4.3), and fast retransmit (see Section 6.3.2.1). Each event carries with it a different type of decrease.

In the case of an idle association, over time the *cwnd* value should degrade to its initial value. A straightforward way to do this is to use the heartbeat timer (discussed in Section 7.2.1) to reduce the *cwnd* by one-half its value each time a destination is idle for a heartbeat period. Notice that the value of *ssthresh* does *not* change in this reduction, because it is a far better estimation than the initial one made at the association startup.

In case of a timeout, *all* data that was in flight gets marked for retransmission: our *cwnd* will be set to 1 MTU, and the *ssthresh* variable will be set to either one-half the old value of *cwnd* or 2 MTU units (whichever is greater). This translates into the formula shown in Figure 6–4.

Note that the expiration of the retransmission timer has the effect of putting the association directly into a slow start. In the case of a fast retransmit, a different algorithm is applied. First we must know what a fast retransmit is.

#### 6.3.2.1   *The Fast Retransmit Algorithm*

Whenever a data sender processes Gap Ack blocks (as described in Section 5.3.3.2) it may recognize a DATA chunk as being potentially missing. Each time this occurs, the data sender should increase a counter of "potential missing reports" for the DATA chunk. When this counter reaches the fourth stroke, a fast retransmit is called for, and the data sender should mark the DATA chunk for retransmission, considering it lost in the network. Note that in doing so, the sender must subtract the size of this DATA chunk from the *flightsize* of the destination address.

The retransmission should be made to an alternate destination address if possible (as discussed in Section 5.5.2.2). This algorithm is termed the **fast retransmit algorithm** because it is hoped that it will retransmit a single missing DATA chunk quickly before the retransmission timer expires. In order to perform this algorithm, a sender must keep a counter for each DATA chunk, initializing this counter to zero upon the first transmission. When a fast retransmit occurs, a less drastic change is made to the *cwnd* variable. In such a case, the *ssthresh* variable is again set to either one-half the old value of *cwnd* or 2 MTU units (whichever is greater). But our *cwnd* variable is set to the value of *ssthresh*. This algorithm translates into the formula shown in Figure 6–5.

$$ssthresh = max\left(\frac{cwnd}{2}, 2 \times MTU\right)$$
$$cwnd = 1 \times MTU$$

**Figure 6–4**  *The cwnd reduction and sstrhresh change due to retransmission timer expiration*

$$ssthresh = max\left(\frac{cwnd}{2}, 2 \times MTU\right)$$
$$cwnd = ssthresh$$

**Figure 6–5**  *The cwnd reduction and ssthresh change due to fast retransmit*

Note that this places the association back into slow start, but it is very close to falling into congestion avoidance. Let us take a closer look at this subtle detail in Figure 6–6.

Here we see the *cwnd* value for a mythical sender. Notice that the first five *cwnd* advancements are happening under slow start (that is, they are below the *ssthresh* line), so we increase our *cwnd* at a rapid rate. At the sixth *cwnd* value we enter congestion avoidance. Here the increase is at a much more moderate rate (1 PMTU for every *RTT* time). We reach the seventh point, and shortly afterwards a fast retransmit occurs. This drops our *cwnd* to one-half of what it was (down to 4 PMTUs) and drops *ssthresh* to the same value. This means our endpoint is once again in slow start, but for only the first acknowledgment after recovery. This is due to the fact that *cwnd* is not greater than *ssthresh*; it is equal to it. Now after the first advancement we once again enter congestion avoidance and increase more slowly.

## 6.4   Interesting Details of the Algorithms

In this section we will present a series of examples using our two endpoints depicted earlier in Figure 6–2 (endpoint A and endpoint Z). We first assume the initial conditions shown in Figure 6–2. We then assume that endpoint A and endpoint Z have the SCTP packet exchanges depicted in Figure 6–7, with an initial PMTU of 1,500 bytes.

Notice point A in Figure 6–7. No *cwnd* increase will occur at this point because Rule 6–2 blocks us from increasing it, due to the fact that we are not using the full 3,000 bytes of *cwnd*. (We only have 2,800 bytes outstanding at the time the SACK arrives.) We now turn our attention to point B; why is this third transmission of data allowed? The key here is that although the *flightsize* after the

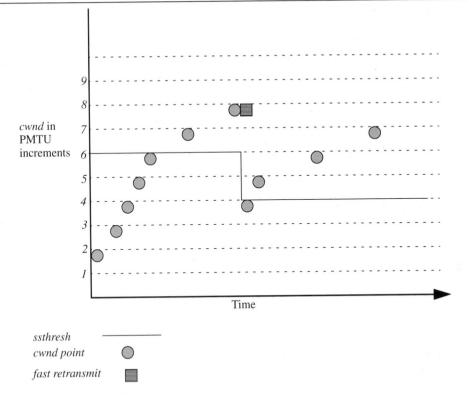

**Figure 6–6**   *Congestion variables over time*

third transmission will go over the value of *cwnd* (3,000 bytes), at the time of the comparison *flightsize* is 2,400 bytes, which makes the transmission allowable.[4] In effect, there is always the ability to slop over the value of *cwnd* by one byte less than the PMTU. At point C, with the arrival of the second SACK, we now increase our *cwnd* variable. Because the association is in slow start, we add 1,500 bytes to the *cwnd* variable even though the SACK acknowledges 2,400 bytes of data. This last SACK arrives at endpoint A (at point D in Figure 6–7). At this point, our view into the association looks like Figure 6–8.

Note that our *ssthresh* variable is still an arbitrarily large value in Figure 6–8, that is, infinity (but in more practical terms it would normally be set to the value of the peer's *rwnd*). This value will not change until we reach some sort of reduction in the *cwnd*, which implies that an association will stay in slow start (ramping up

---

4. Notice that even though the sender "slops" over the *cwnd*, the very next send will *not* be allowed, because at that point *flightsize* would be greater than *cwnd* (no matter how much the slop-over was).

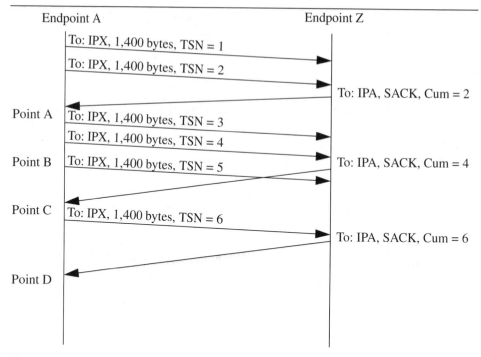

**Figure 6–7**  *Data exchanges with a cwnd increase*

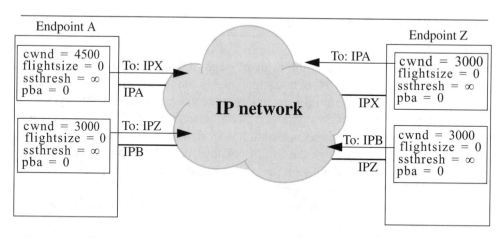

**Figure 6–8**  *Changes after transmitting some data to destination IPX*

its *cwnd* much faster) until it encounters a loss or the *cwnd* value reaches the value of the peer's *rwnd*. Our two endpoints continue data transmission and have the exchange of data shown in Figure 6–9.

Notice point E in Figure 6–9. The sender (endpoint A) first realizes that TSN8 is potentially missing; at this point the "potential missing report" is initialized to one. Note also that no increase is made to the *cwnd* variable (even though we had filled the congestion window). Because the *cumulative TSN* did not advance, no increase can be made. We can, however, send more data because the acknowledgment of TSN9 reduces the *flightsize* to below the *cwnd* value. This sequence continues with each new SACK incrementing our "potential missing report" count on TSN8 until we reach point F. Here the fast retransmit algorithm is induced and TSN8 is retransmitted. Notice that it is sent not to IPX but to the alternate address, IPZ, selected for the retransmit. After the retransmission at point F, our association's variables look as depicted in Figure 6–10.

Note that even after point G, the final SACK completing the sequence, no change will have occurred to any *cwnd* or *ssthresh* depicted in Figure 6–10. When the final SACK arrives, we apportion the SACK between the two destinations, IPX and IPZ, thus yielding a 1,400-byte acknowledgment for both destinations. Neither network is using the full *cwnd* value, so only the *flightsize* variables change, dropping back to zero.

Continuing our example, endpoint A and endpoint Z exchange the SCTP packets depicted in Figure 6–11.

At point H in Figure 6–11, our association increases its *cwnd* from 2,250 (its value after the fast retransmit adjustment) to 3,750. Note that IPX now drops out of slow start and moves into the congestion avoidance phase; at this point *pba* is zero. When the next SACK arrives at point I, the *cwnd* value does not increase (because we are in congestion avoidance); instead *pba* is incremented by 2,800 bytes.

At point J, where TSN19 is acknowledged, *pba* is again incremented by 2,800. We then verify that the *flightsize* before processing of the SACK was larger than our *cwnd*. Because this is true and because our *pba* is also greater than *cwnd*, we increase the *cwnd* by 1 PMTU and decrease the value of *pba* by the same amount. Our association now looks as shown in Figure 6–12.

The congestion avoidance algorithm will attempt to grow the congestion window slowly until it hits a loss condition, a timeout occurs, or the sending endpoint goes idle.

Figure 6–13 depicts an exchange that encounters a timeout.

At point K the retransmission timer expires. Following the normal rules for retransmission (discussed in Section 5.4.3), we find that only one TSN (number 22) will fit in an outbound SCTP packet. Note also that the *cwnd* variable will collapse to 1 PMTU, and *flightsize* will be reduced to zero for IPX. We retransmit this to IPZ (note that the original transmission went to IPX), starting IPZ's

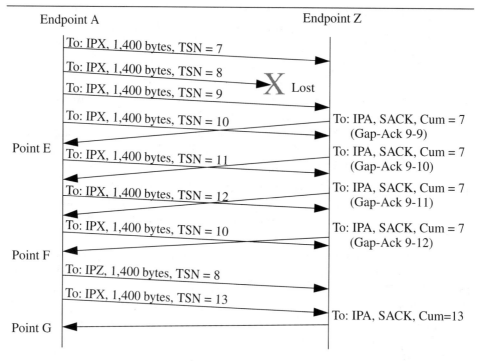

**Figure 6–9** *An exchange with small SCTP packet loss*

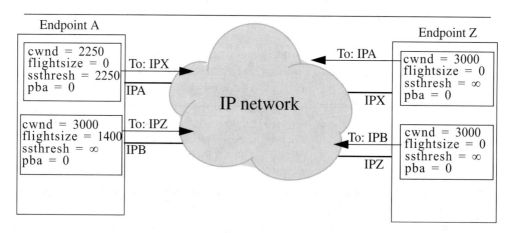

**Figure 6–10**    *Variables at point F*

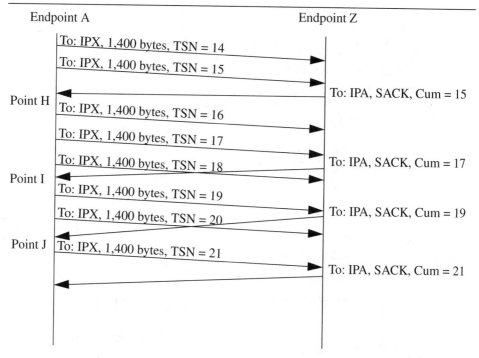

**Figure 6–11**  *Congestion avoidance*

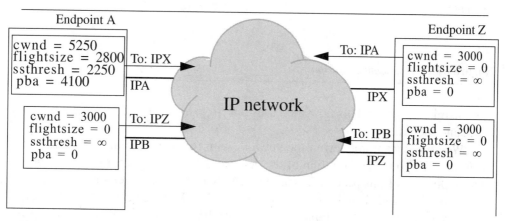

**Figure 6–12**  *Values after congestion avoidance adjustment (point J)*

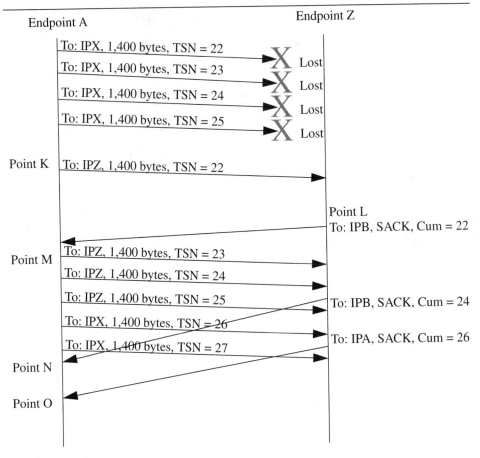

**Figure 6–13**    *A timeout condition*

retransmission timer. This now increases our *flightsize* to 1,400 bytes, but we do *not* send more data.

We do not want to overrun the network with retransmitted data; instead, we now wait for point L (expiration of the delayed-acknowledgment timer) to occur. The expiration of this timer will send the SACK back to IPB, acknowledging the arrival of TSN22. This will then lead us to point M. Here we begin retransmission of the remaining three SCTP packets (based on IPZ's *cwnd*, not IPX's). IPZ does not receive any increase in its *cwnd* for the arrival of the SACK at point M (because we were not using its full 3,000-byte *cwnd*). At point N the SACK arrives from endpoint Z for TSN24. This does advance IPZ's *cwnd* to 4,500 because the full congestion window is in use.

Note also that because our primary address has not changed, we do not clock out any more data, and new data still must go to *IPX*. The next point of interest is point O. Here a split SACK arrives acknowledging TSNs 25 and 26. Here TSN25 was sent to IPZ, and TSN26 was sent to IPX. At this point, IPX was using its full 1,500 byte-*cwnd,* having 2,800 bytes in flight, and thus it receives a *cwnd* increase of 1,500 (its share of the SACK being less than 1 MTU). IPZ, on the other hand, does not receive a *cwnd* update and remains at 4,500 bytes, because at point O it is not using its full *cwnd*.

Figure 6–14 illustrates the new values as of point O.

As you can see in Figure 6–13 and Figure 6–14, a timer expiration causes a significant reduction of our bandwidth and is hopefully a rare event. The fast retransmit is a much friendlier adjustment to the association that helps tune the association to the actual network conditions. No matter which occurs, the routers in the network drop IP datagrams as an indication of congestion. It is a much rarer event to lose an IP datagram due to corruption within the network. If this occurs it cannot be distinguished from a congestion signal. Currently there is ongoing research into the need to distinguish these two types of events, especially when part of the network path travels over a wireless link.

## 6.5   Path MTU Discovery

PMTU discovery is an algorithm and a process that a transport protocol can apply to help it choose the optimal size of data transfer across an IP network. The PMTU value is dynamic in that changes within the routing infrastructure of the network can lead to a different path through the network, and thus to a different value for PMTU. Thus PMTU discovery is a dynamic process itself that if implemented, continually monitors for changes in the PMTU value between any two endpoints.

PMTU discovery is defined in Mogul and Deering (1990) and in McCann, Deering, and Mogul (1996). Two different documents are needed because the original PMTU discovery (Mogul and Deering 1990) was designed for IPv4 and required some minor adjustments for its transition to IPv6 (McCann, Deering, and Mogul 1996). SCTP supports PMTU discovery with very few differences from TCP.

### 6.5.1   A Refresher on How PMTU Works

PMTU discovery is quite simple to implement. Consider the network and two endpoints depicted in Figure 6–15. Here we see a small routed network. Note the number associated with every link. This is the MTU of the interconnection between the routers.

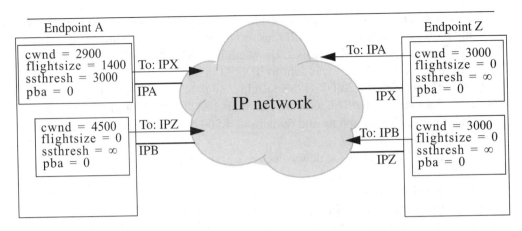

**Figure 6–14**  *Congestion values after a timeout and retransmissions (point O)*

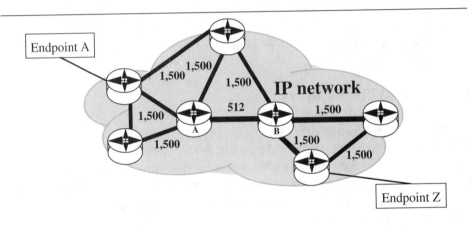

**Figure 6–15**  *A PMTU discovery example*

As IP datagrams travel between endpoints A and Z, dependent on the routing tables, the routers marked A and B may provide a 1,500- or a 512-byte path. To implement PMTU discovery for IPv4, the endpoints mark their IP datagrams with the "Don't Fragment" bit in the IP header. When router A or router B receives a 1,500-byte IP datagram, and the route of choice is over the 512-byte link, the router cannot forward the IP datagram (due to the "Don't Fragment" flag). Instead, the router will return to the sender an ICMP message coded to indicate that the destination is unreachable due to the need to fragment. In most instances, the router will include within the ICMP message the size of the hop that is limiting the IP datagram from being transmitted.[5] Periodically an endpoint may raise its PMTU value, "probing" to see if a change has occurred in the network.

For IPv6 the process is very similar, except there is no "Don't Fragment" bit to set. In IPv6, fragmentation will not be performed by the IP layer anywhere but end nodes (that is, endpoint A and endpoint Z). It becomes the job of the originating IPv6 node to insert fragmentation headers and split IP datagrams that are too large. More precise details can be found in the respective RFCs (Mogul and Deering 1990; McCann, Deering, and Mogul 1996).

### 6.5.2   PMTU Discovery in SCTP

SCTP PMTU discovery, as noted before, is much the same as for TCP. There are some slight differences. One of the biggest differences is that SCTP is multi-homed. So it is quite possible to have two paths to any endpoint. This makes it quite likely that there will exist two different values for the PMTU of the particular path. Having two different values complicates things. Which of the two sizes should I pick? If I only use the primary destination's size, what happens at retransmission when I must send the SCTP packet to the alternate destination address?

One possible implementation choice will be to choose the smallest PMTU of all of its destinations as the size limit for its fragmentation. We will call this value the *"sPMTU."* So, if a peer endpoint has two destination addresses with a 1,500-byte and a 512-byte PMTU, respectively, the *sPMTU* of the peer endpoint would be 512 bytes. When the user application of the local endpoint requests that a 3,800-byte user message be sent to the peer, the local endpoint will fragment the message into pieces to fit the 512-byte *sPMTU*. However, when it is time to transmit to the 1,500-byte path, the local endpoint will bundle multiple chunks together (two in this case) into one SCTP packet to try to optimize the use of the particular destination.

There is another issue that arises with PMTU and SCTP: what happens when I must lower the value of the PMTU?

You may recall that an IP datagram may be dropped by a router (or other device) in the network if the router finds that the size of the datagram exceeds the MTU of the next link in the path. When this happens, the router will send back to the SCTP sender an ICMP message that will contain information such as to whom the datagram was sent and the *Verification tag* carried in the SCTP packet.[6]

---

5.  Some older routers may not include this information. In such a case the sender will need to use heuristics to reduce its IP datagram size and may end up making several unsuccessful sends before "discovering" the PMTU size.

6.  The *Verification tag* that comes back in the ICMP message must be checked before the ICMP message is processed. The SCTP common header was carefully crafted to guarantee that the tag would be present in any returned message so that SCTP would not be easily fooled by a malicious attacker sending ICMP messages.

To handle this ICMP message, the SCTP sender will first lower its internal representation of the PMTU on the destination (and possibly update the *sPMTU* of this association if the lowered PMTU becomes smaller than the previous *sPMTU*). Then, if there are multiple DATA chunks bundled in the dropped SCTP packet, the sender will continue to transmit normally, depending on either a fast retransmit or a timeout to cause the dropped DATA chunks to be retransmitted.

In the case in which only a single DATA chunk was carried in the dropped packet, however, the handling becomes a bit more difficult. If the dropped DATA chunk exceeds the lowered PMTU, the sender must do one of two things (depending on whether the destination address is an IPv4 or IPv6 address).

For IPv4 the sender must remove the "Don't Fragment" bit from the IP datagram that carries the future retransmissions of the chunk. This authorizes the IP layer along the path to perform IP fragmentation on the datagram whenever it becomes necessary. In fact, the sender can immediately mark the chunk for retransmission without affecting the congestion control values (as the timeout surely would).

In the IPv6 case, the IPv6 protocol stack (*not the SCTP stack*) on the sender's machine needs to split the chunk into the correctly sized pieces and create IPv6 fragment headers for each piece so that the peer's IPv6 protocol stack can reassemble the pieces. This is in addition to the normal fragmentation and reassembly that SCTP performs.

## 6.6    Explicit Congestion Notification

ECN, which is defined in Ramakrishnan and Floyd (1999), provides to the network a method of informing endpoints of congestion without dropping IP datagrams.[7] For SCTP, implementing ECN is nearly identical to TCP, with only a few exceptions. For TCP, special bits are defined for use in the SYN and SYN-ACK to indicate that the endpoints support ECN. In SCTP's case, the *ECN capable* TLV for both the INIT and INIT-ACK has been reserved for this same purpose. When an endpoint is ECN-capable, it includes the *ECN capable* TLV in its INIT. If the peer responds with an *ECN capable* TLV as well, then ECN is enabled on the association.

Once ECN is enabled, the same procedures for discovering congestion that are defined in the ECN RFC (Ramakrishnan and Floyd 1999) are used. The ECN bits in the IP header are monitored to see if a network router has marked the IP datagram to indicate that congestion has been experienced. The reporting back to the sender is slightly different than TCP in that no bits or flags are used. Instead,

---

7. ECN was not made a mandatory part of the SCTP standard due to the fact that ECN was still classified as experimental at the time of the publication of SCTP specification *RFC2960*.

two new chunk types have been defined; Congestion Window Reduce (CWR) and Explicit Congestion Notification Echo (ECNE) have been reserved for this purpose. When a receiver recognizes the congestion experienced, it transmits back to the sender an ECNE indicating the numerically lowest TSN number in the SCTP packet marked with the "congestion experienced" bit. This ECNE is continually sent on every outgoing SCTP packet until the sender responds with a CWR notifying the receiver that the sender has reduced its *cwnd*. Other than these minor changes, the handling and processing of ECN is the same as for TCP.

## 6.7  IETF Debate and Issues

The original MDTP specification that was the starting point of SCTP did not include TCP-like congestion control. It was designed only for an engineered network where the SIGTRAN protocols were envisioned to run. The IETF Area Directors (Scott Bradner and Vern Paxson) and some of the working group members of SIGTRAN questioned the ad hoc nature of MDTP's congestion control. They wanted to know why it was not more TCP-like. The working group, thinking in a more limited scope, did not really see the need for such stringent congestion control. After all, this protocol would be running for call control signaling where the network would be carefully engineered, right? After some debate the working group was convinced especially by the argument that "if you run on a well engineered network, not stressing its capacity, then the congestion control procedures of TCP would never be invoked." This started a move to incorporate TCP behavior within SCTP's specification.

The next issue, once the working group was on track to put TCP congestion control into the protocol, was how should this be done? TCP's congestion control is all byte-counting based; SCTP sends messages not bytes. How can we translate these differences? It was noted that even though TCP counted bytes, the MTU size was also applied to translate TCP's congestion control into a number of IP datagrams. But still this did not help, because SCTP was counting chunks not IP datagrams. In the end it was pointed out that even though a sender is transmitting chunks, it still has to maintain the sizes of these chunks. Converting a chunk into a number of bytes is a straightforward application of the knowledge the sender already maintains. This meant a simple translation from chunks to bytes would then let us map directly into TCP's basic algorithms.

Once we were able to equate SCTP to TCP, other notions and questions began to arise, such as the following:

- Why do we wish to retransmit only after four strikes for fast retransmit? Why not sooner? Of course this was shown not to be worthwhile because SACK is incorporated in SCTP, and unless all the SACK's are lost, fast retransmit will get triggered anyway, so the gains are not present when weighed against the spurious and unnecessary retransmissions that such an approach may cause.

- Could we eliminate the *flightsize* variable from the protocol? The *flightsize* variable is really an artifact of implementation. Yes, every efficient implementation will maintain one, but there is no reason to codify it as a protocol variable. An implementation can just as well count all the bytes every time it wishes to know the amount of data still in transit to the remote endpoint. With these thoughts the codification of *flightsize* was removed from the document.

- How do we adjust *rwnd*? The original idea was to do complicated manipulations based on the deliverability of chunks being sent. After much debate on and many illustrations of the aggressive nature of the original proposal by some in the working group, it was finally agreed to simply accept the *rwnd* report included in a SACK and subtract from this the in-flight DATA chunks.

- How do we defeat the "ACK splitting plot"[8] known to be played by some misbehaving TCP endpoints? Placing a limit of 1 MTU per SACK increase in *cwnd* and only increasing *cwnd* by the number of bytes actually acknowledged (if less than a MTU) was put forward by Mark Allman. This was quickly incorporated into the specification.

Multi-homing itself brought up a very important question with respect to congestion control as well. How do we credit potentially multiple *cwnd*s (one for every destination) when a single SACK arrives that acknowledges multiple TSNs sent to different addresses? After some lengthy discussion, it was agreed that these should be credited apportioned to the destinations they were sent to with the restriction that no credit should be given if the *cumulative TSN* did not advance. If the *cumulative TSN* is not advancing, a starvation could occur for the receiver because it could end up always receiving more new data and potentially never be able to get an earlier message that it needed.

Since the publication of *RFC2960* (Stewart et al. 2000), further research by Rob Brennan and Thomas Curran has identified some key weaknesses in the RFC's wording. In particular, fast retransmit as defined will lead to the following issues:

---

8. This plot has been known to be used by some misbehaving TCP implementations in an attempt to gain an unfair share of network bandwidth. Under the plot, those bad implementations intentionally do not report all currently received data in a single ACK. Instead, they send multiple ACKs back, with each reporting only a portion of the received data. This results in an artificial increase in the number of ACKs needed for acknowledging the amount of data being transferred, and thus tricks the TCP data sender into opening up its *cwnd* faster than it would normally.

- The current wording for including Gap Ack blocks in a SACK is "SHOULD." In IETF-speak, this means that it is not a strict requirement. Without Gap Ack blocks reporting in the SACK, the congestion control algorithms do not function as designed. A future version or supplement to the RFC will correct this by changing the "SHOULD" to "MUST."

- DATA chunks being fast retransmitted must wait for room in the *cwnd* before being sent. This could result in a rather long delay while the sender waits for the *flightsize* to drop below *cwnd* on a long-fat pipe.[9] Expect the revised RFC to fix this as well, making it so that a fast retransmit can happen no matter what the *flightsize* or *cwnd* variables are.

- The current wording of the RFC allows a DATA chunk being fast retransmitted to be sent multiple times, each time reducing the *cwnd*. This means once again that a long-fat pipe will be penalized. This is because even if you retransmit the SCTP chunk right away, it will take some time for the SCTP packet to arrive at the receiver, and continued Gap Ack blocks will arrive during this time, reporting the chunk missing. The updated RFC will be changed appropriately to indicate that once a DATA chunk has been retransmitted using fast retransmit, it is not eligible for retransmission again until a timeout occurs.

- A final problem was found that relates to a potential burst of SCTP packets, again in the long-fat pipe category. If a receiver clamps its *rwnd* to zero, due to a lost DATA chunk that will be fast retransmitted, when the SACK arrives for the retransmitted DATA chunk, the *rwnd* has the potential to jump from zero to a full window.[10] This may cause a burst of SCTP packets to be sent in response (if the *cwnd* variable is quite large), more than the network can sustain. A burst limit needs to be added when a SACK that completes a fast retransmit arrives. This burst limit will not effect normal data transfer, because in normal data transfer a fast retransmit is not completed.

## 6.8  Summary

This chapter describes the SCTP congestion control and congestion avoidance mechanism. The guiding principle in the SCTP congestion control design was to make SCTP congestion control behave in a similar way to that of TCP's, so that an SCTP association would compete fairly with a TCP connection for bandwidth

---

9.  A long-fat pipe is a network path that has a large bandwidth-delay product. This can either be the result of high bandwidth and long delay or a smaller bandwidth with a very large delay.

10. This would be due to the receiver delivering all of its data that is being held while awaiting the fast transmission of the missing DATA chunk contained in the SCTP packet.

usage in a network. Therefore, the SCTP congestion control mechanism bears a great deal of similarity to the TCP's, as was shown in this chapter.

Examples were given in the chapter to illustrate how the different SCTP congestion control variables were computed and used during data transfer.

In addition, two congestion control-related mechanisms were discussed, namely the PMTU discovery and the Explicit Congestion Notification mechanisms. Both are built into SCTP.

## 6.9   Questions

1.   When an SCTP endpoint sets up an association with a multi-homed peer with $k$ destination addresses, how many *cwnd* and *rwnd* variables will need to be maintained by the endpoint?

2.   If an endpoint follows the congestion control rules strictly, is it true that *flightsize* will always be smaller than or equal to the *cwnd* value of the same destination address?

# 7

# Failure Detection and Recovery

**O**ne of the important features built into SCTP is the failure detection and recovery mechanism. This is especially useful when the data receiver is multihomed—a typical arrangement found in many high-availability systems. With the failure detection and recovery mechanism, the SCTP data sender can fully take advantage of the redundancy arrangement at the receiver and can normally handle network path failures, without requiring intervention from its user application.

In this chapter we will discuss how the SCTP detects and handles different types of failure.

## 7.1   The Types of Failure SCTP Detects

An SCTP endpoint engaged in data transfer with another endpoint, via an SCTP association, may encounter two types of failure:

1. One or more destination addresses of the peer endpoint become unreachable.

2. The peer endpoint itself becomes unreachable.

### 7.1.1   Unreachable Destination Address

A destination address can become unreachable when a network path from the sender to the receiver breaks due to, for example, some component (such as a router, a cable, or a NIC card) failure along the path. Let us look at an example.

Figure 7–1 shows two multi-homed endpoints (endpoint 1 on machine A and endpoint 2 on machine B), with each machine connected to two separate networks (network 10.1.x.x. and network 160.15.x.x). Let us assume that both machine A and machine B are configured such that all their outbound IP datagrams destined to 10.1.x.x addresses are transmitted through network 10.1.x.x, and all their outbound IP datagrams destined to 160.15.x.x addresses are transmitted through network 160.15.x.x. Furthermore, let us assume that an SCTP association exists between endpoint 1 and endpoint 2.

If, for instance, a cable in network 10.1.x.x fails as shown in Figure 7–1, any SCTP packet sent from endpoint 1 to address 10.1.30.135 of endpoint 2 will not get through, and endpoint 1 will therefore find **address** 10.1.30.135 of endpoint 2 **unreachable**. Similarly, any transmission from endpoint 2 to address 10.1.61.11 of endpoint 1 will fail due to the cable breakage, and that address will be viewed as unreachable by endpoint 2.

However, all 160.15.x.x addresses are not affected by this cable breakage, and the association between endpoints 1 and 2 will remain operational because either endpoint can still reach the other by the peer's 160.15.x.x destination address.

### 7.1.2    Unreachable Peer Endpoint

An endpoint in an SCTP association may find its peer endpoint unreachable if *all* the destination addresses of that peer endpoint become unreachable due to some extensive component or network failures. The peer endpoint itself may have suffered a software failure and gone out of service. Either of these two possibilities will be viewed (from the standpoint of the peer) as an **endpoint unreachable** failure.

Figure 7–2 shows an example of an unreachable peer endpoint, where, with the same network and node configurations as in Figure 7–1, we further assume that a second failure breaks the path through network 160.15.x.x.

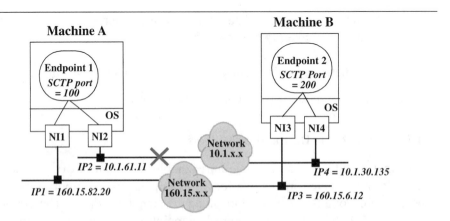

**Figure 7–1**  *Path failure between multi-homed endpoints*

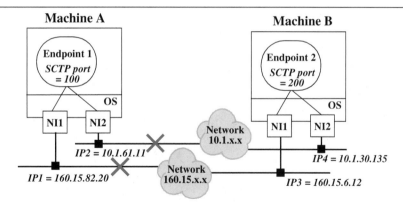

**Figure 7–2**  *Unreachable peer endpoint due to network failures*

With the failures now affecting both network paths, both destination addresses of endpoint 2 will become unreachable from the perspective of endpoint 1. Under such circumstances, endpoint 1 will consider endpoint 2 unreachable. In this example, endpoint 2 will also consider its peer endpoint 1 unreachable for the same reason.

| | |
|---|---|
| *Note* | When an endpoint finds that its peer has become unreachable, it is impossible for the endpoint to make a distinction between whether the failure is in the network or in the peer itself. |

For instance, endpoint 1 will not be able to distinguish the failure depicted in Figure 7–3 from that depicted in Figure 7–2.

## 7.2  How to Detect an Unreachable Address

Every time an SCTP sender sends a DATA chunk or a control chunk that requires a response to a specific destination address of a peer, the sender will get a chance to make a new assessment of the reachability of that destination address.

Along with DATA chunks, the HEARTBEAT chunks are also used in SCTP to assess a destination address' reachability. This will be discussed in detail in the sections that follow.

If, after sending out the DATA or control chunk, the sender receives the expected acknowledgment, it can then conclude that the particular destination address of the peer that the chunk was sent to is still reachable.

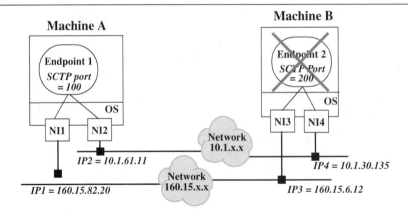

**Figure 7–3** *Unreachable peer endpoint due to peer endpoint failure*

On the other hand, if the sender does not receive a response from the peer in a given period of time (the sender cannot wait forever), the sender may consider that destination address of the peer **possibly unreachable**.

Here we use the phrase "possibly unreachable" to emphasize the fact that this methodology of assessing an address' unreachability is *not* always reliable. This is because, by default, most commonly implemented IP networks are so-called "best-effort" data transfer networks; there is no guarantee that an IP datagram sent through an IP network will be delivered to its intended destination, even when everything in the network is functioning normally without a fault. In other words, a missed response to a DATA or control chunk that requires a response may not indicate a failure at all.

However, if a sender notices that all expected responses are missing for consecutive chunks sent to a destination address of a peer, the sender will then have to conclude that the particular destination address is very likely unreachable now. This leads to the algorithm of unreachability detection in SCTP, which is discussed in Section 7.2.2.

### 7.2.1 Using HEARTBEAT Chunks to Monitor Reachability

When no user data has been sent to a destination address of a peer for a certain period of time, the reachability status of that address can no longer be updated by using user data alone. However, the endpoint can choose to continue the reachability assessment on that address with some special-purpose response-required control chunks generated by the endpoint itself. Particularly, SCTP uses periodic HEARTBEAT chunks for this purpose.

A destination transport address is considered "idle" if no chunk that can be used for updating the path *RTT* of the address has been sent to the address within the current **heartbeat period** of that address.[1] Chunks that can be used for updating the path *RTT* usually include the first-transmission DATA, INIT, COOKIE ECHO, and HEARTBEAT chunks.

This definition of "idle" destination address applies to both **active** and **inactive** destination addresses. (See Section 5.5.2.1 for details on inactive destination addresses.)

The ability to monitor idle destination addresses' reachability is very desirable in many high-availability systems, such as telephone call control systems. In telephone applications it is important to provide notification (alarm) of a failure so that the problem can be addressed immediately and the service will not be disrupted.

Telephone systems often have multi-homed endpoints for redundancy. When the peer is multi-homed, an SCTP endpoint will normally be required to select one of the peer's destination addresses as the **primary destination address**. All other destination addresses of the peer become alternate (or backup) addresses. During normal operation, all the backup destination addresses will be idle and see no user data sent to them.

If the endpoint wants to monitor the reachability status of those idle destination addresses of the peer, it will periodically send HEARTBEAT chunks to those idle destination addresses in order to keep their reachability status updated. The details of using HEARTBEAT chunks to assess the reachability of a destination address are discussed in Section 7.2.2.

### 7.2.2   Address-Unreachability Detection Algorithm

The algorithm used for detecting peer destination address unreachability by an SCTP endpoint is rather straightforward.

For each destination address, $i$, of a peer, the endpoint monitors its reachability state, $S_i$, by keeping track in the error counter, $E_i$, the number of consecutive missed responses to DATA and/or HEARTBEAT chunks sent to that destination address. The endpoint will consider the destination address unreachable and mark it as **inactive** when the number of consecutive missed responses on that address exceeds the threshold set by the protocol parameter *Path.Max.Retrans*. On the other hand, if a DATA or HEARTBEAT chunk sent to the address is responded to by the peer, the endpoint will consider the destination address as reachable and mark it **active**.

---

1. The **heartbeat period** for an address is a configured option with a reasonable default value normally set to 30 seconds. An application is allowed to change this through a socket option or other similar facility.

In particular, the algorithm can be described as follows:

1. Set $E_i = 0$ and $S_i =$ ACTIVE for all destination addresses of the peer when the association is started.

2. Whenever a *T3-rtx* timer expires on an outstanding DATA chunk sent to destination address $i$ and $S_i$ is not set to INACTIVE, set $E_i = E_i + 1$ and, if $E_i > Pat.Max.Retrans$, set $S_i =$ INACTIVE and report this state change of the destination address to the upper layer.

3. Whenever a HEARTBEAT chunk is sent to an idle destination address $i$ and $S_i$ is not set to INACTIVE, set $E_i = E_i + 1$ and, if $E_i > Pat.Max.Retrans$, set $S_i =$ INACTIVE and report this state change of the destination address to the upper layer.

4. Whenever a SACK that acknowledges a DATA chunk last sent to destination address $i$ is received, reset $E_i = 0$ and, if $S_i$ is not set to ACTIVE, set $S_i$ = ACTIVE and report this state change of the destination address to the upper layer.

5. Whenever a HEARTBEAT-ACK is received in response to a HEARTBEAT last sent to destination address $i$, reset $E_i = 0$ and, if $S_i$ is not set to ACTIVE, set $S_i =$ ACTIVE and report this state change of the destination address to the upper layer.

### 7.2.2.1   *Possibility of False Detection*

As we have already indicated at the beginning of Section 7.2, the IP network is only a "best-effort" network, and a single missing response to a DATA or HEARTBEAT chunk may not necessarily mean a failure in the path.

Therefore, to make the detection more reliable, the algorithm described in Section 7.2.2 determines the unreachability of a destination address based on consecutive missing responses.

Even still, the possibility that false unreachability detection can be made by the algorithm does exist. For example, severe network congestion can cause consecutive IP datagrams to be dropped along the path. This may result in the data sender mistaking the destination address as unreachable if the number of consecutively dropped IP datagrams causes the error counter of the destination address to exceed *Path.Max.Retrans*. Another example in which false detection may happen is when the *RTT* of the path corresponding to a destination address suddenly increases dramatically, causing consecutive expirations of the *T3-rtx* timer at the data sender.

When the peer is multi-homed, the alternate destination address(es) of the peer can normally keep the association from failing when a network condition mistak-

> *Note* An implementation must use special caution against false detection events if it chooses to start a *T3-rxt* timer for every outbound SCTP packet. If such an implementation sends out a burst of packets in a very short period of time with the same *RTO*, a sudden change in the *RTT* of the destination address to which the packets are sent could cause all packets in that burst to time out. This would cause a quick rise in the number of errors and could in turn cause a false address-unreachability detection.

enly marks one of the destination addresses **inactive**. In most cases, the error will eventually be corrected at the endpoint when a HEARTBEAT-ACK is received in response to a subsequent HEARTBEAT sent to the **inactive** destination address. The arrival of the HEARTBEAT-ACK will immediately put the destination address back into service and make any necessary adjustment to its *RTO* time.

However, the consequence of a false detection becomes more penalizing when the peer is single-homed—the false detection of unreachability on the single destination address will almost surely cause the association to go down.

By raising the detection threshold (that is, making the protocol parameter *Path.Max.Retrans* larger), one can effectively reduce the chance of false unreachability detection. But the drawback is that it will take longer to detect an actual path failure.

Let us look at an example. Assume that the path failure scenario shown in Figure 7–1 happens and, at the time the failure occurs, endpoint 1 is busy sending data packets to endpoint 2's primary destination address, 10.1.30.135. Furthermore, assume that the initial *RTO* used at the time of the failure is 1 second for destination addresses 10.1.30.135.

If we have *Path.Max.Retrans* set to 4, because of the *RTO* "back-off" procedure (described in Section 5.4.3), it will take at least $1 + 2 + 4 + 8 = 15$ seconds after the occurrence of the failure for endpoint 1 to register four consecutive *T3-rtx* timeouts on destination address 10.1.30.135 and mark it **inactive**.

For *Path.Max.Retrans* = 5, this detection delay will become at least $1 + 2 + 4 + 8 + 16 = 31$ seconds.

To summarize the above discussions, we understand now that the choice of protocol parameter *Path.Max.Retrans* is a trade-off between the reliability of the detection and the speed of the detection. For most applications, a value of 5 for *Path.Max.Retrans*, as recommended in the SCTP specification (Stewart et al. 2000), should be used.

### 7.2.2.2   An Ambiguity in Detecting Address Reachability

Recall that in the algorithm described in Section 7.2.2, an endpoint will immediately mark a destination address as **active**/reachable whenever it receives an acknowledgment for the DATA chunk that was last sent to that destination address. However, if the peer is multi-homed and the DATA chunk being acknowledged has been retransmitted by the endpoint, there will be an ambiguity for the endpoint. Which of the destination addresses of the peer should be credited with this reachability detection? Figure 7–4 illustrates this ambiguity.

In this example, after sending DATA1 to addr1 of the multi-homed peer, the *T3-rtx* timer expired at endpoint A. Therefore, endpoint A will increase the error count of addr1 by one, according to the algorithm described in Section 7.2.2. Then, based on retransmission procedures defined in Section 5.5.2.2, endpoint A retransmits DATA1 to addr2 of the peer. Sometime after this retransmission, endpoint A receives a SACK from endpoint Z acknowledging DATA1. According to our failure detection algorithm, endpoint A will not reset the error count of addr1; instead it will credit this acknowledgment to addr2 because DATA1 was last sent to addr2.

In reality, there exists the possibility that the acknowledgment received may actually be a response from endpoint Z to the first transmission of DATA1 to addr1. In such a case, the strategy defined in our failure detection algorithm will in fact credit the reachability to the wrong address. The root of the problem is that when receiving an acknowledgment to a DATA chunk that has been transmitted more than once, it becomes impossible for the data sender to tell with certainty which copy of the DATA chunk is actually being acknowledged by the data receiver, as shown by the example in Figure 7–4.

However, this ambiguity does not seem to bear any significant consequence for SCTP operation. For example, if the SACK in Figure 7–4 is actually a response to the first transmission of DATA1, addr1 will have an opportunity to clear its error count. Given the *RTO* back-off rule, it is very unlikely that the next data transmission to addr1 will cause another timeout. The error count of addr1 will more likely be cleared when the next transmission is acknowledged.

For addr2, if it is actually unreachable when endpoint A wrongly credits it with the reachability (as a result of the ambiguity), the consequence would be no worse than a few unnecessary retransmissions if endpoint A subsequently sends data to addr2. Thus the drawback to not applying Karn's rule to unreachablility detection is an increase in failure detection time and a resultant delay in any alarm or notification.

In any case, if this ambiguity and its consequences are undesirable, the data sender may choose not to clear the error count if the received acknowledgment is to a DATA chunk that has been retransmitted. This implementation variation is allowed in SCTP.

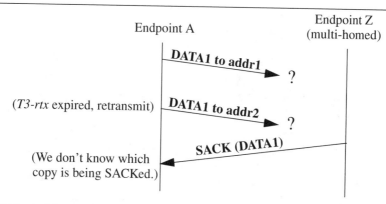

**Figure 7–4** *Ambiguity on reachability detection*

### 7.2.3   More on Using the SCTP HEARTBEAT

As we already mentioned in Section 7.2.1, an endpoint can use the SCTP heart-beat mechanism to continue monitoring the (un)reachability of a destination address even when there is no user data being sent to that address. In this section we give more details on how the SCTP mechanism works and how an endpoint controls this mechanism.

#### 7.2.3.1   User Interface to Control the SCTP HEARTBEAT
SCTP protocol recommends that the implementation provides the following controls to the user application to manage the SCTP heartbeat mechanism:

1. *Disable or re-enable the heartbeat on a specific destination address of a peer*—By default, whenever an **active** or **inactive** destination address of a peer becomes idle (that is, no user data or HEARTBEAT chunk has been sent to that address for *HB.Interval* seconds), the endpoint should send out a new HEARTBEAT chunk to that address. However, the user application can choose to disable (and re-enable later) this default behavior on any given destination address through the use of a primitive interface anytime in the existence of the association.

2. *Change the heartbeat period*—The period for sending HEARTBEAT chunks to each idle destination address is controlled by the protocol parameter *HB.Interval*. The user of SCTP should be able to change the value of this protocol parameter through a primitive interface to suit the nature and requirements of the network and the application better. This is a crucial

variable that an application can use to help tune both failure detection time and network usage during idle periods.

*Note*
> When *HB.Interval* is increased, there is a side effect to the behavior of the association that should be taken into account. In particular, when this value is increased—that is, when the interval between HEARTBEAT chunks becomes longer—the detection of a lost ABORT chunk from the peer will take longer as well. This is because if the peer for any reason is trying to tear down the association, and its ABORT chunk is lost, the local endpoint will not discover the lost ABORT until it sends the next DATA or HEARTBEAT chunk (which in turn will cause the peer to send another ABORT).

3. *Trigger a single HEARTBEAT chunk to be sent to a specific destination address of a peer*—A primitive interface should exist to allow the user of SCTP to trigger the SCTP stack to send out a single HEARTBEAT chunk to a specific destination address of a peer, regardless of whether the address is idle or not at the moment. This interface may be used by the SCTP user to take over the control of the timing of HEARTBEAT chunks so that it can be coordinated with certain application activities.

### 7.2.3.2   *What the Sender of a HEARTBEAT Should Do*

#### 7.2.3.2.1   *Managing the Error Count*
As defined in our (un)reachability detection algorithm in Section 7.2.2, the HEARTBEAT sender increments the error count of a destination address every time a HEARTBEAT is sent to that address; whenever a HEARTBEAT-ACK arrives, the sender clears the error count of the destination address to which the HEARTBEAT was sent.

An alternative implementation approach the sender can use is to increase the respective error count only after a HEARTBEAT sent to that address is not acknowledged for one *RTO*.

Furthermore, whenever the value of this error count reaches the protocol parameter *Path.Max.Retrans*, the endpoint will mark the corresponding destination address as **inactive** if it is not so marked, and optionally report to the SCTP user the reachability change of this destination address.

### 7.2.3.2.2 Timing for Sending out HEARTBEAT Chunks

On an idle **active** destination address $i$ that is allowed to heartbeat, the endpoint normally sends out a HEARTBEAT chunk every $H_i$ seconds, which is determined using the following formula:

$$H_i = RTO_i + HB.Interval \times (1 + \delta)$$

where $RTO_i$ is the latest $RTO$ of destination address $i$ calculated using the algorithm defined in Section 5.4.1.2, and $\delta$ is a random value between -0.5 and 0.5 designed to add some jitter into the timing of each individual HEARTBEAT so that the traffic created by all the HEARTBEAT chunks in the network will not become too clumpy.

Furthermore, at the time the current HEARTBEAT is sent, if the previous HEARTBEAT sent to the same destination address $i$ was never acknowledged, $RTO_i$ should be doubled in the same way as if a *T3-rtx* timer expiration had happened on that address (see Section 5.4.3).

On an idle **inactive** destination address that is allowed to heartbeat by the SCTP user, because the $RTO$ of the destination address is no longer meaningful, one reasonable way of determining $H_i$ for that address is to substitute the protocol parameter *RTO.Initial* in for $RTO_i$:

$$H_i = RTO.Initial + HB.Interval \times (1 + \delta)$$

For implementers, one convenient way of timing this heartbeat mechanism is to run a heartbeat timer for each destination address, and to start the timer to expire in $H_i$ seconds every time a DATA or HEARTBEAT chunk is sent to that destination address. In particular, if a new DATA or HEARTBEAT chunk is transmitted to that address before the timer expires, clear the timer and restart it with an updated $H_i$; however, if the timer ever expires, send out a HEARTBEAT chunk and then restart the timer with the updated $H_i$.

It is also possible for an implementation to control the heartbeat timing of an entire association with a single heartbeat timer. This approach may require fewer resources than the one just described; the timer will be used to cover all the destination address(es) of the peer. However, when there are multiple destination addresses to monitor, the design following this approach should try to spread over the time the outbound HEARTBEAT chunks sent to different idle destination addresses so that they will not create bursts of HEARTBEAT traffic into the network.

In particular, the endpoint should avoid sending multiple HEARTBEAT chunks each time the heartbeat timer expires. One simplified method of preventing this is to start the heartbeat timer with an interval of $H_i/m$, where $m$ is the current number of destination addresses of the peer that have HEARTBEAT chunks enabled by the SCTP user. Select one of the *m* destination addresses in a round-robin fashion to send out a single HEARTBEAT chunk every time the timer expires. However, it is not hard to show that the heartbeat timing control with this simplified approach will be far less than ideal if the *m* destination addresses have *RTO*s that differ widely from one another.

### 7.2.3.2.3   Including Useful Information in HEARTBEAT Chunks

In order to make assessments on the reachability of a destination address, the endpoint will need to know exactly whether a HEARTBEAT sent to that particular destination address has been acknowledged by the peer. Because there may be multiple destination addresses to monitor for the same peer, the sender needs to be able to tell by examining the HEARTBEAT-ACK where the original HEART-BEAT was sent. This can be achieved by including the destination address (or an internal index of it) to which a HEARTBEAT is sent as part of the HEARTBEAT chunk. The receiver of a HEARTBEAT always copies this address or address index information from the HEARTBEAT into the HEARTBEAT-ACK when it responds. In this way, upon the reception of the HEARTBEAT-ACK, the endpoint can easily identify the correct destination address to credit the reachability assessment.

The sender of a HEARTBEAT chunk may also want to include a timestamp in the chunk to indicate the time the chunk is sent. This information will also be copied out and sent back in the corresponding HEARTBEAT-ACK by the peer if it is present in the received HEARTBEAT. Upon receiving the HEARTBEAT-ACK, the sender of the HEARTBEAT can use this information to update the *RTT* of the destination address.

The sender of the HEARTBEAT chunk should carry the above destination address and timestamp information in the *HEARTBEAT Sender Specific Information* field of the chunk (see Section 3.2.7).

### 7.2.3.3   What the Receiver of a HEARTBEAT Should Do

The receiver of a HEARTBEAT chunk should immediately respond to the sender with a HEARTBEAT-ACK. More importantly, the IP address the receiver should use to send the HEARTBEAT-ACK to must be the source IP address found in the IP datagram header that carried the HEARTBEAT chunk.

Furthermore, the receiver of the HEARTBEAT must copy the information in the *Sender Specific Heart Beat information* field out from the arrived HEART-BEAT and insert this information, without any alteration, into the *Sender Specific Heart Beat information* field of the corresponding HEARTBEAT-ACK (see Section 3.2.8). A very simple way for an implementation to do this is to overwrite the HEARTBEAT chunk type with that of a HEARTBEAT-ACK type. This overwriting of the chunk type will turn the original HEARTBEAT into a HEARTBEAT-

ACK, which can then be transmitted back to the source IP address found in the IP packet carrying the HEARTBEAT.

### 7.2.4 Handling an Unreachable Primary Destination Address

As you may recall from Section 5.5, when a peer is multi-homed, one of the destination addresses for that peer will be selected (either by the endpoint at the association initialization or by later user primitives) as the primary destination address. By default the local endpoint will automatically transmit user data to this primary destination address.

When the primary destination address is detected as unreachable, the local endpoint will mark it **inactive** and report the reachability change to the SCTP user, as discussed in Section 7.2.2. In addition the local endpoint will automatically pick a temporary primary destination address for that peer if an alternate destination address exists and is in the **active** state for that peer. Subsequent user data will be transmitted to this temporary primary destination address until one of the following occurs:

1. The association is closed.

2. The user changes the primary destination.

3. The original primary destination becomes **active** again.

The selection policy for the temporary primary destination address is not specified in SCTP protocol and is an implementation decision.

In practice, upon receiving the primary destination address unreachable notification, the SCTP user will probably instruct the SCTP stack to switch to the most suitable alternate address as the new permanent primary address for that peer.

If, before the SCTP user selects a new permanent primary address, the old primary destination address recovers and becomes reachable again (for example, a HEARTBEAT to the old primary address is answered), the local endpoint will retain the original primary destination address and automatically switch data transmission back to it.

## 7.3 How to Detect an Unreachable Peer

The local endpoint will consider a peer unreachable if too many consecutive packets sent to the peer fail to get any acknowledgment back. An unreachable peer is normally the result of either of the following:

- The peer endpoint itself has suffered a failure (for example, a software crash of the peer SCTP stack or a hardware shutdown of the host machine where the peer runs).

- The network connecting the local endpoint to the peer has a severe problem that cuts all the communication paths to the peer.

It is evident that the local endpoint will not be able to distinguish between these two different types of failure.

For each peer with which the local endpoint has an association, the local endpoint keeps a counter on the total number of consecutive timeout-induced retransmissions to its peer (including retransmissions to all the destination transport addresses of the peer if it is multi-homed). The endpoint will also increase this error counter every time a HEARTBEAT is not acknowledged.

During normal operation, this total retransmission counter is reset to zero every time a DATA chunk sent to that peer endpoint is acknowledged (by the reception of a SACK from the peer) or a HEARTBEAT-ACK is received from that peer.

However, if the value of this counter exceeds the limit indicated in the protocol parameter *Association.Max.Retrans*, the local endpoint will mark the peer endpoint as unreachable. This will in effect bring an end to the association; that is, the association will enter the CLOSED state.

When this happens, the endpoint will report the loss of communication with the peer to the SCTP user and will optionally pass back to the SCTP user all pending user data remaining in its outbound queue.

Figure 7–5 shows the event sequence of detecting the failure of a multi-homed peer. We assume that the peer (endpoint Z) has two destination addresses and that the *RTO* for both addresses is 1 second at the time of failure. We also assume that the protocol parameter, *Association.Max.Retrans*, for the local endpoint (endpoint A) is set to 5.

When the peer failure occurs, the DATA chunk sent to destination address addr1 will cause a timeout at endpoint A. This timeout event will increase the *total error counter* (*tec*) of the peer by one and will trigger a retransmission of the DATA chunk to destination address addr2. This will also cause the *RTO* of the first address to be doubled (see Section 5.4.3).

Similarly, this retransmission to addr2 will time out, and the events described above will be repeated again and again, as shown in Figure 7–5, each time with longer *RTO*s and an increased *tec* value. Finally, the value of *tec* will exceed the value of *Association.Max.Retrans*, and endpoint Z will be marked as unreachable.

In the end, each of the two destination addresses will have experienced three timeouts, and the total detection delay of the peer failure in this example will be $(1 + 1 + 2 + 2 + 4 + 4) = 14$ seconds, as shown in Figure 7–5.

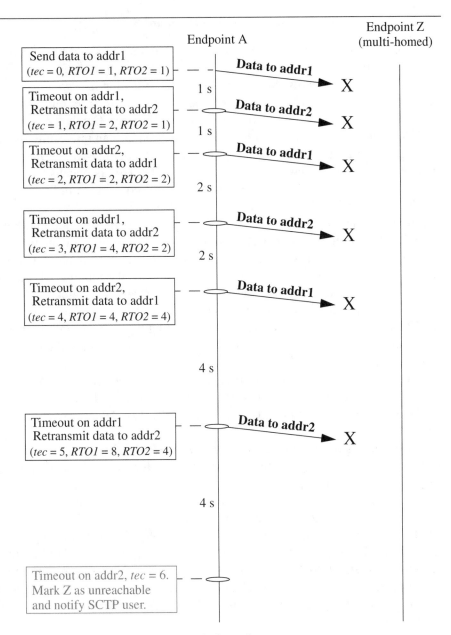

**Figure 7–5** *Detecting the failure of a multi-homed peer*

### 7.3.1　When an Association Enters the Dormant State

It is worth noting that in the current SCTP standard, the threshold for detecting the peer failure (that is, *Association.Max.Retrans*) and the threshold for detecting the failure of each of the individual addresses of the peer (that is, *Path.Max.Retrans*, see Section 7.2.2) are independent protocol parameters of an endpoint. Each parameter can be separately configured by the SCTP user. Careless configuration of these protocol parameters can lead the association into an interesting **dormant** state in which all the destination addresses of the peer are found unreachable while the peer still remains in the reachable state. This is because the overall retransmission counter for the peer (that is, the *tec* counter, as in Figure 7–5) is still below the set *Association.Max.Retrans* threshold.

To avoid this **dormant** state, when configuring the SCTP endpoint, the user should avoid setting the value of *Association.Max.Retrans* higher than the summation of the values of *Path.Max.Retrans* for all the destination addresses for the peer. This will guarantee that, *if the peer fails*, the local endpoint will detect the failure before all the destination addresses of the peer become unreachable.

However, if the unreachable peer is a result of network problems, even if the SCTP user follows the above precaution on setting the protocol failure detection thresholds, there will still be a possibility that the association will end up in the **dormant** state.

Let us look at an example. In Figure 7–6 we assume that multi-homed endpoint Z has two destination addresses (addr1 and addr2) and that endpoint A has its *Association.Max.Retrans* set to 5 and its *Path.Max.Retrans* set to 3 for both addr1 and addr2.

Initially, as shown at the top of Figure 7–6, addr1 failed due to, for instance, an interface card problem at endpoint Z. After four timeouts on addr1, endpoint A detects this failure and marks addr1 as unreachable.

Later, another network problem causes addr2 to become unreachable. After four timeouts on addr2, we have both the address error counter for addr2 (*aec2*) and the total error counter of the association (*tec*) equal to 4. Following the algorithm in Section 7.2.2, endpoint A marks addr2 as unreachable. But because the value of *tec* is still below *Association.Max.Retrans*, which is set to 5, endpoint A will not consider the peer unreachable. This is in spite of the fact that both destination addresses of the peer are now unreachable. The association enters the **dormant** state.

How the endpoint should handle associations in the **dormant** state is not completely specified by SCTP standards, but the endpoint will continue sending HEARTBEAT chunks to all the unreachable destination addresses. If any one address comes back into service again (that is, a HEARTBEAT is acknowledged

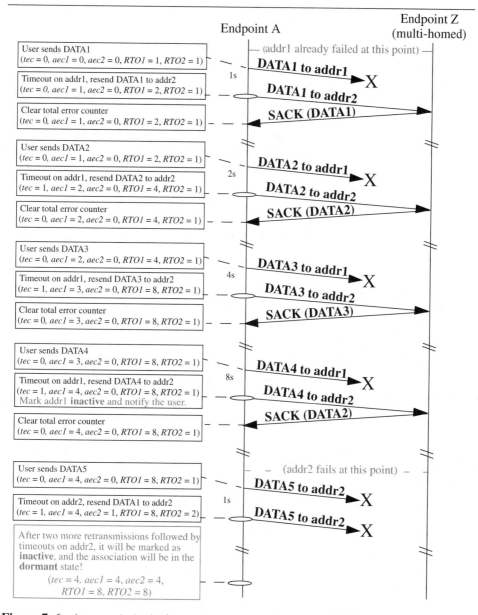

**Figure 7–6**  *An association's dormant state caused by network failures*

by the peer or a SACK arrives), the endpoint will bring the association out of the **dormant** state.

The implementation, therefore, must decide what to do with all the outstanding data in its retransmission queue and how to deal with new user messages passed from the SCTP user when the association is in the **dormant** state. In practice, when the association enters the **dormant** state, the SCTP user will likely become aware of the situation through some application-level events (for example, time expirations on application messages), and may accordingly take necessary actions. In this state, the SCTP implementation **may** still choose one of the addresses and attempt to retransmit data (at timer expiration) to the remote endpoint in the hope that one of the addresses becoming active again.

## 7.4   Fault Resilience Communication and Routing Configuration

In this section we will show that fault management mechanisms built into the SCTP can detect an unreachable peer destination address. When a peer is multi-homed, SCTP can automatically switch the subsequent data transmission to an alternative address.

However, using multi-homed endpoints with SCTP does not automatically guarantee resilient communications. One must also design the intervening network(s) properly. This section discusses some of the issues in network design that must be considered to take full advantage of multi-homing.

### 7.4.1   Maximizing Path Diversity

To achieve fault resilient communication between two SCTP endpoints, one of the keys is to maximize the diversity of the **round-trip** data paths between the two endpoints. The reason that we emphasize **round-trip** data paths is because, for example, if endpoint A has two different paths to reach endpoint Z, but endpoint Z only has one path to reach endpoint A, the communication will be lost whenever the only path from endpoint Z to endpoint A breaks.

Under an ideal situation, we can make the assumption that every destination address of the peer will result in a different, separate path towards the peer. Whether this can be achieved in practice depends entirely on a combination of factors that include path diversity, multiple connectivity, and the routing protocols that glue the network together. In a normally designed network, the paths may not be diverse, but there may be multiple connectivity between two hosts so that a single link failure will not fail an association.

In an ideal arrangement, if the data transport to one of the destination addresses (which corresponds to one particular path) fails, the data sender can migrate the data traffic to other remaining destination address(es) (that is, other paths) within the SCTP association.

Figure 7–7 shows such an ideal routing arrangement for two multi-homed endpoints.

In the diagram we use a simplified network address notation $x.y$, where $x$ represents the network number and $y$ the host number.

As you can see in Figure 7–7, the arrangement that achieves maximum path diversity between the two endpoints is made possible by the fact that two separate paths are maintained (by the network routing protocols)—between router 1.1 and router 3.1, and between router 2.1 and router 4.1—and by the host routing table settings shown in Table 7–1.

With this routing arrangement, it is easy to see that when endpoint 1 sends a data packet to destination address 3.2 of endpoint 2, the packet will take the following route:

host A interface 1.2 $\Rightarrow$ router 1.1 $\Rightarrow$ router 3.1 $\Rightarrow$ host Z interface 3.2

Because the source IP address carried with the packet will be 1.2, the acknowledgment from endpoint 2 will take the same path in the opposite direction; that is,

host Z interface 3.2 $\Rightarrow$ router 3.1 $\Rightarrow$ router 1.1 $\Rightarrow$ host A interface 1.2

Similarly, for data packets sent from endpoint 1 to destination address 4.2 of endpoint 2, the following route will be taken:

host A interface 2.2 $\Rightarrow$ router 2.1 $\Rightarrow$ router 4.1 $\Rightarrow$ host Z interface 4.2

The acknowledgment from endpoint 2 will take the same route in the opposite direction:

host Z interface 4.2 $\Rightarrow$ router 4.1 $\Rightarrow$ router 2.1 $\Rightarrow$ host A interface 2.2

We can get similar routing results for data packets sent from endpoint 2 to endpoint 1.

This routing arrangement effectively creates a completely different and separate path for each different destination address of the peer, and if one of those paths breaks (for example, gateway router 1.1 fails), both endpoints will find one of its peer's destination addresses becoming unreachable. But because the other path will still be able to transfer data packets and the corresponding acknowledgments in both directions, the association will survive the failure.

To set up the routing tables shown in Table 7–1, a host may be statically configured, or the administrator may need to run a routing protocol that host machines

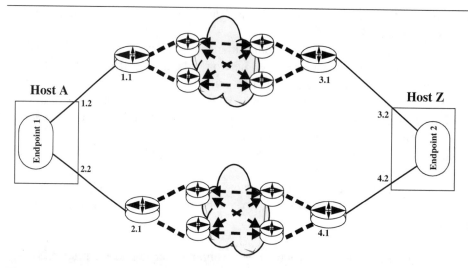

**Figure 7–7**   *Ideal routing arrangement for two endpoints with redundant networks*

**Table 7–1** A Fault-Resistant Routing Tables

| Host A | | Host Z | |
|---|---|---|---|
| Destination | Gateway | Destination | Gateway |
| 3.0 | 1.1 | 1.0 | 3.1 |
| 4.0 | 2.1 | 2.0 | 4.1 |

"monitor" only. The endpoints on each end of the communication should bind all of the addresses into their associations to utilize this maximum diversity.

## 7.4.2   Asymmetric Multi-homing Configuration

In practice, many network layouts may be less than ideal, as in Figure 7–7, and the endpoints engaged in communications may have an asymmetric number of network addresses assigned to them.

Figure 7–8 is an example in which an SCTP association is set up between multi-homed endpoint 1 and single-homed endpoint 2.

In such a case, the redundant network addresses at endpoint 1 will help very little in providing fault resilience to the communication if the routing tables depicted in Table 7–2 are in use.

First, due to the lack of redundancy, it is obvious that if the path between gateway router 3.1 and host Z interface 3.2 breaks in either direction, the association

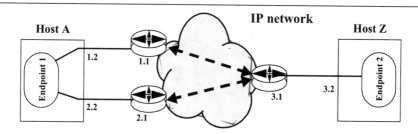

**Figure 7–8** *An asymmetric SCTP association*

**Table 7–2** Sample Routing Tables for the Asymmetric SCTP Association

| Host A | | Host Z | |
|---|---|---|---|
| Destination | Gateway | Destination | Gateway |
| 3.0 | 1.1 | 1.0 | 3.1 |
| | | 2.0 | 3.1 |

between endpoints 1 and 2 will break. What is less obvious is that if the path between host A interface 1.2 and gateway router 1.1 breaks in both directions, the association will not survive either. This is because of the setting in host A's routing table. The setting forces *all* of its outbound traffic destined to the 3.x network to use interface 1.2, which leads to our broken router, 1.1. In other words, this particular routing arrangement is preventing the association from taking advantage of the existence of the second interface, 2.2, on host A.

This example also tells us that because of the fact that the number of possible different paths that can be used to route data between two endpoints can never be larger than the minimum of IP addresses used by the endpoints. It is often beneficial in terms of fault resilience for both endpoints to use all the IP addresses available to them when setting up the association.

However, with some minor modification, the fault resilience (or the lack of it) of the system in Figure 7–8 can be improved. The modification will require the assignment of a second network address to the sole interface on host Z, as shown in Figure 7–9.

With this additional address, 4.2 on host Z (as well as the necessary changes to router 3.1 to service this new 4.x address), we can then make some changes to the routing tables, as depicted in Table 7–3 (changes shown in shaded box).

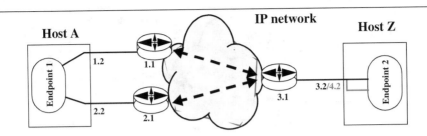

**Figure 7–9**  *Modification to improve fault resilience on an asymmetric association*

**Table 7–3** Changed Routing Tables for the Asymmetric Association

| Host A | | | Host Z | |
|---|---|---|---|---|
| Destination | Gateway | | Destination | Gateway |
| 3.0 | 1.1 | | 1.0 | 3.1 |
| 4.0 | 2.1 | | 2.0 | 3.1 |

With these modifications, the association between endpoints 1 and 2 will be able to survive failures in either the path

host A interface 1.2 ⇔ router 1.1 ⇔ router 3.1

or the path

host A interface 2.2 ⇔ router 2.1 ⇔ router 3.1

The fault resilience coverage includes the interfaces and routers themselves at both ends of the path.

### 7.4.3    Effects of Source Address Selection

Source address selection is another factor that will interact with routing in SCTP. The SCTP sender uses the following general rules:[2]

---

2.  Note that these rules are not imposed by the SCTP specification; instead they are made up by the authors from their experience implementing SCTP. The rules for source address selection and SCTP are, as yet, unspecified. Currently, work specifying rules for the scoping of IPv6 addresses within the IETF is ongoing.

**Rule 7–1**   Whenever a packet is emitted, use a source address in the IP packet that is associated with the network adaptor from which the packet is being emitted. For IPv6 that source address should be of a scope equal to or more global than that of the destination.[3]

**Rule 7–2**   When the source address cannot be made to match the NIC that the packet is emitted from, rotate the source address among all the other bound addresses or, alternatively, make sure that all networks can be reached from all sources (that is, ensure network resilience).

Rule 7–1 cannot always be followed if the implementation is allowing specific binding of subsets of addresses or if virtual interfaces are being used inside of a router sourcing SCTP packets. Let us consider the effects of source address selection when this rule either is not or cannot be followed. For our example, we will use the scenario depicted in Figure 7–7 and assume that the routing tables defined in Table 7–1 are in use.

We first examine what will happen if the sender selects the source address using the policy defined in Table 7–4.

In Table 7–4 we see that each endpoint specifies the source address of the IP packet as that of the opposite network from which it is emitted. This leads to a dependency on both networks being available and reachable.

When one of the destination addresses becomes unreachable, the selection policy in Table 7–4 will not become a severe problem if, upon detecting duplicate data packets, the data receiver implementation is smart enough to ignore the source address seen in the arrived data packets and select an alternate address to return the SACK. Nonetheless, the performance of the SCTP association operating under such a condition would be severely hampered. It could become worse, however, if the receiving side's implementation does not recognize the duplicate data condition and then switch to an alternate address to return the SACK. This would cause the association to fail.

These problems can be basically avoided if both endpoints simply follow Rule 7–1.

In our next example (see Figure 7–10) we will take a closer look at the interplay between source address selection and whether or not all addresses on the hosts are used by the association.

We assume that the host routing table setting for the two endpoints is as is shown in Table 7–5. As you can see, it is set up to route packets between the same

---

3. For IPv6 various types of addresses exist with different scope. Each address's scope defines its routability. A **global** address can be accessed from anywhere; a **site-local** address is only valid and routeable within a specific site; a **link-local** address can only be used on a particular link (or local area network segment).

**Table 7–4** Inefficient Source Address Selection Policy

| Sending Node | Destination Address | Source Address to Use |
|---|---|---|
| Endpoint 1 | 3.2 | 2.2 |
|            | 4.2 | 1.2 |
| Endpoint 2 | 1.2 | 4.2 |
|            | 2.2 | 3.2 |

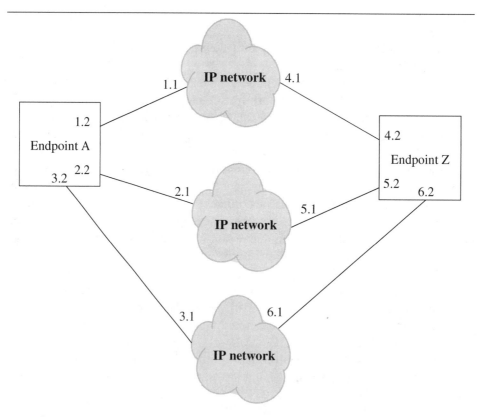

**Figure 7–10**  *An association involving three networks*

**Table 7–5** Routing Tables for an SCTP Association with Three Networks

| Host A | | Host Z | |
|---|---|---|---|
| Destination | Gateway | Destination | Gateway |
| 4.2 | 1.1 | 1.2 | 4.1 |
| 5.2 | 2.1 | 2.2 | 5.1 |
| 6.2 | 3.1 | 3.2 | 6.1 |

sets of interface cards so that if all interfaces on each endpoint bounded all the addresses, we would have complete triple redundancy for the association.

For the purpose of our discussion, let us assume that endpoint Z has bound all the IP addresses (4.2, 5.2, and 6.2), but that endpoint A has bound only two interfaces (1.2 and 2.2).

As endpoint A sends data to endpoint Z, everything will be fine as long as the selected destinations are 4.1 and 5.1 and we use Rule 7–1. The question is, what source address should we use when we need to send an IP packet to 6.2? With the host routing tables configured for fault tolerance, packets bound for 6.2 will be emitted out of interface 3.2. This of course makes it impossible for endpoint A to invoke Rule 7–1, because local address 3.2 is not part of the association. This is where Rule 7–2 can be applied.

If we applied Rule 7–2, we would, upon the first transmission to destination 6.2, set the source address as 1.2; upon the second transmission to destination 6.2, we would set the source address as 2.2; and so on. In other words, the source address for packets destined to 6.2 would rotate between the two available local addresses (that is, 1.2 and 2.2) on every other transmission. This would allow the association to still function even if one of the paths to these addresses broke. If such a breakage did occur, performance would suffer, but data transfer would continue to function.

## 7.5 IETF Debate and Issues

During the early stages of SCTP's development, there was a large volume of discussion on message revocation. What happens when a signaling message is delayed for too long and is no longer valid? Should SCTP attempt to cancel this message somehow? What sense does it make to keep attempting to deliver an old message?

Heartbeating was also an item of some debate on the list. One of the original contentions was to heartbeat every destination address each *RTO* (with a small random jitter added to this timer). This would help ensure a proper *RTO* estimate as well as the reachability of the remote destination address. After some discussion it was pointed out that this could lead to an overwhelming number of HEARTBEAT chunks being sent across a network, especially if you have hundreds of endpoints, each with associations interconnecting them. This discussion led to changes in the heartbeat definition as follows:

- Send a HEARTBEAT to only one peer destination address every *RTO* seconds.

- After each HEARTBEAT is sent to a destination address, wait a certain amount of time before sending the next one to the same destination. This time should be decided using the destination's *RTO* + a user-set heartbeat delay (*HB.interval*) + some random jitter.

- Set the default *HB.interval* to 30 seconds.

- Allow the upper layer to disable and re-enable the heartbeat on all destinations or on any particular destination.

## 7.6    Summary

This chapter discusses a key feature of SCTP—the communication fault detection and recovery mechanism.

We first defined the two types of communication failures that an SCTP endpoint can detect, namely an unreachable destination address and an unreachable peer endpoint. Then we discussed how the individual data transmission and heartbeat failures are tracked and used by an endpoint to determine the reachability of a given destination address of a peer or the reachability of the peer itself.

We also discussed the issue of false detections, the guidelines on how to properly use HEARTBEAT chunks, and how to properly set the detection thresholds.

Finally, we pointed out that the failure detection and recovery mechanism of SCTP was just one piece of the puzzle of achieving fault resilience communications, and that other factors such as routing configuration and network path diversity also played a crucial role. Several examples were given to show the impact of different routing configurations on the fault resilience of an SCTP association.

## 7.7    Questions

1.    When is a destination address considered idle?

2.  What is the **dormant** state of an association and how can it be avoided?

3.  What does path diversity mean?

4.  Will making both the SCTP endpoints in an association multi-homed be enough to provide communication fault tolerance? If not, what other factors need to be taken into consideration?

# 8

# Auxiliary SCTP Packet Handling Functions

In this chapter we will discuss how the SCTP endpoint handles **out-of-the-blue** SCTP packets and the *Verification tag* rules for an endpoint that sends and receives SCTP packets.

## 8.1   Handling Out-of-the-Blue SCTP Packets

When an endpoint processes a received SCTP packet, finding the peer (and thus the corresponding association) from which the SCTP packet comes is normally the next step after the endpoint confirms the integrity of the received packet (by verifying the *Adler-32 checksum* carried in the SCTP common header).

Typically the endpoint will try to identify the peer that originated this SCTP packet by comparing the source and destination transport addresses[1] carried in the SCTP packet to the destination address(es) of all of its known peers.

If the receiver is unable to find a known peer to associate the received SCTP packet with, it will consider the SCTP packet an out-of-the-blue (OOTB) packet.

The arrival of an OOTB SCTP packet can be an indication of some erroneous conditions (such as race conditions, delayed/out-of-order SCTP packets, etcetra), but some normal SCTP operations will also result in OOTB SCTP packets. Therefore, when handling an OOTB SCTP packet, the receiver must first examine the content of the SCTP packet in an attempt to determining the possible cause of the OOTB packet. The receiver will then decide what to do with the packet.

---

1. Recall that the source and destination transport addresses are defined as the combination of the source and destination port numbers carried in the SCTP common header, and the source and destination IP addresses found in the IP datagram that contains the SCTP packet.

The following rules are the guidelines for an SCTP receiver to follow when deciding how to process an OOTB SCTP packet:

**Rule 8–1**   If the OOTB SCTP packet is sent to or comes from a non-unicast address (for example, a multicast or broadcast address), it must be silently discarded. This is because non-unicast addresses are not only illegal for an SCTP endpoint to send messages to, but also dangerous to reply to. (For example, replying to such an SCTP packet could assist in a denial-of-service attack because non-unicast addresses amplify the number of IP datagrams in the network.)

**Rule 8–2**   If the OOTB SCTP packet contains an ABORT chunk, it must be silently discarded. The reason for this is that the only sensible handling the receiver could do in this circumstance would be to reply with an ABORT of its own. But replying to an ABORT with another ABORT can cause an infinite message loop and therefore must be avoided.

**Rule 8–3**   If the OOTB SCTP packet contains an INIT chunk *and* if the *Verification tag* field in the SCTP common header has a value equal to zero, the receiver must treat it as a request for an association by a new peer endpoint. The procedures for setting up a new association are discussed in Chapter 4.

**Rule 8–4**   If the first chunk in the OOTB SCTP packet is a COOKIE-ECHO chunk, the receiver must process it following the procedures described in Section 4.4. This is because the OOTB SCTP packet is most likely the third message of the four-way handshake association setup process (see Chapter 4 for more details).

**Rule 8–5**   If the OOTB SCTP packet contains a SHUTDOWN-ACK chunk, it is very likely that the local endpoint (that is, the receiver of the OOTB SCTP packet) has gone through the three-way handshake association termination process with the remote endpoint (that is, the sender of the OOTB SCTP packet). However, the last message of the three-way handshake (a SHUTDOWN-COMPLETE sent by the local endpoint to the remote endpoint) was lost, and the remote endpoint retransmitted its SHUTDOWN-ACK. This lost SHUTDOWN-COMPLETE scenario is discussed in full detail in Section 9.1.4.

When handling this OOTB SCTP packet, the local endpoint should reply to the remote endpoint with a SHUTDOWN-COMPLETE. Moreover, when sending this SHUTDOWN-COMPLETE, the local endpoint will copy the *Verification tag* value found in the SCTP common header of the OOTB SCTP packet into the *Verification tag* field of the outbound SCTP packet and set the *T flag* to 1 in the outbound SHUTDOWN-COMPLETE. The *T flag* will indicate that the TCB of the old association is no longer existent at the local endpoint and that the receiver will not find its expected *Verification tag* (instead it will find its own *Verification tag*).

**Rule 8–6**    If the OOTB SCTP packet contains a SHUTDOWN-COMPLETE chunk, the receiver should silently discard the SCTP packet.

The scenario that this rule tries to cover is a variation of the scenario discussed in Rule 8–5. The current scenario can occur when the retransmission of the SHUTDOWN-ACK by the remote endpoint in the previous case turns out to be unnecessary. The first SHUTDOWN-COMPLETE sent out by the local endpoint was simply delayed but not lost, and it arrived at the remote endpoint after the endpoint retransmitted its SHUTDOWN-ACK. Therefore, when the second SHUTDOWN-COMPLETE reaches the remote endpoint (per Rule 8–5 above), it appears to the remote endpoint as an OOTB SHUTDOWN-COMPLETE.

**Rule 8-7**    If the OOTB SCTP packet contains a COOKIE-ACK chunk or an OPERA-TIONAL-ERROR chunk with a *Stale cookie* cause code, the receiver should silently discard the SCTP packet. Such an SCTP packet can only be triggered by certain stale SCTP packets from an old association that no longer exists.

**Rule 8–8**    For all the other cases that are not covered by the preceding rules, the receiver of the OOTB SCTP packet will respond to the sender of the OOTB SCTP packet with an ABORT. Furthermore, when sending the ABORT, the receiver of the OOTB SCTP packet will copy the *Verification tag* value found in the SCTP common header of the OOTB SCTP packet into the *Verification tag* field of the outbound SCTP packet, and set the *T flag* to 1 in the ABORT chunk. The *T flag* indicates to the receiver that no TCB exists for the association. After sending this ABORT, the receiver of the OOTB SCTP packet will discard the OOTB SCTP packet and take no further action.

## 8.2   SCTP Packet Verification Tag Rules

The *Verification tag* carried in every SCTP packet plays an important role in the four-way association setup handshake procedure and in the handling of duplicated SCTP control messages (see Section 4.7); it is used, for example, to discover complicated race conditions like a peer restart.

The *Verification tag* also provides an inexpensive line of defense against the so-called "blind attack," where the attacker only has "write-only" access to the target network. In such a scenario, the attack cannot be effective unless the attacker can guess the correct value of the 32-bit *Verification tag* of the target endpoint, which is basically impossible in practice.[2]

In this section we will discuss the rules and procedures for *Verification tag* that an endpoint should follow.

### 8.2.1   Basic Verification Tag Rules

The basic *Verification tag* rules apply when sending or receiving SCTP packets that do not contain an INIT, SHUTDOWN-COMPLETE, COOKIE-ECHO, or ABORT chunk. The rules for sending and receiving SCTP packets containing one of these chunk types are discussed separately in the next section. These rules are applied to unrecognized chunk types as well as to all other chunks not specifically excluded.

The following are the basic *Verification tag* rules:

**Rule 8–9**   When sending an SCTP packet to a peer, the sending endpoint must put the peer's tag value in the *Verification tag* field of the outbound SCTP packet. The peer's tag value is recorded from the *Initiate tag* parameter of the INIT chunk (or the INIT-ACK chunk, depending on who was the initiator of the association) received from the peer when the association started.

**Rule 8–10**   When receiving an SCTP packet from a peer, the receiving endpoint must ensure that the value carried in the *Verification tag* field of the received SCTP packet matches its own tag. This is the tag the endpoint assigned to the association and sent to the peer in the *Initiate tag* parameter in the INIT chunk (or the INIT-ACK chunk) when the association was set up. If these two tag values do not match one another, the receiver will silently discard the received SCTP packet.

*Note*   This does not conflict with Rule 8–8 in that, Rule 8–8 applies when the receiver fails to identify, among all its existing peers, the sender of the received packet, while this rule applies *after* the sending peer is successfully identified but the verification tags are found mismatching.

### 8.2.2   Special Verification Tag Rules

Rules different from those defined in the previous section are used when sending and receiving SCTP packets containing one of these chunks: INIT, COOKIE-ECHO, SHUTDOWN-COMPLETE, and ABORT.

---

2.  It is critical for an SCTP implementation to select a good-quality random number for its *Verification tag*. An implementer should consult Bellovin (1996) for advice on how to select random numbers.

The primary reason for this is that the peer's *Verification tag* value may not always be available when an endpoint is sending or receiving these chunks. These special rules are discussed in the following section, organized according to what the SCTP packet carries.

### 8.2.2.1   SCTP Packet Carrying an INIT

An endpoint only sends an INIT chunk to set up an association with a new peer. This means that when the INIT is sent, the association does not exist, and hence there is no way the sender of the INIT will know its future peer's *Verification tag*. In such a case, the following special rules will be used:

**Rule 8–11**   The sending endpoint of an INIT chunk must set the *Verification tag* of the outbound SCTP packet carrying the INIT chunk to zero.

**Rule 8–12**   The receiving endpoint, when receiving an SCTP packet whose V*erification tag* is set to zero, should *never* discard the SCTP packet without further checking whether the SCTP packet is carrying a single INIT chunk. If it is, the receiver will accept the INIT chunk following the procedures described in Section 4.2. Otherwise, the receiver *must* send an ABORT to the sender with the *T flag* set to indicate that no association exists. The endpoint will also copy the *Verification tag* from the received SCTP packet (that is, zero) to the outbound SCTP packet carrying the ABORT.

### 8.2.2.2   SCTP Packet Carrying an ABORT

The ABORT chunk can be used by an endpoint either to terminate abruptly an association in any state, or to respond to a received OOTB SCTP packet (see Section 8.1). In the former case, the sender normally knows the *verification tag* of the peer endpoint because the association to be aborted exists. But in the latter case, the endpoint sending the ABORT will have no knowledge about the peer's *verification tag*. Therefore, special rules are needed for sending and receiving SCTP packets carrying an ABORT chunk:

**Rule 8–13**   When sending an ABORT chunk, the sender will always fill the *Verification tag* field of the outbound SCTP packet with the peer's *verification tag* whenever it is available.

**Rule 8–14**   If the peer's *verification tag* is not available (such as in the case of responding to an OOTB SCTP packet in which the peer is unidentifiable), the sender of ABORT will follow Rule 8–8, as described in Section 8.1; that is, it will use the *Verification tag* value found in the SCTP common header of the received OOTB SCTP packet and set the *T flag* to 1 in the outbound ABORT chunk.

**Rule 8–15**    When an ABORT chunk is present in a received SCTP packet, the receiver must accept and process the SCTP packet if the *Verification tag* of the SCTP packet matches its own *verification tag*, *or* if the *T flag* of the ABORT is set to 1 and the *Verification tag* of the SCTP packet matches the peer's *verification tag*.

### 8.2.2.3   SCTP Packet Carrying a SHUTDOWN-COMPLETE

When an endpoint sends out a SHUTDOWN-COMPLETE, there exists the possibility that the sending endpoint may not know the *verification tag* of its peer (that is, the receiving endpoint of the SHUTDOWN-COMPLETE message). This can happen, for example, in the error case described for Rule 8–5 in Section 8.1. Therefore, special *verification tag* rules similar to those for handling ABORT chunks are designed for SHUTDOWN-COMPLETE:

**Rule 8–16**    When sending a SHUTDOWN-COMPLETE in response to a SHUT-DOWN-ACK, if the sending endpoint has no knowledge of the *verification tag* of the peer endpoint, the sender must fill the *Verification tag* field of the outbound SCTP packet with the *Verification tag* value found in the SCTP common header of the received SHUTDOWN-ACK, and then set the *T flag* to 1 in the outbound SHUTDOWN-COMPLETE.

**Rule 8–17**    When a SHUTDOWN-COMPLETE chunk is present in an arrived SCTP packet, the receiver will need to accept and process the SCTP packet if the *Verification tag* field of the received SCTP packet matches its own *verification tag*, *or* if the *T flag* in the received SHUTDOWN-COMPLETE is set to 1 and the *Verification tag* field of the SCTP packet matches its peer's *verification tag*.

*Note*    Regardless of the result of the *verification tag* comparison, the receiving endpoint will ignore the SHUTDOWN-COMPLETE if it is not in the SHUTDOWN_ACK_SENT state.

### 8.2.2.4   SCTP Packet Carrying a COOKIE-ECHO

Sending and receiving a COOKIE-ECHO are part of the process of establishing an association. Some cautions should be taken regarding the handling of the *verification tags*:

**Rule 8–18**    When sending a COOKIE-ECHO in response to an arrived INIT-ACK, the sending endpoint will fill the *Verification tag* field of the SCTP common header of the outbound SCTP packet with the value found in the *Initiate tag* field of the received INIT-ACK.

**Rule 8–19**    The receiver of a COOKIE-ECHO will first follow the procedures in Section 4.4 to authenticate the cookie and unpack it into a TCB. Then it will compare the value in the *Verification tag* field of the received SCTP packet (found in the SCTP common header of the SCTP packet) with its own *verification tag* (discovered in the newly created TCB).

## 8.3    IETF Debate and Discussion

OOTB SCTP packet handling has been under some discussion during SCTP's development. All the discussion has centered around a few basic questions:

- How do we precisely define an OOTB SCTP packet?

- Should we or should we not send back an ABORT in response to an OOTB packet?

- What *verification tag* should the outbound SCTP packet carry when it sends an ABORT in response to an OOTB SCTP packet?

The first and third questions, of course, have now been fully defined in the SCTP specification (Stewart et al. 2000) and discussed in the preceding pages of this section. But the second question is one that was debated at length. The alternative to responding with an ABORT is to silently discard the received OOTB packet. Some thought that would be a better approach to help minimize traffic and to avoid a potential denial-of-service attack. In the end the desire to help the remote endpoint (that is, the sender of the OOTB packet) to clean up its protocol state more quickly won out over the desire to minimize traffic on the network.

Another interesting side note is that the fact that ABORT messages are sent in response to OOTB SCTP packets has ramifications for the IP layer and ICMP. In the case of UDP, if no application is attached to a port, the UDP stack will recognize this and send back an ICMP message to indicate the problem. With SCTP, instead of an ICMP message, the stack must generate an ABORT message. TCP accomplishes the same function by sending back a *RESET*, or *RST flag*. A good implementation will recognize either the ICMP or ABORT message because it is always possible that the implementation of the remote endpoint will miss this subtle point and that both types of messages (ICMP or ABORT) can be recognized by the *Verification tag* found within the first 64 bits of the SCTP common header.

## 8.4   Summary

This chapter described some special packet handling rules used by SCTP. The first set of rules were designed to deal with the reception of a so-called **out-of-the-blue** SCTP packet. We discussed that the handling procedures will differ depending on the types of SCTP chunks carried in the packet. The second set of rules discussed in this chapter define how the value of the *Verification tag* field in the SCTP common header is set by the sender and examined by the receiver in various cases.

## 8.5   Questions

1.   What is an OOTB packet? If a UDP datagram is erroneously sent to an SCTP endpoint, will it be considered an OOTB packet? Why or why not?

2.   What is the advantage of sending back an ABORT in response to an OOTB packet?

# Close of an Association

$\mathbf{A}$ny reliable protocol needs a methodology not only to bring up a communication (as we saw in Chapter 4), but also to bring that communication to a close. This chapter will detail the procedures for closing SCTP associations.

SCTP has two basic methods for bringing an association to a CLOSED state.[1] We will refer to these as the "graceful shutdown" and the "abortive shutdown." In the graceful shutdown, each endpoint assures that all data in the queue is delivered and acknowledged. After all data is delivered, the association enters the CLOSED state. This graceful shutdown shares some similarities with the graceful shutdown used in TCP, with one major exception: while TCP supports a "half-closed" state, where one side is CLOSED and not accepting new data to transfer, and the other side is still open and able to send new data; SCTP does not.

SCTP uses a three-message handshake to gracefully close the association. A simple diagram of the three messages can best illustrate the similarities and differences between TCP and SCTP (see Figure 9–1).

Notice point A in the diagram; from this moment forward, no new user data will be accepted from the upper-layer protocol[2] (ULP) of the SCTP stack at endpoint A. All messages that may have been in the queue to endpoint Z will have been sent before the SHUTDOWN chunk is transmitted to endpoint Z. (For simplicity, Figure 9–1 depicts the simplest case, where neither side has SCTP packets

---

1. In most implementations, the CLOSED state of an association simply means that all resources allocated to the association will be reclaimed and all record of the association will be erased by the endpoint. In other words, the association no longer exists.

2. What runs above the SCTP stack will be either a higher-layer protocol (such as HTTP) or the user communications application. Here we simply refer to this higher-layer protocol as the upper-layer protocol because these two cases are not (and need not be) distinguishable, from the SCTP stack's viewpoint.

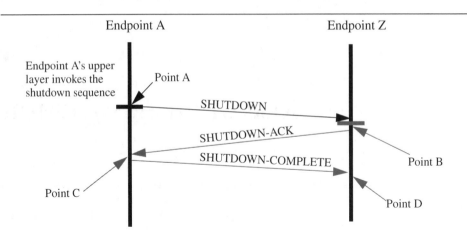

**Figure 9–1**  *A simple overview of the graceful shutdown sequence*

in the queue.) At point B (the arrival point of the SHUTDOWN chunk at endpoint Z), endpoint Z will no longer accept new user messages from its ULP to be sent to endpoint A. Points C and D are where the association enters the CLOSED state. We will look at this case in Section 9.1 in more detail.

The other type of shutdown that may occur in an SCTP endpoint is what is known as an abortive shutdown. This consists of simply sending an ABORT chunk to the peer and removing the TCB. We take a closer look at this case in Section 9.2.

## 9.1   The Graceful Shutdown

As discussed earlier, the graceful shutdown sequence involves a three-way hand-shake. This graceful shutdown sequence is never triggered by the SCTP stack itself; it is only triggered by the ULP of one of the endpoints. At some point during the exchange of messages, one of the endpoints will be notified by its upper layer that it wishes to tear down the association and stop communication with its peer.

At the point when the SCTP stack at an endpoint is notified by its ULP to start a shutdown, it may still have outbound user data in various transmission states. The endpoint may have some user data that it has sent to the peer but for which it has not yet received acknowledgment (we call this outstanding user data), and/or it may have outbound user data queued for its ULP but never sent (we call this pending user data). Or, as in the previous example, the endpoint may have neither situation.

In cases in which user data is still outstanding or pending, the SCTP stack will mark the association as shutting down and stop accepting new user data from its UPL. The SCTP stack then enters what is known as the SHUTDOWN_PENDING state.

The endpoint will continue to send its DATA chunk(s), using the rules discussed in Chapter 5, until all pending as well as outstanding data has been delivered and acknowledged by the peer. While in this state, new user data from the upper layer will be rejected by the SCTP stack.

Once the SACK arrives, indicating to the SCTP stack that the last pending DATA chunk has been received, the SCTP stack will then send a SHUTDOWN chunk to the peer and enter the SHUTDOWN_SENT state.

If an endpoint had no data in the queue when the ULP issued the shutdown request, the endpoint will send the SHUTDOWN chunk and enter the SHUTDOWN_SENT state, bypassing the SHUTDOWN_PENDING state. Figure 9–2 illustrates an endpoint entering both the SHUTDOWN_PENDING and SHUTDOWN_SENT states.

### 9.1.1  Sending SHUTDOWN

The SHUTDOWN chunk (see Section 3.2.9) is quite simple. The chunk is made up of just the standard chunk header and the current *Cumulative TSN*. The *Cumulative TSN* is the same value that is sent in the SACK message (see Section 5.3). This counter indicates to the peer which data messages have been received and helps the receiver of the SHUTDOWN chunk with retransmission decisions. Once the SHUTDOWN chunk is sent, the sending endpoint does the following:

- Starts a *Shutdown* timer and initializes the association error counter to zero.

- Every time an SCTP packet containing one or more DATA chunks arrives, the endpoint acknowledges the DATA chunk(s) with a SHUTDOWN chunk if no gaps exist in the received TSN sequence space. If gaps exist between the *Cumulative TSN* and the newly arrived TSN(s), then the data receiver *must* respond with both a SHUTDOWN chunk and a SACK chunk.[3]

- Along with acknowledging the DATA chunk(s), the endpoint also clears any error counter on the association and restarts the *Shutdown* timer.

This ensures that the SHUTDOWN chunk is received by the peer and that the peer stops accepting new data from its application. This is done because if a SHUTDOWN chunk were not required to be sent upon the reception of every data packet, it would be easy to envision a case in which the peer would continually send new data, never becoming aware that the sender of the SHUTDOWN wished to terminate the association.

---

3. The two chunks are normally bundled together and sent in a single SCTP packet.

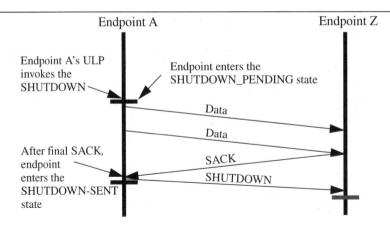

**Figure 9–2**  *The graceful shutdown sequence from SHUTDOWN_PENDING to SHUTDOWN_SENT*

If the *Shutdown* timer expires, the endpoint should do the following:

1. Resend the SHUTDOWN chunk with the current *Cumulative TSN* value (this may be different than what was sent in the previous SHUTDOWN chunk). When sending this chunk, if the receiver is multi-homed, choose a different address than the one to which the chunk was previously sent (if possible). See Section 5.5.2.2 for details on alternate address selection.

2. Stroke an error counter for the association *and* for the destination address to which the last SHUTDOWN chunk was sent.

3. If the destination error counter exceeds its preset maximum, mark the destination as **inactive**.

4. If the association error counter exceeds a preset threshold, report the peer as unreachable, destroy the TCB, and move the association into the CLOSED state.

The sender of the SHUTDOWN chunk must continue this procedure until either the association fails or a SHUTDOWN-ACK chunk is received. When the endpoint receives a SHUTDOWN-ACK, it should do the following:

1. Stop its *Shutdown* timer.

2. Send a SHUTDOWN-COMPLETE chunk.

3. Remove the TCB, which moves the association into the CLOSED state.

This sequence is depicted in Figure 9–3.

## 9.1.2   Receiving SHUTDOWN

When an endpoint receives a SHUTDOWN chunk from the peer, the endpoint will first move the association to the SHUTDOWN_RECEIVED state and then perform the following:

1. Notify the ULP that a SHUTDOWN chunk has been received.

2. Stop accepting new user messages from the ULP.

In the SHUTDOWN_RECEIVED state, the endpoint will continue to follow the rules defined in Chapter 5 to finish the transportation of all outstanding and pending user data. The endpoint will use the *Cumulative TSN* in the SHUTDOWN chunk to mark off any newly acknowledged DATA chunks.

Once all user messages have been acknowledged, the endpoint will send a SHUTDOWN-ACK chunk and enter the SHUTDOWN_ACK_SENT state. Once the SHUTDOWN-ACK chunk is sent, the sending endpoint will take the following actions:

1. Clear the association error count.

2. Start a *Shutdown* timer.

If the *Shutdown* timer expires, the endpoint should do the following:

1. Resend the SHUTDOWN-ACK chunk. When sending this chunk, if the receiver is multi-homed, choose a different address than the one to which the chunk was previously sent (if possible).

2. Stroke an error counter for the association *and* for the destination to which the last SHUTDOWN-ACK chunk was sent.

3. If the destination error counter exceeds its preset maximum, mark the destination as **inactive**.

4. If the association error counter exceeds a preset threshold, report the peer as unreachable, destroy the TCB, and move the association into the CLOSED state.

The sender of the SHUTDOWN-ACK chunk must continue this sequence (resending the SHUTDOWN-ACK chunk when the timer expires) until either the association error counter is exceeded or the endpoint receives a SHUTDOWN-

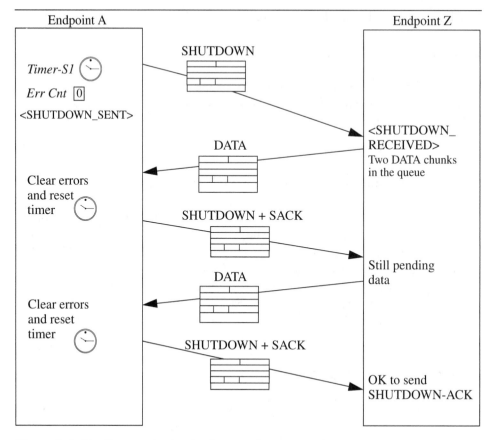

**Figure 9–3** *The first step in the shutdown exchange*

COMPELTE chunk. When the endpoint receives the SHUTDOWN-COMPLETE, it should do the following:

1. Stop its *Shutdown* timer.

2. Delete its TCB and move the association into the CLOSED state.

This sequence is depicted in Figure 9–4.

### 9.1.3   Sending SHUTDOWN-COMPLETE

When you formulate the SHUTDOWN-COMPLETE chunk, you must take one special consideration into account. This chunk, unlike most other chunks, may be

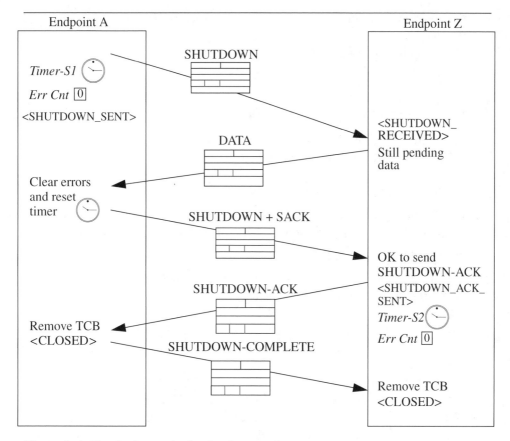

**Figure 9–4** *The final steps in the shutdown exchange*

sent when no TCB exists for the association. We will provide more details on the cause of this condition in the next section.

When a SHUTDOWN-COMPLETE chunk is sent in the normal case (that is, when the sender endpoint still has an association that it is being removed), all flag bits are set to zero, and the *Verification tag* in the outbound SCTP common header is set to the correct *Verification tag* value of the peer of the association.

However, when a SHUTDOWN-COMPLETE chunk is sent when *no* TCB exists for the association, the sending endpoint cannot know the peer's *verification tag*. *In such a case*, in the common header of the outgoing SCTP packet that carries the SHUTDOWN-COMPLETE chunk, the endpoint will use the *Verification tag* from the SCTP common header of the chunk that caused the SHUTDOWN-COMPLETE chunk to be sent (that is, the SHUTDOWN-ACK that was received).

In addition, the endpoint will set a flag bit in the chunk header to 1. This bit is referred to as the *T flag*, or "no TCB flag."

How would this sequence unfold? This leads us into the topic of our next section: race conditions and lost messages.

### 9.1.4   Race Conditions and Lost Messages

You may have noticed a few potential problems in the shutdown sequence discussed in the last few sections, namely the following:

- What happens when a SHUTDOWN-COMPLETE is lost?

- What happens when a SHUTDOWN-COMPLETE is lost and then the endpoint that sent the SHUTDOWN-COMPLETE attempts to bring up a new association by sending an INIT chunk?

- What happens if an endpoint does not enter the SHUTDOWN_RECEIVED state and continues to accept new user messages from its ULP?

Two of these conditions have not been overlooked and are handled by some special properties and procedures that the SHUTDOWN-COMPLETE chunk has. The third case becomes an implementation issue, as will be discussed in this section.

Let us first see how a lost SHUTDOWN-COMPLETE chunk is handled. Figure 9–5 depicts what happens when a SHUTDOWN-COMPLETE chunk is lost. The *Shutdown* timer that endpoint Z was running expires, causing the endpoint to retransmit the SHUTDOWN-ACK chunk.

Now this puts endpoint A in a situation in which it has received a chunk "out of the blue," or OOTB, from its perspective. The normal handling would yield an ABORT chunk, as discussed in Section 8.1.

However, in this case, a special exception is made as part of the OOTB handling. In this case endpoint A responds with a subsequent SHUTDOWN-COMPLETE chunk, but, as mentioned previously, the endpoint sets the *T flag* in the chunk header. Because the endpoint has no information about the peer's verification tag, it populates the *Verification tag* field in the common header of the outgoing SCTP packet holding the SHUTDOWN-COMPLETE with the same *Verification tag* value found in the SCTP packet holding the SHUTDOWN-ACK. Endpoint Z must be prepared to handle this situation (that is, having the *T* flag set to "1" and the *Verification tag* set to the value it dispersed in the outbound SCTP packet). This allows the shutdown to be completed gracefully, even in the event of a lost message.

The second possibility also covered in the SCTP specification (Stewart et al. 2000) is what happens when not only is the SHUTDOWN-COMPLETE chunk

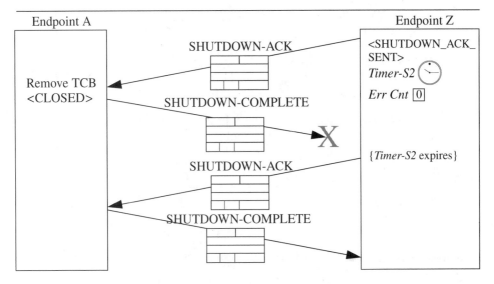

**Figure 9–5** *A lost SHUTDOWN-COMPLETE*

lost, but the endpoint sending it decides to start a new association with its peer. This situation is depicted in Figure 9–6.

Here, once again, the SHUTDOWN-COMPLETE sent by endpoint A is lost; not only that, but also endpoint A's upper layer decides it was too hasty in terminating the association and immediately sends an INIT chunk, gets back an INIT-ACK, and then sends off the cookie in a COOKIE-ECHO chunk. All this occurs before endpoint Z has a chance to retransmit a SHUTDOWN-ACK chunk. In this situation endpoint Z must do the following:

1. Retransmit the SHUTDOWN-ACK.

2. Restart the *Shutdown* timer.

3. Send an OPERATIONAL-ERROR indicating a *Cookie received while shutting down* error cause code.

Endpoint A should react in the following way:

- Treat the arrived SHUTDOWN-ACK as an OOTB packet (Rule 8–5 in Section 8.1) and send a SHUTDOWN-COMPLETE with the *T flag* set to 1, copying the *Verification tag* from the inbound packet that carries the

SHUTDOWN-ACK into the common header of the outbound packet that carries the SHUTDOWN-COMPLETE.

- Optionally, recognize the OPERATIONAL-ERROR and use this to reset itself to the INIT state. This will cause the endpoint to send a new INIT and thus receive a new INIT-ACK with a different cookie.

- Alternatively, the endpoint may wish to just let the *T1-cookie* timer expire and cause a retransmission of the cookie, hoping that the cookie has not expired during the delay.

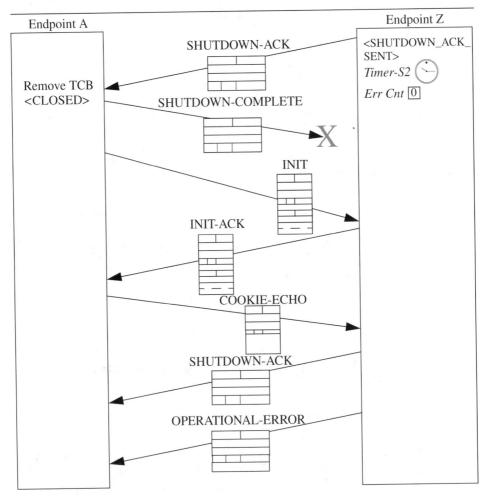

**Figure 9–6** *A lost SHUTDOWN-COMPLETE and quick restart*

Our final case to examine is what happens when an endpoint does *not* stop accepting new user messages from its ULP. This case may occur if the peer's implementation is incorrect or noncompliant with the SCTP protocol specification (Stewart et al. 2000). In such a case the specification itself does not give any advice on what to do. However, there are two simple approaches that an implementation may wish to put in place to prevent this situation. The first is as follows:

1. Upon sending a SHUTDOWN chunk to a peer, start a second timer that we will call the "Shutdown-error" timer. Set this timer to a larger value such as 30 times the current *RTO* of the primary destination address.

2. Continue with the normal shutdown sequence just described.

If the Shutdown-error timer expires, do the following:

1. Send an ABORT chunk to the peer.

2. Destroy the TCB and move the association into the CLOSED state.

Following these procedures will ensure that the association will enter the CLOSED state in a timely fashion. An implementation, however, may not wish to go to the extra expense of coding an extra timer for this purpose. In such a case, a second alternative can be followed as well:

1. Create an additional variable, *TSN shutdown maximum*.

2. Set this variable, upon sending a SHUTDOWN, to the value of the *Cumulative TSN* plus some predetermined number of messages that the implementation is willing to accept after sending a SHUTDOWN.

3. When in the SHUTDOWN_SENT state, when updating the *Cumulative TSN* value of the association (through the arrival of new data), verify that the new *Cumulative TSN* is smaller than the *TSN shutdown maximum*.

4. If the *Cumulative TSN is* larger than the *TSN shutdown maximum*, destroy the TCB and enter the CLOSED state.

This method, though possibly less expedient, does not require a timer. Both methods will work, and one of them *should* be implemented to protect against incorrect peer implementations.

## 9.2   The Abortive Shutdown

The abortive shutdown is an unreliable best-effort attempt to tell a peer that the association is going away. The ABORT is also used, at times, to refuse an association or in response to certain invalid parameters. Both the SCTP stack and the user may generate an ABORT.

### 9.2.1   ABORT Usage

The application may use the abortive shutdown procedure when it wishes to immediately terminate an association. This could occur for a number of reasons:

- The application does not wish any messages currently in the queue to be sent, and instead wants the communications immediately terminated.

- The application fails and "dumps core," causing an abortive close of the socket. As part of the socket close procedures, the operating system then sends an ABORT chunk to all open associations.

The SCTP stack will use the abortive shutdown for a number of reasons, including the following:

- There are no resources to begin an association upon the arrival of a cookie.

- The INIT message contains invalid mandatory parameters. (For example, if the *Initiate tag* is set to zero, the receiver *must* respond with an ABORT.)

- A catastrophic failure causes the operating system to need to release association resources. This should be a very rare event but it is allowed.

### 9.2.2   Sending an ABORT

The procedures for sending an ABORT are quite simple. Figure 9–7 depicts a typical abortive shutdown.

As you can see, endpoint A simply formulates an ABORT and sends it, after which endpoint A removes its TCB. Endpoint A may optionally include one or more error causes to indicate why it is aborting. If an error cause is included, the receiver may wish to pass this information to its upper layer.

If an ABORT does not reach the peer, the association, from the peer's perspective, will still be up and in service. However, the sender of the ABORT will have no record of the association. The next message of any kind that arrives from

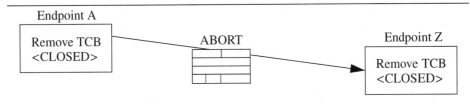

**Figure 9–7**  *An abortive shutdown*

the peer will be treated as an OOTB message by the sender of the ABORT, usually causing a new ABORT to be sent. Consult Section 8.1 for further details.

### 9.2.3   Receiving an ABORT

Notice that the receiver in Figure 9–7 simply removes the TCB corresponding to the association being aborted and moves the association into the CLOSED state upon reception. Of course, this is only after all the following occur:

1. It is verified that the receiver does have a TCB corresponding to the association that the sender of the ABORT is trying to terminate.

2. The *Verification tag* field in the common header of the SCTP packet that carries the ABORT is valid; that is, it matches the receiver's own *Verification tag* value for the association.

Otherwise, the ABORT is silently discarded.

> *Note*  Just like with the SHUTDOWN-COMPLETE chunk, the SCTP packet that carries the ABORT chunk may hold either endpoints' *Verification tag*. The receiver must be prepared to accept either verification tag as valid if the *T flag* in the ABORT chunk is properly set.

Normally the common header of the SCTP packet carrying the ABORT will contain the receiver's *Verification tag*. But in some instances, it is possible that the sender is responding to an SCTP packet sent to a nonexistent association. In such a case, the *T flag* in the ABORT chunk will be set to 1, and the outbound SCTP packet carrying the ABORT will contain the *Verification tag* copied from the SCTP common header of the SCTP packet that arrived and caused the ABORT chunk to be sent.

You may have noted that there are no procedures specified for a lost ABORT. This is because they are imbedded within the OOTB handling, as detailed in Section

8.1. In effect, once an endpoint sends an ABORT, any contact by its peer (due to a lost ABORT) will cause it to send a new ABORT with the *T flag* set. This effectively provides a guarantee that the peer endpoint will eventually receive the ABORT.

## 9.3   IETF Debate and Issues

It was not until quite late in the review process that any issues arose on the close of an association. Originally SCTP used only a two-way handshake to gracefully shut down an association. This was brought out and discussed in some detail within the working group. In the end the graceful association-close procedure was turned into a three-way handshake so that both sides could be fully assured that the association closed gracefully.

The abort procedures were also discussed in some detail. One particularly interesting proposal was to make the ABORT more reliable. However, as was pointed out earlier, this completely defeated the purpose of the ABORT. It was also noted that if an endpoint continued to send SCTP packets (such as HEART-BEATs) to a sender of an ABORT, the ABORT would be resent with the *T flag* set (because the receiver of the SCTP packet would not have a TCB, having sent an ABORT and thus having entered a CLOSED state). This in effect makes the abort procedure reliable without using timers or adding any additional complexity to the procedure.

## 9.4   Summary

We have discussed in this chapter how an SCTP association closes down. Two different styles of terminating an SCTP association have been described, namely the graceful shutdown and the abortive shutdown. The former approach employs a three-way handshake procedure that guarantees that any data pending for transmission at both endpoints will be transferred to the other end before the final closure of the association. The latter approach can be used in some more urgent situations in which a speedy termination of the association is more important, while data integrity becomes less a concern.

We also analyzed some potential race conditions that may occur during the three-way handshaking of a graceful shutdown, and described the corresponding handling procedures.

## 9.5  Questions

1.  What are the main differences between the SCTP graceful shutdown and TCP shutdown procedures?

2.  If an endpoint has received a SHUTDOWN from its peer, will the application at that endpoint be allowed to send more new user data?

# 10

# IANA and Future Extension of SCTP

The Internet Assigned Numbers Authority (commonly known as IANA) assigns Internet numbers. This means that all common protocol numbers and values of global significance to the Internet are administrated and assigned by IANA to help maintain interoperability among implementations and by all standards-track IETF protocols.

The IP protocol identifier 132 has been assigned to SCTP by IANA.

IANA has assigned TCP and UDP the IP protocol identifiers 6 and 17, respectively, and has assigned well-known port numbers for a large range of common IP applications (such as *TELNET* and *FTP*) that use TCP or UDP. For example, if one wished to contact the *TELNET* server on a host within the Internet, the assigned *TELNET* port number 23 would be contacted.

When a new common IP application requests a well-known port number, IANA in many cases assigns both a TCP and a UDP port number to the application. For example, *TELNET* has been assigned both the UDP and TCP port number 23, even though *TELNET* typically runs over TCP.

## 10.1 SCTP Port Number Assignment

SCTP, like TCP and UDP, needs similar port number administration services from IANA.

SCTP's specification (Stewart et al. 2000) continues the tradition of IANA in number assignment in that it calls for all current TCP-application well-known port numbers to be preassigned to SCTP for the same common IP applications. This means that for instance, the well-known *TELNET* port number 23 (as well as all other well-known port numbers already assigned to *TELNET* over TCP) is also reserved in SCTP for *TELNET* applications if someone decides to implement the *telnet* service over SCTP.

Currently, allocation of a well-known port from IANA is a very simple process. You just go to the IANA Web page and fill out a simple form specifying your name, e-mail address, and a brief description of the "well-known" port's purpose. No RFC is required to allocate a well-known port number. In the well-known port number request, you must specify the transport protocol (UDP or TCP) with which the port number will be used. Generally even if only one of the two protocols is specified, the port number will be reserved for both UDP and TCP.

With the advent of SCTP, IANA will be adding a third choice to the protocols (that is, SCTP) for which the port will be used. It is to be expected that IANA will continue its current assignment practices and that soon you will receive your port in three protocols (that is, UDP, TCP, and SCTP).

## 10.2   IETF Chunk Extensions

Unlike TCP and UDP, SCTP is a protocol in which extensibility has been designed. As such, the *Chunk type* field allows new and additional features to be added to the SCTP protocol. The control of the chunk number assignment will also now be a responsibility of IANA. However, unlike with port numbers, you will need to supply more than a contact list and a general description of the usage of the proposed *Chunk type* in order to get a chunk assignment. It is required that IANA have an IETF standards-track RFC that fully describes the extension and its use. This means that *any* new feature added to SCTP must go through the full IETF review process and be part of IETF's standards-track protocol process. Requiring a standards-track RFC is necessary in order to maintain true interoperable implementations of SCTP. The IETF review process is required to control functionality explosion in order to maintain protocol stability.

If no control were placed on SCTP *Chunk type*, it would soon become impossible to have different vendors of SCTP interoperate, because each would be adding their own special chunks to perform possibly similar features. IANA will not assign a *Chunk type* that has not been through the IETF standards process. This, of course, will not stop a vendor from randomly grabbing a *Chunk type* and using it for some special purpose. Of course, if a vendor does do this, the vendor's SCTP implementation will become noncompliant with the protocol standard.

There are four specially reserved IETF *Chunk type* values: 31 (0x2f in hexadecimal), 63 (0x3f in hexadecimal), 127 (0xbf in hexadecimal), and 255 (0xff in hexadecimal). These numbers are reserved for when the particular chunk range is depleted. Remember that the upper two bits of the *Chunk type* hold special meaning, as discussed in Section 3.1.4. Each of these special bit patterns holds a reserved *Chunk type* to allow for extension. If a *Chunk type* runs out of space in a particular range, then it is expected that the extension into the next range of chunks will look *similar* to the one depicted in Figure 10–1.

In Figure 10–1 the *Type*, of course, would be either 255, 127, 63, or 31, depending on the which chunk range was exhausted.

Here we see how a mythical extended *Chunk type* (0xff)0x01 can be potentially added. The IETF extension "0xff" is used as the base chunk type. This means that the extended chunk requires both the "report" and "skip this chunk and continue processing" treatments when a receiver of this chunk does not recognize the extended chunk type.

Of course, this extension will only happen after all the base *chunk types* for this particular range—that is, base types 192 through 254 (0xC0 through 0xFE, in hexadecimal)—are exhausted.

Currently no format is defined for a *Chunk type* extension; the preceding example is just for illustrative purposes.

## 10.3   IETF Parameter Extensions

SCTP parameter numbers are also assigned and controlled by IANA. They too require a standards-track RFC in order to gain an assignment. Of course, the *Parameter type* space is much larger than the *Chunk type* space because the *Parameter types* allow 16 bits, or 65,535 different parameter types. Each of these *Parameter types* is associated with a particular *Chunk type*. This means that every specific *Chunk type* can, in theory, have 65,535 unique parameters. For this reason, no extension was reserved in the base protocol for extension.

To date, all parameter values across all *Chunk types* are unique. This means that even though there is the capability to assign the same *Parameter type* in two different chunks (each containing a different meaning), this has not currently been done. A software implementation cannot currently depend on uniqueness across all chunks; for now all parameters are unique across *Chunk types*. However, this uniqueness may soon become a requirement of the protocol when it moves to draft standard (from proposed standard), because movement is currently underway within the IETF to formalize this number-assignment policy.

## 10.4   IETF Extensions to Error Causes

The fourth assignment that can be made by IANA for SCTP is error causes. Error causes are used across both ABORT and OPERATIONAL-ERROR chunks. They specify some error that has occurred and is being reported to the remote endpoint.

| Base Type = 0xff | Base Chunk Flags | Chunk Length = X |
|---|---|---|
| Ext Type = 0x01 | Ext Chunk Flags | Other extension information |
| Chunk data | | |

**Figure 10–1**  *An example of an extended chunk type*

Here again, a formal consensus process must be undergone via the IETF. This means that an IETF standards-track RFC must be produced in order to add new error causes.

## 10.5   Payload Protocol Identifier

Inside every DATA chunk is a *Payload protocol identifier*. This 32-bit number is neither used nor checked by SCTP. It is present in the DATA chunk solely for the benefit of some network devices and the applications at both ends of the association. As such, no formal standards-track RFC process is required for the addition of a new *Payload protocol identifier*.

It is anticipated that specific protocols being developed to run over SCTP will request the assignment by IANA of a *Payload protocol identifier*. The assignment policy will be similar to the assignment of protocol port numbers. That is, a general description of what the *Payload protocol identifier* is used for will be required, but no formal specification will be needed to get an identifier.

As of this writing, several requests have been made for the SIGTRAN working-group protocols, M3UA, IUA, M2UA, M2PA, and SUA. Other protocols expected to also request a *Payload protocol identifier* are ITU-T Recommendations H.248, ITU-T Recommendations Q.2150.3, etcetera.

## 10.6   Summary

In this chapter we discussed the relationship between SCTP definition and the Internet Assigned Numbers Authority (IANA). We noted that for an Internet protocol, all the standard numbers, such as the *Chunk type* values, SCTP protocol identifier, error cause values, etcetera, will need to be registered with or assigned by IANA. Moreover, any future extensions to SCTP protocol will probably also need new number registrations with IANA.

# 11

# A Sockets API for SCTP

So far this book has presented to you information on SCTP. We have covered many of the features of SCTP and a lot of the details on how SCTP works "on the wire." One question that may have occurred to you as read about the features of SCTP is, "How will I write code to use this feature?" This chapter will try to answer that by detailing work that is currently underway to expand the "sockets" interface to include and account for some of the unique features of SCTP.

One note on this chapter is that the sockets API, as of the writing of this book, is a "work in progress." As such, some of the details may change as the work evolves, so you may wish to consult the latest SCTP sockets API specification. This chapter is meant to give you a "taste" of how you will use SCTP with a sockets interface.

The SCTP sockets expansion work has three main goals as its central focus:

1. *Maintain consistency with the existing sockets APIs*—The SCTP sockets API extension must stay consistent with the existing UDP, TCP, IPv4, and IPv6 sockets APIs.

2. *Support a UDP-style interface*—The purpose behind this goal is to provide an easy and efficient method to exploit all the features in SCTP. A UDP-style interface allows us to do this in a way that is superior to the TCP interface. Because SCTP is connection-oriented (through its use of associations), this interface cannot support multicast or broadcast communications like UDP.

3. *Support a TCP-style interface*—The purpose behind this goal is to provide an easy migration path for existing TCP applications to SCTP. Maintaining a

direct mapping from a TCP user interface to an SCTP user interface will allow many TCP-based applications to move to SCTP with few changes. Of course, those applications that wish to exploit some of the unique features of SCTP will need to be enhanced and will need to use the UDP-style interface.

We will begin by doing a short review of the "typical" connection-oriented sockets API. After this quick review we will examine the mapping of the TCP sockets interface to SCTP. After reviewing how the TCP sockets API maps onto SCTP, we will examine another alternative that more fully supports the features of SCTP and that is a UDP-style interface.

## 11.1   A Quick Review of the TCP Sockets API

The typical IPv4 TCP sockets API segregates client and server applications into two distinct paradigms. Each side must be aware (to a small degree) of the state of the transport and take part in setting up a TCP connection. We thus divide this review into two distinct parts: the server-side application and the client-side application.

### 11.1.1   The Server-Side Application

The server-side application typically performs the following steps in order to use the TCP sockets API:

1. *Open a socket*—This step returns a descriptor used in all subsequent calls.

2. *Bind a port number to the socket*—This step associates a well-known port number with the socket so that clients can foreknow where to contact a particular server. Each server or service offered by a machine will use a different port. (For example, *telnet* uses port 23.)

3. *Listen for connections*—This step tells the TCP stack that the application will be accepting connections.

4. *Accept a connection request when it arrives*—This step will pull off a new descriptor from the old one, placing the "new" connection into its own separate descriptor.

5. Add the new connection to its "receiving from" set of connections, *or* fork off a thread (or service process) to handle the task of reading from the new descriptor.

6. Go back to the listening step on the original descriptor. These steps (listen, accept, service) are repeated until the process is exited.

As you can see, the application is aware at all times of the transport state and can manage the transport connections with a state machine. In Figure 11–1 we present a small segment of C code that illustrates these steps.

Here we see the initial setup of the socket through the **socket()** call. Note the use of AF_INET to indicate to the sockets API that the type of socket is an IPv4 domain socket. Also note the use of *SOCK_STREAM* and *IPPROTO_TCP*. These two arguments specify the use of TCP. We then see the setup of a socket address reserving port 2960 for the use by this "well-known" service. With the bind completed, the application calls the **listen()** system call to tell the TCP stack that it is ready to accept a connection request. Note that the value "10" in *listen()* specifies that the operating system should queue up to ten simultaneous connection requests if the server fails to keep up with the number of arriving inbound requests for service. We then go in to a "forever" loop waiting for a connection request. Once a request arrives, we "accept" the connection onto a new file descriptor with the **accept()** call, discovering in the process who is connecting to us. (The operating system fills in the "who" address on return from the accept call.) Then after pulling off the new connection, we call the **Start_Service_Thread()** routine (not shown), which presumably starts a thread (or in some cases may fork a new process), passing to the new thread the connection identification (that is, the descriptor returned from the accept call). Upon return from the "service starter," we go back to the top and do this same loop all over again.

### 11.1.2   The Client-Side Application

The client side must make the effort to "connect" to the server. It must have some foreknowledge of the port number of the service, so it goes through the following steps:

1. *Open a socket*—This step returns a descriptor used in all subsequent calls.

2. *Optionally, bind a port number, not a specific port (as in our server) but any port that is available*—This is often called an **ephemeral** port number.

3. *Issue a* **connect()** *call to "bring up" the connection so that communication may begin*—This is true whether or not the client binds a port.

In the case of our client, no state machine is needed; instead the client must be aware of the connection state to our server. Only after the connection comes up may the application send data. Figure 11–2 shows a sample set of C code that illustrates a connection to our server (described in the previous section).

The client first creates a socket. Next it binds itself to an available port.[1] (It uses INADDR_ANY in both the address and the port fields to indicate that an ephemeral port is sought.) After binding to the port, the client sets up the IP

```
int fd,ret,newfd;
struct sockaddr_in s,who;
fd = socket(AF_INET,SOCK_STREAM,IPPROTO_TCP);
if(fd == -1){
    exit(0);
}
s.sin_family = AF_INET;
s.sin_addr.s_addr = INADDR_ANY;
s.sin_port = htons(2960);
ret = bind(fd,&s,sizeof(s));
if(ret == -1){
    exit(-1);
}
ret = listen(fd,10);
if(ret == -1){
    exit(-1);
}
while(1){
      newfd = accept(fd,&who,sizeof(who));
        if(newfd < 0)
            continue;
      Start_Service_Thread(newfd,&who);
}
```

**Figure 11–1**  *A sample set of TCP server code*

address and port to specify the server and then calls **connect(),** which again, in this example, is a blocking call. After the **connect()** call returns successfully, the client calls the **send()** routine to send off the first user message. Presuming a successful data transmission (that is, that the return value from the **send()** call is not "–1"), the client next calls the **recv()** function to obtain the response message from the server.

The client may continue to converse with the server through the file descriptor, *fd*, until its communication to the server is finished. At the end of the conversation (not shown in the example), the client would either call **shutdown()** or simply **close()** the *fd*. These calls would normally cause the connection to close down. But in the case in which the application does call **shutdown()**, it may cause a "half-closed" state in the TCP, in which the caller can no longer send data but can still receive data. As mentioned in Chapter 9, this behavior is not supported in SCTP.

---

1.  As noted previously, the binding of a port is an optional step for the client. If a client does not bind a port, the operating system will provide an **ephemeral** port for the connection.

```
      int fd,ret,newfd;
      struct sockaddr_in s, whoTo;
      fd = socket(AF_INET,SOCK_STREAM,IPPROTO_TCP);
      if(fd == -1){
          exit(0);
      }
      s.sin_family = AF_INET;
      s.sin_addr.s_addr = INADDR_ANY;
      s.sin_port = INADDR_ANY;
      ret = bind(fd,&s,sizeof(s));
      if(ret == -1){
          exit(1);
      }
      whoTo.sin_family = AF_INET
     whoTo.sin_addr.s_addr = inet_network("10.1.1.1");
      whoTo.sin_port = ntohs(2960);
      ret = connect(&whoTo,sizeof(whoTo));
      if(ret == -1){
         printf("Failed to connect .. out of here\n");
          exit(-1);
      }
      ret = send(fd,aNewRequest,len_of_request);
      if(ret == -1){
        printf("Failed to send the request\n");
          exit(-1);
      }
      ret = rcv(fd,aResponse,sizeof(aResponse));
```

**Figure 11–2**  *A sample set of TCP client code*

## 11.2   The TCP-Style SCTP Sockets API Extension

The sockets API usage examples just discussed can be easily modified to access
SCTP transport using SCTP's TCP-style sockets API extension. To make this
modification, you would need to make only one slight change to the server code in
Figure 11–1. All other API function calls would work as currently defined, with
the exception of the **shutdown()** call (because SCTP does not support the "half-
closed" state). We see in Figure 11–3 a server similar to the one presented in Figure 11–1, but this server uses an SCTP's TCP-style socket.

Note that the only difference presented here is in the **socket()** call. Here we
see a different protocol type, that is, IPPROTO_SCTP in place of IPPROTO_TCP.

The SCTP client side is using an SCTP's TCP-style socket, which is presented
in Figure 11–4, and is also very similar to the TCP client shown in Figure 11–2.

You may have noticed that the two examples of the TCP-style interface to
SCTP shown in Figure 11–3 and Figure 11–4 do not really gain all the advantages

```
int fd,ret,newfd;
struct sockaddr_in s,who;
fd = socket(AF_INET,SOCK_STREAM,IPPROTO_SCTP);
if(fd == -1){
    exit(0);
}
s.sin_family = AF_INET;
s.sin_addr.s_addr = INADDR_ANY;
s.sin_port = htons(2960);
ret = bind(fd,&s,sizeof(s));
if(ret == -1){
    exit(1);
}
ret = listen(fd,10);
if(ret == -1){
    exit(-1);
}
while(1){
    newfd = accept(fd,&who,sizeof(who));
        if(newfd < 0)
                continue;
        Start_Service_Thread(newfd,&who);
}
```

**Figure 11–3**  *The modified server-side code using an SCTP TCP-style socket*

of SCTP. In these examples, you will not be able to send messages to different streams without inserting additional system calls (as we will see) or without using different calls in place of the **send()**/**recv()** call. The next section will present a UDP-style SCTP sockets interface and will include some new extended sockets calls (that is, the **sendmsg()**/**rcvmsg()** calls) that may also be applied to the SCTP TCP-style interface shown in Figure 11–3 and Figure 11–4.

## 11.3   The UDP-Style SCTP Sockets API Extension

We now turn our attention to a new style of interface being proposed by SCTP to enhance the sockets API. It still uses all the traditional sockets API calls, but it presents methods that free the programmer from tracking the state of the various associations that the application may have open.

In this section we describe a "UDP-style" interface that does not use the **accept()**, **connect()**, or **listen()** calls. Instead, a client application simply sends data to a peer (or server) after the socket has been created. If the client does not have an association with the destination, then one is automatically set up. User messages sent before the association finishes its initialization are queued and held until the association is up. In many systems that optimize bundling, this method

```
int fd,ret,newfd;
struct sockaddr_in s,whoTo;
fd = socket(AF_INET,SOCK_STREAM,IPPROTO_SCTP);
if(fd == -1){
    exit(0);
}
s.sin_family = AF_INET;
s.sin_addr.s_addr = INADDR_ANY;
s.sin_port = INADDR_ANY;
ret = bind(fd,&s,sizeof(s));
if(ret == -1){
    exit(1);
}

whoTo.sin_family = AF_INET
whoTo.sin_addr.s_addr = inet_network("10.1.1.1");
whoTo.sin_port = ntohs(2960);
ret = connect(&whoTO,sizeof(whoTo));
if(ret == -1){
    printf("Failed to connect .. out of here\n");
    exit(-1);
}
ret = send(fd,aNewRequest,len_of_request);
if(ret == -1){
    printf("Failed to send the request\n");
    exit(-1);
}
ret = rcv(fd,aResponse,sizeof(aResponse));
```

**Figure 11–4**  *The modified client-side code using an SCTP TCP-style socket*

also results in the first DATA chunk being "piggybacked" or bundled with the COOKIE-ECHO chunk (see Section 4.3.2).

Note that this model especially lends itself to a true peer-to-peer world[2] where clients and servers do not exist in the typical sense, and instead peers talk to each other. At any one moment a peer may be acting like a server or client, its role changing only in the sense of what information it wishes to ask for or provide to one of its peers.

### 11.3.1   A View of a Client Using a UDP-Style SCTP socket

A client using a UDP-style SCTP socket will typically perform the following steps in order to communicate with a server:

---

2.  A peer-to-peer model can be obtained using TCP or UDP, but the authors do have a bias for SCTP, having developed it for peer-to-peer communications.

1. Open the SCTP UDP-style socket.

2. Optionally bind a port number.

3. Optionally set up the automatic close feature so that there is no need to track associations.

4. Send off a request to the peer.

Note in Figure 11–5 that this is exactly what is being performed. The process presumably has a message, *message*, of length *lenOfMsg* to be sent to a peer. It composes the address it wishes to send this message to in *whoto* and calls the sockets API call **send()**. The process in this case does not need to call the **connect()** call. Also notice the special flag being used to create this descriptor in the **socket()** call. The *SOCK_SEQPACKET* flag is used to request this UDP-like behavior on the socket.

An interesting effect of this methodology is that all the associations reside on one socket descriptor. There is not a profusion of socket *fd*s that the application must track. We will now turn our attention to the "server" or peer that receives the request. After examining its steps we will then turn our attention to an interface function that is specifically meant for this model, and to some additional interface functions that can be used in both models to access the additional features of SCTP.

```
int fd,ret,newfd,time2close;
struct sockaddr_in s,whoto;
fd = socket(AF_INET,SOCK_SEQPACKET,IPPROTO_SCTP);
if(fd == -1){
    exit(0);
}
s.sin_family = AF_INET;
s.sin_addr.s_addr = INADDR_ANY;
s.sin_port = htons(2960);
ret = bind(fd,&s,sizeof(s));
if(ret == -1){
    exit(1);
}
time2close = 100; /* 100 second of idle closes */
setsocketopt(fd,SCTP_AUTOCLOSE,&time2close);

whoto.sin_family = AF_INET;
whoto.sin_addr.s_addr = htonl(peersAddress);
whoto.sin_port = htons(peersPort);
ret = sendto(fd,&whoto,message,lenOfMsg);
```

**Figure 11–5**  *A typical SCTP client using the UDP-style SCTP socket*

## 11.3.2 A View of a Server Using a UDP-Style SCTP Socket

A server using a UDP-style SCTP socket performs only two extra steps in setting up the socket. It typically performs the following steps:

1. Open the UDP-style SCTP socket.

2. Bind a port number to the socket.

3. Issue a socket option call to enable automatic receiving of associations.

4. Issue a socket option call to enable automatic closing of associations.

5. When the socket description "wakes up for receiving," receive the message.

In Figure 11–6 we see this very behavior in a simple receiver that is doing a blocking **recvmsg()**. It first opens the socket and then binds the port number to it. After this it sets the socket option *SCTP_RECVASOCEVNT* with a backlog of "10," and it also sets up the default initialization parameters for all associations it creates. The backlog represents how many associations can be queued to it before it receives the notification of the new association by reading a message and its associated *CMSG_HDR*[3] from the socket. For our default initialization parameters we request 100 outbound streams and no more than 100 inbound streams. The attempts and timeout value we leave to the system default values by setting them to zero.

After this the program enters a blocking **recvmsg()** and waits for someone to send a message to it. Also note the *AUTOCLOSE* option in use. This socket option will force idle associations to close after 100 seconds of idle time. This obviates the need to track any information on the clients being communicated with other than their address, much like is done in a UDP server.

In a more complex receiver, this **recvmsg()** call would be part of a **poll()** or **select()** loop. The loop would await the socket descriptor to "wake up" for reading and then **recvmsg()** the newly arrived message. This then raises the question of how one would do a multi-threaded application in this model. This is why a new call has been added to assist the developer. You may have also noted that in the preceding descriptions, neither the client nor the server was able to make use of the "SCTP streams" feature.

In order to support this SCTP model better, a new call is needed to "peel off" a busy file descriptor so that it can be handed to a thread in a multi-threaded program.

---

3. CMSG, or the *CMSG_HDR* structure, is a format used in socket APIs to parse control messages. It is normally a set of macros that a programmer uses to access the ancillary data passed up with a **recvmsg()** call.

```
int fd,ret,newfd,on,time2close;
struct sockaddr_in s,whofrom;
struct sctp_initmsg im;
int on = 10;
im.sinit_num_ostream = 100;
im.sinit_num_instreams = 100;
im.sinit_max_attempts = 0;
im.sinit_max_init_timeo = 0;


fd = socket(AF_INET,SOCK_SEQPACKET,IPPROTO_SCTP);
if(fd == -1){
    exit(0);
}
s.sin_family = AF_INET;
s.sin_addr.s_addr = INADDR_ANY;
s.sin_port = htons(2960);
ret = bind(fd,&s,sizeof(s));
if(ret == -1){
    exit(1);
}
setsocketopt(fd,IPPROTO_SCTP,SCTP_INITMSG,&im,
             sizeof(im));
setsocketopt(fd,IPPROTO_SCTP,SCTP_RECVASOCEVNT,on,
             sizeof(on));
time2close = 100; /* 100 second of idle closes */
setsocketopt(fd,SCTP_AUTOCLOSE,&time2close);
ret = recvmsg(fd,msghdr,flags);
```

**Figure 11–6**  *A typical SCTP server using a UDP-style SCTP socket*

Programs that use a single-threaded, event-driven model will not necessarily need to use this function.

The SCTP sockets API calls for the new call **sctp_peeloff**(). This call will take an existing socket descriptor and an address. The call detaches the association from the original socket descriptor into its own unique socket descriptor. Once an association is "peeled off" of its main socket descriptor, its fate is no longer tied to the main descriptor, and the descriptor must be tracked and closed separately. Remember that in the UDP-style socket operation model, all associations share a common socket descriptor and thus a similar fate. This shared fate means that closing the one socket will cause all the associations attached to that socket to close as well. The new descriptor that the **sctp_peeloff**() call returns is not tied to the original socket descriptor and takes on the properties of a traditional TCP compatibility socket.

We see an example of the **sctp_peeloff**() call in use in Figure 11–7.

This example looks much the same as our earlier receiver, with the addition of the new call. At the termination of the **sctp_peeloff**() call, the program has two socket descriptors, *fd* and *newfd*. The original descriptor may have multiple asso-

```
int fd,ret,newfd;
struct sockaddr_in s,whofrom;
fd = socket(AF_INET,SOCK_DGRAM,IPPROTO_SCTP);
if(fd == -1){
    exit(0);
}
s.sin_family = AF_INET;
s.sin_addr.s_addr = INADDR_ANY;
s.sin_port = htons(2960);
ret = bind(fd,&s,sizeof(s));
if(ret == -1){
    exit(1);
}
setsocketopt(fd,SCTP_RECVASSOCEVNT,10);
ret = recvmsg(fd,msghdr,flags);
newfd = sctp_peeloff(fd,&whofrom);
sendto(fd,&otherpeer,othermsg,lenOfmsg2);
startThreadWith(newfd,&whofrom);
```

**Figure 11–7**  *Peeling off an association*

ciations still tied to it, whereas the newly returned descriptor only has the association with *whofrom* (found inside the *msghdr* structure) attached to it. The *newfd* descriptor can use the **sendmsg()** and **recvmsg()** calls, like *fd*, but any address passed with it is ignored. In the case of our original socket descriptor, the subsequent **sendto()** call shown in the figure will possibly create a new association (if one did not exist), sending perhaps a notification message to the *otherpeer* that it is starting a thread in the next call, **startThreadWith()**.

As you have seen, UDP-style sockets allow a flexibility to the application that frees it from the constraints of dealing with a huge number of socket descriptors. It also provides a simpler mechanism, where a server or client does not need to track the state of the transport before message passing can begin. But as we have noted, there are still a number of deficiencies that keep us from harnessing the full potential of SCTP. How does one send to different streams? How can you set up associations with different initialization parameters? How can you receive all the event notifications that are provided for in the SCTP specification? We address these questions and a few others in the next section.

## 11.4   Common API Mechanisms for Both Models

Two new mechanisms are being introduced with SCTP for both API models. These mechanisms use an existing and little-used set of calls, that is, **sendmsg()** and **recvmsg()**. The ancillary data provided by these calls will be used to help access the full potential of SCTP. We now turn our attention to the **sendmsg()** and **recvmsg()** calls.

### 11.4.1   Using the sendmsg() and recvmsg() Calls with SCTP

The **sendmsg()** and **rcvmsg()** calls have been a little-used part of the sockets interface. Their primary purpose is to allow a scatter/gather array to be passed to/from
the operating system. A scatter/gather array allows an application to compose (or
receive) a message in several non-contiguous buffers and yet have them all considered as one message. The typical formats of the **sendmsg()** and **rcvmsg()** calls are
as follows:

```
sendmsg(int socket, struct msghdr *msg, int flags)
rcvmsg(int socket, struct msghdr *msg, int flags)
```

The socket is our socket descriptor created by the **socket()** call or by an
**sctp_peeloff()** call. The *msghdr* structure is the key element that allows us the
extensibility as well as the traditional ability to use a scatter gather array. The format of the structure is shown in Figure 11–8.

This structure has several elements of note. The *msg_name* is the pointer to a
socket to which you wish to send data or from which data was received. The
*msg_len* is the length of the socket contained in *msg_name*. The *msg_iov* is the
scatter gather array that contains the one message to be sent, or it is a collection of
buffers in which to receive the single message. The *msg_iovlen* is the length of the
scatter gather array. The element we will concentrate on is the *msg_control*
pointer. This pointer is set to a bundle of data that contains CMSG[4] header structures, sometimes termed **ancillary** data. Each message (there can be more than
one in the buffer) has a CMSG header that identifies the protocol to which it is
directed. (In cases of receiving, this would be the protocol from which the information is coming.) It also holds the length of the message (so you know where the
next CMSG structure begins) and a type. This is much like SCTP's Type-Length-
Value format used on the wire. The SCTP sockets interface defines several of
these structures; of particular interest to us are the *sctp_initmsg* structure and the
*sctp_sndrcvinfo* structure.

In Figure 11–9 we see these two structures. When sending information, you
can include these to direct the SCTP stack to set specific parameters. Upon completion of the setup of a SCTP association, an endpoint will receive the
*sctp_initmsg* structure. This tells the endpoint specific information about how
many streams the endpoint has coming into it from its peer, and how many
streams the endpoint has available going out to its peer. By default an endpoint
sends and receives a preset number of streams. This can be changed with various

---

4. CMSG, or the *CMSG_HDR* structure, is a format used in socket APIs to parse control messages. It is normally a set of macros that a programmer uses to access the ancillary data passed up with a **recvmsg()** call.

```
struct msghdr{
  void            *msg_name;
  socklen_t        msg_len;
  struct iovec    *msg_iov;
  size_t           msg_iovlen;
  void            *msg_control;
  socklen_t        msgcontrollen;
  int              msg_flags;
}
```

**Figure 11–8** *The msghdr structure*

```
struct sctp_initmsg{
  uint16_t           sinit_num_ostreams;
  uint16_t           sinit_max_instreams;
  uint16_t           sinit_max_attempts;
  uint16_t           sinit_max_init_timeo;
}


struct sctp_sndrcvinfo{
  uint16_t           sinfo_stream;
  uint16_t           sinfo_ssn;
  uint16_t           sinfo_flags;
  uint32_t           sinfo_ppid;
  uint32_t           sinfo_context;
  uint8_t            sinfo_dscp;
  sctp_assoc_t   sinfo_assoc_id;

}
```

**Figure 11–9** *The sctp_initmsg and sctp_sndrcvinfo structures*

socket option calls to set up these default values. With a UDP-style socket the *sctp_initmsg* structure can also be included on the first transmission to a peer. When used in this manner, the default values of the association are **overridden** with the values included here. Note that if it is not the first transmission, the SCTP stack will ignore this structure (if it is included).

You can use the *sctp_sndrcvinfo* structure to control which stream you wish to send to by filling in the *sinfo_stream* parameter. This field will also tell you which stream the inbound data arrived on when the *sctp_sndrcvinfo* structure is found in the ancillary data on a **recvmsg()** call. The *sinfo_ppid* is how one specifies the *Payload protocol identifier* that is attached to this message. On reading a message with the **recvmsg()** call, the *sinfo_ppid* value will be filled in with what the peer application specified in the *sinfo_ppid* field in its **sendmsg()** call. The *sinfo_context* is useful for error handling. A sender of a message attaches this 32-bit value, which the

SCTP stack will retain with the message until it is acknowledged. If the message cannot be sent (due to association failure), when the endpoint reads back the unacknowledged and un-sent messages, this information can be used for application-specific purposes such as correlation of a state machine or some other application-specific function. The *sinfo_dscp* field allows a sender to change the IP Code Point (sometimes called the TOS value) value on a per-transmission basis. A receiver can also get a picture of the last DSCP value that was used on the network by examining this information upon data reception. The *sinfo_flags* field is used to indicate various options to SCTP, including the following:

- The sending and reception of unordered data

- A request to close an association with a UDP-style socket

- A request to abort an association

- A request to override the primary address to the one specified in the *msg_name* field of the *msghdr* structure

The last field, *sinfo_assoc_id*, is a unique identifier that is assigned on a per-association basis. Every time a message on a particular association arrives, this value will contain a unique identifier for the association upon which the message arrived. This can be useful to applications that do wish to track the various associations.

As you can see, the addition of these two ancillary data structures solves all the SCTP interface issues except how to deal with all the various notifications. In particular the ancillary data formats are not ideal for delivering variable-length data structures such as failed-message notifications. For some applications it is crucial to get back the data that was queued and never attempted to be sent, as well as data that was transmitted yet never acknowledged (right before an association went down). If only the CMSG structures are used, we need to have the variable-length data messages be read back from a failed association. To get around this problem, the SCTP sockets API defines a new flag that is returned from a **rcvmsg()** call. If upon return from the **recvmsg()** call the *msg_flags* field of the *msghdr* structure holds the value MSG_IS_NOTIFICATION, the message just read is a notification and *not* data from the remote endpoint.

### 11.4.2 Notification Information

At the time of this writing the structures of all the notifications are still being formed in a pending RFC (Stewart et al. forthcoming). The exact syntax and semantics of how one interprets all the notifications are still being refined. We urge readers to acquire this RFC to get the most up-to-date information on the various notifications.

As mentioned earlier, when a notification or other event arrives from SCTP, a user can read the event much like it would read an incoming user message. We call this reading of the notification via the **recvmsg()** call "using the **normal data channel**." To enable reception of events however, a user process *must* set the specific socket option(s) corresponding to the event it wishes to receive. These socket options "turn on" the event(s) in which the user is interested. Table 11–1 summarizes the socket options and includes a short description of their uses. To turn on or off any of the particular options, the **setsocketopt()** function is called with the desired option, and with an integer flag that is set to "1" to enable the option or zero to disable the option.

**Table 11–1** Socket Options and Associated Events

| Socket Option | Description |
| --- | --- |
| *SCTP_RECVDATAIOEVNT* | This option will enable the reception of information on each inbound message via the CMSG header's ancillary data of **recvmsg()** calls. See Section 11.4.1 for more information. |
| *SCTP_RECVASOCEVNT* | This option will enable the association's change event information to be passed in the normal data channel (that is, not as a CMSG header). This option must be set in a UDP-style socket to allow incoming associations (that is, server-side behavior). See Section 11.4.2.1 for more details. |
| *SCTP_RECVPADDREVNT* | This option will enable the reception (via the normal data channel, not the CMSG header) of association events. See Section 11.4.2.2 for details. |

**Table 11–1** Socket Options and Associated Events (cont'd)

| Socket Option | Description |
|---|---|
| *SCTP_RECVPEERERR* | This option will enable the reception of any errors encountered on the association via the normal data channel. See Section 11.4.2.3 for details. |
| *SCTP_RECVSENDFAILEVNT* | This option will enable the reception of failed messages via the normal data channel. The user will receive the entire message that could not be transmitted, accompanied by a *SCTP_RECVDATAIOEVNT* message structure describing the details that were supplied when the user data was sent. See Section 11.4.2.4 for more information. |
| *SCTP_RECVSHUTDOWNEVNT* | This option will enable the reception of shutdown events. This notification informs the user when the peer begins the graceful shutdown procedures. Once this event is received, no new data will be accepted for transport to the peer endpoint. See Section 11.4.2.5 for details. |

Each of the options that enable events has a data structure that is associated with that particular event. We will now describe the details of the structures passed in these notifications. Note that *none* of the listed events in the subsequent subsections will be received *unless* the corresponding socket option is enabled.

### 11.4.2.1    The SCTP_ASSOC_CHANGE Structure
Whenever an association has a change of state, the user that has enabled this option will receive the structure depicted in Figure 11–10.

The fields are defined as follows:

- *sac_type*—This field identifies the inbound message and should be set to SCTP_ASOC_CHANGE.

- *sac_flags*—This field is currently unused.

- *sac_length*—This field will hold the total length of this notification (including the header).

```
struct sctp_assoc_change{
  uint16_t          sac_type;
  uint16_t          sac_flags;
  uint32_t          sac_length;
  sctp_assoc_t  sac_assoc_id;
  uint16_t          sac_state;
  uint16_t          sac_error;
  uint16_t          sac_outbound_streams;
  uint16_t          sac_inbound_streams;
}
```

**Figure 11–10**  *The association change structure*

- *sac_assoc_id*—This field will identify the association. Every notification that arrives for this association will have the same value in the association identifier. For a TCP-style socket, this field is ignored.

- *sac_state*—This field holds the event that has transpired on the association. Events include the following:

  - COMMUNICATION_UP—A new association is now ready to send and receive data.

  - COMMUNICATION_LOST—The association is now failed and has entered the CLOSED state. If send failure notifications are enabled (SCTP_RECVSENDFAILEVNT), following this notification a series of SCTP_SEND_FAILED notifications may occur (based on the number of user messages that were in the queue and could not be delivered).

  - RESTART—This indicates that the association with this peer has restarted.

  - SHUTDOWN_COMPLETE—This indicates that the association has finished the graceful shutdown procedure and is now in the CLOSED state.

  - CANT_START_ASSOC—An association could not be started with the peer. This notification may also be followed by multiple SCTP_SEND_FAILED notifications (if user messages were in the queue awaiting the association's startup).

- *sac_error*—This will hold any error information for events that indicate an error has occurred.

- *sac_outbound_streams* and *sac_inbound_streams*—These two fields will hold the number of outbound streams and the number of inbound streams that were set up in the association.

With UDP-style sockets, the application is *required* to enable the association change event in order *to accept associations* from peers. Failure to enable this option will cause an ABORT chunk to be sent in response to any inbound INIT chunk.

### 11.4.2.2   The SCTP_PADDR_CHANGE Structure

Whenever a destination address on a peer encounters a change, this notification (if enabled) will be sent to the user. The data structure shown in Figure 11–11 will be passed with this notification.

The fields are defined as follows:

- *spc_type*—This field identifies the inbound message and should be set to SCTP_PEER_ADDR_CHANGE.

- *spc_flags*—This field is currently unused.

- *spc_length*—This field will hold the total length of this notification (including the header).

- *spc_assoc_id*—This field will identify the association. For the TCP-style socket, this field is ignored.

- *spc_addr*—This field holds the destination IP address that encountered the state change described in this notification.

- *spc_state*—This field represents the event that occurred at the address carried in this notification. The events are as follows:

  - ADDRESS_AVAILABLE—This state indicates that the address is now a reachable destination.

  - ADDRESS_UNREACHABLE—This state indicates that the address is no longer reachable.

  - ADDRESS_ADDED—This state indicates that the address has been added to the association.

  - ADDRESS_REMOVED—This state indicates that the address has been removed from the association.

  - ADDRESS_MADE_PRIM—This state indicates that the address has been made primary.

- *spc_error*—If this state was reached due to an error, this field will hold any relevant error information.

```
struct sctp_paddr_change{
    uint16_t              spc_type;
    uint16_t              spc_flags;
    uint32_t              spc_length;
    sctp_assoc_t   spc_assoc_id;
    struct sockaddr_storage spc_addr;
    uint16_t              spc_state;
    uint16_t              spc_error;
}
```

**Figure 11–11**  *The peer address change structure*

### 11.4.2.3   The SCTP_REMOTE_ERROR Structure

If the remote peer sends an OPERATIONAL-ERROR, this notification will communicate the error to the user in the form of the full Type-Length-Value. When an OPERATIONAL-ERROR is received, the data structure shown in Figure 11–12 will be passed along with the notification to the user.

The fields are defined as follows:

- *sre_type*—This field identifies the inbound message and should be set to SCTP_REMOTE_ERROR.

- *sre_flags*—This field is currently unused.

- *sre_length*—This field will hold the total length of this notification (including the header).

- *sre_assoc_id*—This field will identify the association. For the TCP-style socket, this field is ignored.

- *sre_error*—This field will hold the operational error cause as defined in any of the SCTP specifications.

- *sre_len*—This field will hold the length of the Type-Length-Value. This includes the *sre_error* and the *sre_len* fields, as well as the *sre_data* field.

- *sre_data*—This field contains the payload of the OPERATIONAL-ERROR chunk as defined in any of the SCTP specifications.

### 11.4.2.4   The SCTP_SEND_FAILED Structure

When an SCTP association cannot deliver a message, this notification will be sent to the user. The structure defined in Figure 11–13 will be used to pass back this notification.

```
struct sctp_remote_error{
    uint16_t            sre_type;
    uint16_t            sre_flags;
    uint32_t            sre_length;
    sctp_assoc_t    sre_assoc_id;
    uint16_t            sre_error;
    uint16_t            sre_len;
    uint8_t              sre_data;
}
```

**Figure 11–12**   *The remote error structure*

The fields are defined as follows:

- *ssf_type*—This field identifies the inbound message and should be set to SCTP_SEND_FAILED.

- *ssf_flags*—This field will take one of the following values:

  - SCTP_DATA_INQUEUE—This indicates that the message was in the queue to the remote peer but was never transmitted.

  - SCTP_DATA_INTMIT—This indicates that the message was sent but left outstanding with no acknowledgment when the association failed.

- *ssf_length*—This field will hold the total length of this notification (including the header).

- *ssf_assoc_id*—This field will identify the association. For the TCP-style socket, this field is ignored.

- *ssf_error*—This field specifies the reason that the transmission failed.

- *ssf_info*—This field holds the transmission information for this failed message. It identifies the stream and other information that the sender specified.

- *ssf_data*—This is the actual message that could not be sent.

### 11.4.2.5   The SCTP_SHUTDOWN_EVENT Structure

When an SCTP peer begins a graceful shutdown of the association (that is, when the local SCTP association has entered the SHUTDOWN_RECEVIED state), the information shown in Figure 11–14 is passed to the user (if the option is enabled).

```
struct sctp_send_failed{
    uint16_t            ssf_type;
    uint16_t            ssf_flags;
    uint32_t            ssf_length;
    sctp_assoc_t  ssf_assoc_id;
    uint16_t            ssf_error;
    struct sctpsndrcvinfo ssf_info;
    uint8_t             ssf_data;
}
```

**Figure 11–13**  *The send-failed structure*

```
struct sctp_shutdown_event{
    uint16_t            sse_type;
    uint16_t            sse_flags;
    uint32_t            sse_length;
    sctp_assoc_t  sse_assoc_id;
}
```

**Figure 11–14**  *The shutdown event structure*

The fields are defined as follows:

- *sse_type*—This field identifies the inbound message and should be set to SCTP_SHUTDOWN.

- *sse_flags*—This field is not currently used.

- *sse_length*—This field will hold the total length of this notification (including the header).

- *sse_assoc_id*—This field will identify the association. For the TCP-style socket, this field is ignored.

## 11.5   Summary

This chapter gave a brief introduction to the sockets work currently underway in the IETF. It introduced a compatibility mode interface for TCP applications and a new interface mode that resembles UDP. This chapter by no means gave much more than an overview of a complicated subject that deserves a book of its own.

## 11.6    Questions

1.    What are the major differences between the TCP-style and UDP-style SCTP sockets interface operations?

2.    What advantages as well as drawbacks do you see with using the TCP-style SCTP sockets interface?

3.    What advantages as well as drawbacks do you see with using the UDP-style SCTP sockets interface?

4.    If an endpoint needs to communicate with thousands of different peer endpoints at different times, what interface mode would you recommend to be used and why?

# 12

# Comparing SCTP to TCP

There are distinct differences between SCTP and TCP, yet many similarities as well. This chapter will first take a close look at the similarities between the two protocols, and then move on to the differences between them. We will finish this chapter with a short conclusion and a set of questions.

## 12.1 The Similarities between SCTP and TCP

### 12.1.1 Startup

Both protocols go through a startup exchange of messages in order to bring up the end-to-end relationship between the two endpoints. There are differences in the ways these messages are exchanged and their format, but they do hold the same purpose, that is, to bring up an end-to-end connection or association.

### 12.1.2 Reliability and Ordering

Both SCTP and TCP provide a mechanism for a user to send data reliably from one application to another over an IP packet network. Most IP networks are "best effort" and provide no assurance to a user application that its message will arrive at the remote endpoint to which it is being sent.[1] Both TCP and SCTP provide the necessary reliability to assure users that all of their messages are successfully transmitted to a peer endpoint. They provide for ordered delivery of messages as

---

1. Even in a Quality-of-Service-enabled (QoS-enabled) network, the IP layer itself is unreliable.

well. Ordered delivery becomes necessary when, for instance, an application asks a remote peer to perform an "add" operation followed by a "delete" operation. Without the assurance of message ordering, the result of the operation at the remote peer would vary depending upon which message arrived first.

### 12.1.3   Congestion Control

Another important similarity is the provision of congestion control. Both SCTP and TCP hold the same congestion control mechanism—Additive Increase, Multiplicative Decrease (AIMD) congestion window management. With the Internet of today (as discussed in Chapter 6), congestion control is a critical element in any transport protocol. Without congestion control the Internet would collapse (as in the past, see Nagle [1984]) and become unusable by most if not all users. The same basic methods defined in Allman, Paxson, and Stevens (1999) are used by both TCP and SCTP as the basis of their congestion control algorithms. This ensures fairness for both protocols as they work together on the Internet of tomorrow.

### 12.1.4   Closing Down

Both protocols have a graceful close procedure (as well as an abortive one). The graceful close procedure can be used to shut down an association or connection. It will assure the user that all data in the queue at the time of the close is reliably delivered to its peer before the end-to-end relationship with the peer is terminated.

## 12.2   The Differences Between SCTP and TCP

On the surface both protocols look very similar, so why would one want to use SCTP? Looking at the differences between the two protocols will be useful in finding an answer to this question.

### 12.2.1   Differences at Startup

As we mentioned, TCP and SCTP do have an exchange of setup messages at the initiation of the end-to-end communication. However, SCTP does differ from classic TCP. SCTP uses a four-way handshake (as discussed in Chapter 4), whereas TCP uses a three-way handshake. At first glance this would make it seem that TCP minimizes the number of messages that must be exchanged before data can flow. However, upon closer examination we can see that SCTP actually can exchange data upon the delivery of the third SCTP packet, or after one complete round trip. This is an improvement over most typical TCP implementations and their sockets APIs, which wait for the completion of the three-way handshake before the user is allowed to send data.

Another difference that is not so apparent has to do with protection against a blind SYN attack. SCTP uses its four-way handshake with a **signed state cookie** to protect against this form of attack. Some more modern TCP implementations also use a cookie mechanism. However, these implementations usually do *not* use a signed cookie, and, of course, the cookie mechanism is not built directly into the protocol; only some TCP implementations have this mechanism as an option. SCTP, on the other hand, requires that a cookie mechanism be used, with a signed and verified cookie exchange.

### 12.2.2 Head-of-Line Blocking

Once an association is established there are some fundamental differences between TCP and SCTP. One of these differences is head-of-line blocking. When you send several messages on a TCP connection, you receive a strict head-of-line blocking paradigm. What this means is that if you end up sending three TCP segments, and the first TCP segment is lost while the other two are received, even though the two TCP segments of data are available at the receiver, this data is held until the first TCP segment is retransmitted and received. This ensures that the order of delivery is the same for what the user sent and what the peer receives. There are some applications for which this strict head-of-line blocking causes a problem, by adding unnecessary and unwanted delay.

For example, if an application is performing several different transactions in parallel, holding the delivery of data for unrelated transaction 2, due to a lost TCP segment that only relates to transaction 1, may be undesirable. Many applications have attempted to get around this problem by opening multiple TCP connections to the peer. The World Wide Web (HTTP) generally opens two connections, and in some cases more. This has the undesirable consequence of causing the following:

- Multiple connections for each peer to manage

- Unfairness, by getting $x$-$m$ths of the bandwidth between two hosts instead of 1-$m$th (where $x$ is the number of user connections and $m$ is the number of total connections between the two endpoints)

SCTP has incorporated a concept called streams to alleviate this problem. Each stream will provide ordered delivery within the stream; however, two streams being transmitted over the same association are designed not to block each other. Consider Figure 12–1.

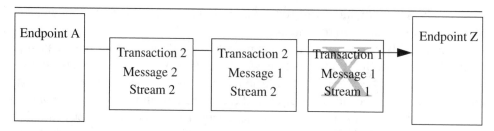

**Figure 12–1** *An example of head-of-line blocking avoidance using SCTP*

Here we see the application sending each unrelated transaction on different streams. Transaction 1's first message is lost. This, however, does not prevent Transaction 2's first message (nor its subsequent messages) from being delivered to the application with SCTP. TCP, however, would hold all subsequent messages, awaiting the retransmission timeout or fast retransmit from endpoint A's TCP stack.

### 12.2.3   Message Boundaries

Another difference between SCTP and TCP is the fundamental paradigm of message delivery. For TCP the data transported between two peers over a connection is a stream or sequence of bytes.[2] For SCTP, user message boundaries are preserved. This seems like a small difference, but in reality it provides a huge benefit to the application in that in-stream message delineation is not needed. Consider the example in Figure 12–2.

Here we see an application, endpoint A, write three distinct messages to the TCP stack destined to endpoint Z. Note the shading of the three outbound messages. The data is serialized on the wire and sent by TCP as a stream of bytes. It arrives in pieces at endpoint Z's TCP stack and is read in four separate pieces. The first read returns part of message 1. The second read returns the rest of message 1 and the first part of message 2. The third read picks up the rest of message 2 and the first part of message 3. Finally on the fourth read all of message 3 arrives. Now, in order to process these messages correctly, the applications must embed in the message a length that tells the receiver how much to read. Also, the receiver will need a reassembly buffer because at any time either more or less data than is expected may show up. The result of all this is as follows:

---

2. Note that this "stream of bytes" should *not* be confused with an SCTP stream. For TCP a stream of bytes is just a consecutive sequence of data bytes on the wire. In SCTP a stream is an ordering mechanism for messages.

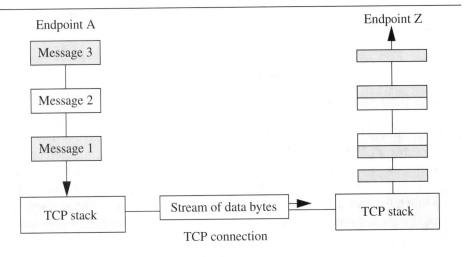

**Figure 12–2** *Message boundaries and TCP*

- Extra information being carried on the wire

- The receiving application needing to do a complex buffering and framing task (application-level framing, or ALF)

Some applications have tried to get around this by using the PUSH or URGENT pointers, only to discover that there is only one such mark (for each mechanism) and that TCP, in the face of congestion, will collapse a PUSH or an URGENT mark as it sees fit. Applications that take this shortcut will find themselves failing in strange and unusual places, normally under heavy loads, when things are hardest to troubleshoot.

In SCTP a message is delivered in a complete read. The only exception is when a message is very large, that is, larger than the peer's initial *rwnd*. In this exceptional case, if the implementation supports a partial-delivery mechanism, the partial-delivery API will be invoked. However, even in this case an application-level read always returns either a whole message or part of a message, but never two messages mixed together.

### 12.2.4  Unordered Delivery

One additional advantage of SCTP over TCP is SCTP's ability to deliver all data completely unordered yet still reliably. In some applications such an option is of great benefit when dealing with a large number of independent transactions. When a message is marked as unordered by the user, it is placed in the application delivery queue upon arrival. There is no implicit or explicit order placed on any un-ordered message[3].

### 12.2.5   Selective Acknowledgment

Another slight difference between SCTP and TCP is the use of SACK. SACK, or Selective Acknowledgment, allows a receiver to report its exact condition to the sender, informing the sender of all disjointed pieces that may have arrived at the receiver. For TCP this is an option, and it may be present in some implementations. For those implementations that support the use of SACK, only four TCP segments may be reported in its SACK information (carried in IP options). SCTP has a much larger limitation (dictated by the PMTU), allowing a large number of SACK blocks to be reported in every SACK, and thus may have better performance than the retrofitted TCP implementations.

### 12.2.6   Multi-homing

One of the key features of SCTP is the direct support of multi-homing by SCTP. Multi-homing is when more than one IP address is assigned to a host. Usually this also entails having multiple network interface (or NIC) cards. Consider Figure 12–3, which shows an SCTP association *and* a TCP connection between two hosts.

Processes 1 and 3 hold an SCTP association between them. Processes 2 and 4 hold a TCP connection. The small circles represent NIC cards with their IP addresses (1 to 4) contained inside the circle. If, as the diagram illustrates, IP2 fails, the TCP connection is broken. There is no recovery for this connection because it holds the single point of failure, IP2, in either the source or destination address of every IP datagram, and this NIC is unusable. Now consider the SCTP association. Because an association is a broader concept, it encompasses *all four* IP addresses; it can survive this failure and continue to transfer data over the alternate path between IP1 and IP3. Another interesting note is that the application can be completely unaware of the failure if it so chooses. The SCTP stack will take care of all the details, hiding the network errors from the user.

---

3. Note that in the past to achieve unordered service, most applications had to use UDP. UDP is not only unordered but also unreliable. Thus the application would have a need to build in a reliability mechanism (on top of UDP) in order to achieve reliable delivery in an unordered set of messages.

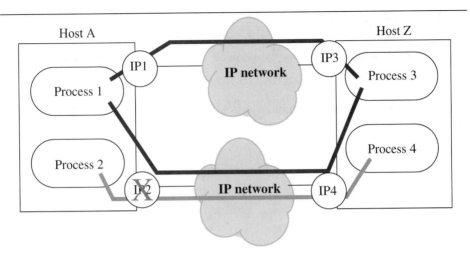

**Figure 12–3**  *A multi-homing comparison*

### 12.2.7   A Closing Difference

There is one function that SCTP lacks, and it does so in the close procedure. We already noted that both TCP and SCTP have a graceful close mechanism. But there is a difference in the two mechanisms. TCP allows one side to close a connection, but the connection stays open. The side that closed the connection cannot send data but will continue to receive data until its peer closes its side of the connection. This state, when one side has closed but the other remains open, is known as the "half-closed" state. TCP explicitly allows this, whereas SCTP does not. With SCTP, when either endpoint issues the graceful shutdown primitive, both sides of the SCTP association will de-queue their data and shut down the association.

   One of the main reasons that SCTP did not add this "half-closed" state is the little use that this function has received in TCP. Very few applications require this type of service. The extra complexity was not thought to be worth the addition of the feature.

## 12.3   Summary

We have examined some of the similarities and differences between TCP and SCTP and shown that SCTP has many advantages over and improvements to TCP. Many of these improvements have been brought about by experience and research within the TCP community. SCTP just brings these experiences into a focal point, that is, a new reliable transport protocol.

## 12.4   Questions

1. Name some applications in which head-of-line blocking may be a critical issue.

2. How does the message boundary-preservation feature of SCTP help an application?

# 13

# Using Streams in SCTP

**I**n this chapter we will take a close look at the ways in which SCTP streams can be used to help an application provide more efficient utilization of the association.

It is worthwhile to note that the application examples used in this chapter are mostly imaginary and may bear little practical significance because our intention here is to show the usage of the multi-stream feature of SCTP.

We will take a look at three examples:

- File Transfer Protocol-like (FTP-like) application

- Call control application

- Web browser

## 13.1    A File Transfer Application

For many years FTP (Postel and Reynolds 1985) has been used in the Internet for the bulk transfer of files. In a typical FTP session a user follows these steps (as depicted in Figure 13–1):

1. Set up a TCP connection with the server on which the file is located.

2. Log into the server, supplying credentials to verify that the user is allowed access to the server.

3. Request via specific commands (**get**, **mget**, **put**, **mput**, etcetera) to transfer files.

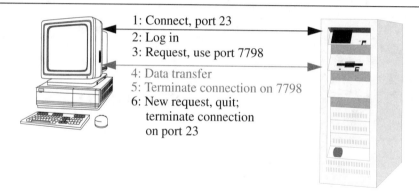

1: Connect, port 23
2: Log in
3: Request, use port 7798
4: Data transfer
5: Terminate connection on 7798
6: New request, quit;
   terminate connection
   on port 23

**Figure 13–1**  *A classic FTP session*

4. Each time a file is transferred, open a new TCP connection to send the specific file. The specifics of which port, who listens, and who connects to
   whom are part of the "behind the scenes" negotiation that FTP performs for
   the user.

5. When the file has been completely transferred, the TCP connection used
   for transferring the file is terminated.

6. Make new requests or, if the user logs out, terminate the initial connection.

One thing to note about this methodology is that through the "command channel" (the original connection used to send and receive commands and responses),
the FTP session negotiates the details of the addresses to which to send the
requested file. This provides a bit of a problem for NATs and firewalls because the
actual details of which addresses and ports are used are placed in the data stream
of the control connection. This means that if a NAT or firewall will let FTP sessions pass through, they also must monitor and translate addressing information
presented on the original connection.

Now we will show a **mythical** SCTP-based file transfer application (see Figure 13–2) that provides services similar to the classic FTP but without the need for
multiple connections. In place of each connection we will use an SCTP stream.
The steps for using this SCTP-based FTP would be similar to those for using the
classic FTP.

1. Set up the association with 100 streams.

2. Log in, using stream 0 to communicate credentials.

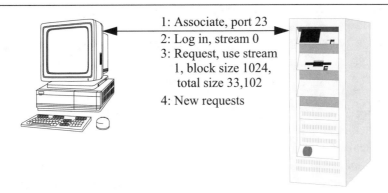

1: Associate, port 23
2: Log in, stream 0
3: Request, use stream
   1, block size 1024,
   total size 33,102
4: New requests

**Figure 13–2** *An SCTP file transfer*

3. Use stream 0 to request a file transfer on stream 1, specifying that the block size will be 1,024 bytes and the total file size will be 33,102 bytes.

4. Enter any new requests, which would either terminate the association or use additional streams.

Note that in the SCTP-based file transfer application, we only use one association. We use the streams SCTP provides in place of the TCP connections that would normally be used by the classic FTP to transfer files to or from the server. Note also that we no longer exchange addressing information; instead we specify the message block size (because each message sent will be a part of the file) and the total size of the file. We could also start parallel transfers, if we so desired, by using additional streams even while the first transfer was occurring. Each stream number on the inbound side would be used to demultiplex the file to which the data belonged.

## 13.2 A Telephone Call Control Application

Telephone call control applications present other requirements for SCTP. Instead of the need to transfer a "file" of data, we have a number of messages that need to be exchanged in a timely manner between the two endpoints. Each phone call will be represented by a sequence of messages that set up and tear down the phone call. Note that a call control engine may have hundreds or thousands of phone calls that it is maintaining at any single instance between it and a particular peer.

This creates an interesting situation. On any one particular call, we wish to start the setup and proceed with the call as soon as we can. However, each call that we process has a sequence of messages that must be exchanged in a set order. One would not want to receive the "disconnect" of a call before the setup request. If we were to use a typical TCP connection, call 1 might lose a message in the transmission, yet call 2, call 3, and call 4 might have messages in the queue that do not get lost but are held up by TCP awaiting the retransmission of the lost message (the one associated with call 1). This creates on all calls a domino effect of delay, which is not desired. SCTP provides a convenient mechanism to get around this problem, that is, streams.

In the example in Figure 13–3 we have endpoints A and endpoint Z exchanging call control information. Notice that the endpoints use a different stream number for each call traveling across the association. This allows any of the messages traveling across the network to be lost without affecting any other call. For practical reasons a call control application may spread the calls over a smaller range of streams. For example, the application may take a set number of streams and modulo a call reference number over them. This would spread most of the calls evenly across a smaller number of streams and provide a minimum of head-of-line blocking.

Call control applications for carrier-grade service require highly reliable communication with no single point of failure. SCTP can help here as well with the use of its multi-homing feature. By providing different paths through the network over separate and diverse means, the goal of "no single point of failure" can be achieved by proper network engineering.

## 13.3   A Web Browser

Another possible use of SCTP is for a Web browser. Currently a Web browser will create a TCP connection to a specific server on a well-known port (usually 80). It will then send a message requesting a specific page. The Web server will respond with the page. Often if there are multiple images and various multimedia objects, separate TCP connections will be created to transfer these objects in parallel. This way, if a piece of an object is lost during transfer, the other objects will continue loading while the lost piece is retransmitted. This gives better response to the user and provides a primitive escape for the head-of-line blocking issue. However, there is a problem with these actions. With multiple connections the Web browser may get more than its fair share of the bandwidth between the two endpoints (assuming other traffic such as FTP is competing for that bandwidth).

SCTP could be used to help solve this problem. If in place of a TCP connection the Web client used SCTP, the server could use individual streams to transfer the objects or images. Each object, up to 65,535 of them, could be sent down a separate SCTP stream. Thus the browser and client would achieve the highest

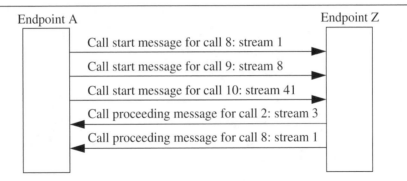

**Figure 13–3**  *An example of call processing with SCTP*

amount of parallel transfer without acquiring more than their fair share of the bandwidth between two endpoints.

## 13.4  Summary

This chapter has shown SCTP streams in action in several application examples. SCTP streams are, in general, used to escape the head-of-line blocking problem. Each application must consider if head-of-line blocking will cause undesirable effects for it. In most cases this determination can be made by understanding each message's relationship to any previous message that was sent. When messages do not have any interdependency, SCTP streams can be of great assistance.

Other instances and possibilities also exist for stream usage. An application may wish to use an SCTP stream to provide an index into a particular application instance. An example of this would be if an application had a number of state machines. Each one of the state machines on occasion sends a message to a peer endpoint. If each state machine uses a specific stream, the stream can be used as either an index or a reference into the state machine itself. The stream concept imbedded in SCTP provides a powerful tool to help applications.

## 13.5  Questions

1.  In what situations would multiple streams *not* be helpful?

2.  Will the use of multiple streams gain an unfair advantage for an application in terms of network bandwidth usage? Why or why not?

# 14

# A User Space Implementation of SCTP

This chapter will document the user-space reference implementation. It will attempt to detail the basic code flow and overall design of the implementation. For those who only want to understand SCTP, this may be a good chapter to skip. For those interested in how an SCTP implementation is put together, this chapter will serve as a guide to the CD that comes with this book.

The implementation included in this CD should run on Linux, FreeBSD, Net-BSD, Lynx O/S, and Solaris. In general it works with most UNIX-like systems that provide two basic things: a classic sockets API and a method for sending raw IP datagrams.

## 14.1   The Big Picture

The implementation is structured in such a way as to make it possible for any application to link in a library and run the user space implementation of SCTP. However, there is a fundamental trade-off that is made to make this library version possible. All the UNIX-like operating systems that this implementation runs on require Set User IDentification (SUID) to root[1] in order to have access to a "raw"

---

1.  Root is the "super user" that has access to everything. As such, it is very dangerous to allow casual access to this account.

IP socket. There are two options that one has when confronted with this "root" dilemma:

- Require *all* users of SCTP to have the *SUID* bit set to "make them root" when they run.

- Require *all* users to tunnel their IP datagrams to a daemon that has its *SUID* set to root.

The advantage of forcing applications to set *SUID* to root is that no tunneling or additional overhead is required. With only one application using SCTP, this can be a tremendous savings. The sender is the actual library composing the SCTP packets, making debugging easier and cutting overhead to a minimum. The downside to this choice is two-fold: first there is the inconvenience that every process that wants to use SCTP must be started and owned by the root and have its *SUID* bit set. Second is the overhead of opening a raw SCTP IP socket. When you open a raw IP socket, you get every IP datagrams of that type. This means that every process using the library will get a copy of every SCTP packet sent to the machine.

The second choice, that of using a daemon, has an equal trade-off to consider. You free the application from the need to be owned by root and have its *SUID* bits set, but you now must tunnel IP datagrams to the daemon. The daemon still requires the *SUID* bits set, so you don't escape asking your system administrator to let one of your processes run as root. But you do *not* need to set every one of your processes to be owned by root and to have the *SUID bit set*. The tunneling of IP datagrams forces every SCTP packet to be sent first to the daemon and then resent to the IP network by the daemon. This obviously creates additional overhead. The implementation included with the book is of this type; that is, a daemon is set up to run and the library tunnels IP datagrams to the daemon[2]. Also, the choice of IPC mechanisms to actually tunnel IP datagrams to the daemon creates another side effect. We use UDP to send the IP datagrams between the daemon and the local library. To take a shortcut when writing this daemon, we require that the user's SCTP port match that of the UDP port that the library has bound. This means that every SCTP port taken uses a port from the UDP space. The overall architecture of a process running the reference implementation can be seen in Figure 14–1. The dashed line represents the route that SCTP packets take on their way to the "IP" wire.

The daemon itself is a small program that does not comprise a lot of code. As such, we will leave it to you to go and examine how it operates and what it does. We

---

2.  For BSD users this implementation also holds an option that moves the user space daemon into the kernel and thus avoids the extra data copies. Using this option avoids the overhead discussed here.

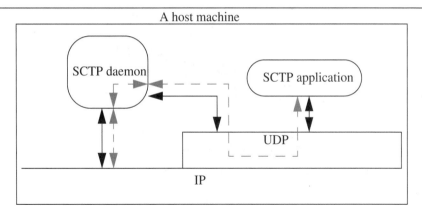

A host machine

SCTP daemon

SCTP application

UDP

IP

**Figure 14–1**  *SCTP reference implementation: a high-level view*

will instead turn our attention to the user library and how it functions and relates to the topics discussed in this book. However, before we dive in, let us take a look at how the reference implementation itself inside a process is structured. Figure 14–2 illustrates the process structure in the program *sctp_test_app* found on the included CD.

The distributor provides a reactor-type model in which events are passed to subscribed functions. It also provides timer services for any interested "object."[3] The user interface "object" receives any events associated with the standard input (sometimes called "stdin"), that is, the user input. It knows how to interface to the SCTP library to send various messages and association requests. The SCTP adaptor provides an interface between the more generic SCTP library (and what it requires) and the distributor's framework. We will focus the discussion in this chapter on the SCTP library. The adaptor and the rest of the framework, including the user interface, are left for you to explore on your own.

## 14.2  Data Structures

Three basic files are included throughout the reference implementation:

- *sctpHeader.h*
- *sctpStructs.h*
- *sctpConstants.h*

---

3. We use the term object here even though the program is written in "C." The reference implementation is object oriented in that all functions have an "object" of data that is always associated with them, if you will, a "this" pointer in C++ terms.

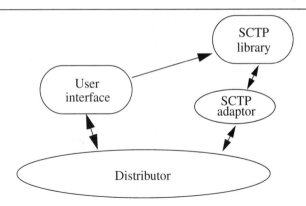

**Figure 14–2** *The internal structure of the library*

The file *sctpHeader.h* encapsulates all the "bits on the wire" that can be easily defined in structures. All the structures discussed in Chapter 3 can be found here, with the exception of elements like the cookie, which is privately created and concatenated together from a number of sources.

The file *sctpStructs.h* contains all the detailed tracking and management structures that the library uses to keep track of what is going on in the SCTP library. Each application that links the SCTP library gets its own copy of the SCTP code. When an endpoint is initialized by the user, it binds itself to a UDP port (which is usually specified by the user) and then registers with the local SCTP daemon. Subsequently SCTP packets are tunneled to the daemon for transmission. This daemon's sole job is to drop the tunneled IP datagrams onto a raw IP socket.[4] In the opposite direction, the daemon receives SCTP packets and tunnels them to the respective application. When the library is initialized, it does so using the structures found in *sctpStructs.h*. Defined here is the key "object," *struct SCTP*. This structure is required to be present in all library interface calls and represents the endpoint. Multiple "objects" of this type can be created, thus creating multiple SCTP endpoints in a single process.

The file *sctpConstants.h* contains various constants and defaults used by the SCTP endpoint at startup. Many of these parameters are able to be set further by the user via SCTP calls. Not all the parameters listed within this file can be configured. Some, such as *RTO-MIN* and *RTO-MAX*, are constants that when changed, require that the whole library be recompiled.

---

4. The daemon is a SUID process that has the needed permissions to send raw IP datagrams.

## 14.3    Events and the API

The user of the SCTP library will access the various SCTP functions by including the *sctp.h* header file and calling the functions defined therein. The *sctp.h* header file contains all the "visible" function calls and provides the API to the library. It closely matches Stewart et al. (2000) and attempts to provide the services discussed therein.

When initializing an endpoint (the first step in setting things up), a pointer is passed to a number of functions in the initialization routine:

- *Timer function*—This function can supply a timer start/stop service.

- *Event mask update*—This can change the event mask, that is, those events that the SCTP stack is looking for on its file descriptor. These are in terms of the **poll()** function call.

- *Notification*—This is a callback function that provides notification events from the SCTP stack to the user process.

- *Time access*—This function gets the time of day in a posix timespec format.

After initializing the endpoint data structure, the **sctpINITIALIZE()** routine will do the following:

- Create a UDP socket.

- Register with the SCTP daemon.

- Return to the user a pointer to the *struct SCTP* that all calls to access this endpoint should use.

The library expects the caller to then use the **getSCTPfileDescriptor()** call to find and register the file descriptor(s) to be watched for events. The functions in *sctpAdaptor.c* perform this by calling the appropriate distributor functions to set up any file descriptors found using the **getSCTPfileDescriptor()** call.

Once the SCTP stack is initialized, events will flow in one of three ways into the SCTP library:

- The user will type a command, which the user interface module will translate into one of the SCTP library calls that provide the API to the user (all defined in *sctp.h*).

- A file descriptor will awaken with an event, calling through **sctpFdInput()** in *sctpAdaptor.c* to the main **sctpfdEvent()** routine, where all input from the network arrives.

- A timer will expire, calling the main timer entry point to the library **sctptimerExpires()**.

This event flow is illustrated in Figure 14–3.

There are many other support utilities defined in *sctp.h* that allow a user application to control various aspects of the SCTP stack, such as timing, thresholds, and heartbeating. We do not show these in Figure 14–3 because these do not cause event or data flow within the SCTP stack. With this background in mind, we will now turn our attention to association setup.

## 14.4   Association Setup

Two methods of association setup can occur in an SCTP endpoint:

- The upper layer may issue an associate call, causing the SCTP endpoint to send an INIT chunk to its remote peer. This can be in the form of either the associate function call **sctpASSOCIATE()**, or in the implicit form, when the user application sends a message to a peer for which no association exists, with the **sctpSEND()** function call.

- The SCTP endpoint may also receive an INIT chunk from a peer. This will occur in the reference implementation as a **sctpfdEvent()** call from the distributor/adaptor, which in turn causes a message to be read. The event-processing routine, **sctpfdEvent()**, will service the file descriptor, reading any message that may arrive. The routine will pass off any ICMP messages to **SCTPhandleICMP()** and any inbound SCTP packet to **SCTPprocessInbound()**.

As we examine association setup within the reference implementation, we will follow both paths through the code. We will first take a closer look at our local endpoint being the initiator of the association.

### 14.4.1   When an Upper Layer Issues an Associate Primitive

As mentioned earlier, our local endpoint may send an INIT message on one of two stimuli: first, if the upper layer issues **sctpASSOCIATE()**, or, as an alternative, if the user just calls **sctpSEND()** to a peer address with which no association has been set up.

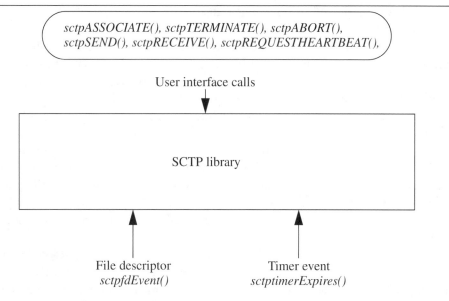

**Figure 14–3**  *Library event flow*

If the user issues **sctpASSOCIATE()**, the implementation will translate this call into a lower-level subcall, **SCTPstartInit()**. The **SCTPstartInit()** call is found in *sctpinitiate.c*, where a large majority of the INIT processing code resides. **SCTP-startInit()** will allocate an association TCB (by calling **SCTPalocAssociation()**, found in *sctputil.c*), formulate and send off the INIT message (by calling **SCTPsen-dInitiate()**, found in *sctpsenders.c*) set up the TCB's internal state, start a timer (by calling **timerWork()**, found in *sctputil.c*) and return the newly created association.

If the user calls the **sctpSEND()** module instead, a special restriction is applied. The user must be sending to stream 0. This is the only stream that is guaranteed to be created in every association. If the user is not sending to stream 0 and no association exists, the **sctpSEND()** function will return an error. Otherwise a special function, **sendToStream0()**, is called (still within the base interface file *sctp.c*). This special module will first attempt to find the association (using **SCT-PfindAssociation()**, found in *sctputil.c*). If the association is not found, then special handling is employed to first call the **SCTPstartInit()** function. This builds the association and begins the INIT sequence (as just described) and returns the association TCB. This TCB is then used to queue the user data, ensuring that the data will be piggybacked upon the COOKIE-ECHO. The data is queued and possibly sent through the normal functions that are described in Section 14.5. Figure 14–4 illustrates the basic call flow just described.

At this point the SCTP stack will wait for either of two events: a timeout that occurs from the timer started in **SCTPstartInit()**, or an INIT-ACK returned by the peer endpoint. If a timer expires, the **sctptimerExpires()** routine is called. This routine will figure out the type of timer that expired and call one of the timeout handling functions found in *sctphandleto.c*. In our case an INIT-type timer would expire, causing the **SCTPhandleInitTimer()** function to be called. This routine will first check to make sure that the maximum number of retransmissions has not yet been reached; if it has, the upper layer is notified and the association TCB is removed. To remove an association, the function **SCTPfreeAssociation()** is called. As you may have guessed, it is also found in *sctputil.c*. If the maximum number of retransmissions has not been reached, a simple callback to **SCTPsendInitate()** will retransmit another INIT message to the peer. After another INIT message is sent, the timer is once again restarted, and we again wait for either a timeout or an INIT-ACK.

If the peer does return an INIT-ACK, the message is read in by **sctpfdEvent()**, which in turn calls **SCTPprocessInbound()**. SCTPprocessInbound is the module that performs two functions: it calls the control chunk handling function, and it processes all DATA chunks contained within a SCTP packet. The data processing portion is described in Section 14.5. Control chunks are always first within an SCTP packet, so the first thing to do (after finding any association TCB) is to call the function **SCTP_handleControlPortion()**. This function can be found in *sctpinitiate.c*. All control chunks and validations (with a few exceptions) are preformed in this module. After doing any out-of-the-blue handling, as described in Section 14.8, this function processes all control chunks contained within an SCTP packet. One of three conditions will terminate its processing: the end of the SCTP packet, encountering a chunk that is always required to be singular, or encountering a DATA chunk. For our current discussion, an INIT-ACK message should have no other chunks included with it; if it does the rest of the IP datagram is ignored. Once the control processing function finds the INIT-ACK, it then calls the function **SCTP_handleInitiateAck()**.

**SCTP_handleInitiateAck()** will first do a special case test. If the association was not found during **SCTP_handleControlPortion()**'s normal association lookup, using **SCTPfindAssociation()**, it will use a special lookup procedure, **SCTPspecialFindAssociation()**. This function will look within the actual INIT-ACK for IP address parameters. For each address parameter it finds, it will issue a lookup call to attempt to find the association. This is necessary because it is possible that the source address of the SCTP packet that contains the INIT-ACK will not match the address to which the INIT was sent. In this case the only way to find the association TCB is to look within the INIT-ACK and find the address to which the INIT was actually sent. If the association is not found, the function returns a NULL to indicate that no association exists, terminating processing of this SCTP

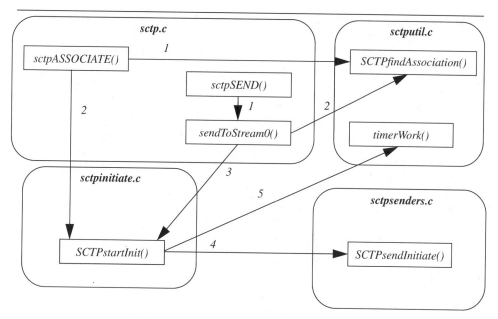

**Figure 14–4** *Basic INIT call flow*

packet. If the association TCB is found, then various checks are performed on the
SCTP packet, including the following:

- Make sure the *Verification tag* is valid and matches the Initiation tag sent in
  the INIT.

- Check to be sure the peer's *Initial tag* is not zero.

- Make sure the peer has met the minimum *a_rwnd* requirement.

- Make sure that a minimum of at least one stream is allowed by the peer in its
  *MIS* value.

- Verify we are in the correct state, anticipating the arrival of an INIT-ACK.

If all of these conditions are met, then the INIT-ACK is adopted, and the association TCB values are updated from the INIT-ACK. This adoption of variables is
performed by **SCTPadoptThisInitAck()**.

**SCTPadoptThisInitAck()** will first pull out the cookie and place it in a special holder inside the TCB. Placing it in the special cookie pointer causes the
return function call path to send out the cookie at the completion of **SCTPpro-
cessInbound()** through its call to **SCTPsendAnyWeCan()**. **SCTPadoptThisInit-**

**Ack()** will call the function **SCTPadoptThisInit()** to actually pull in the values and build all appropriate structures inside the association TCB to align with the peer. It can do this because the INIT and INIT-ACK have nearly identical structures and thus have a common set of processing that can be applied to both an INIT and an INIT-ACK. Figure 14–5 illustrates the call flow just described.

As noted earlier, the pulling out of the cookie will cause it to be sent in a COOKIE-ECHO to our peer. This places us in the COOKIE_ECHOED state. Here we again run a timer to ensure that the COOKIE-ECHO arrives at our peer. Two events may occur that will cause the next set of logic to execute: either we will timeout, again flowing into similar timeout handling, or we will receive a COOKIE-ACK message. If a timeout does occur, the call flow is almost identical to that described for the previous flow, with the only minor exception being the end function called. Instead of **SCTPhandleInitTimerUp()**, the function **SCT-PhandleCookieTimerUp()** is called. This function performs similarly to the former function, that is, incrementing the overall error count and verifying that it does not exceed the maximum retransmission threshold. If it does exceed the threshold, the function terminates the association and reports the termination to its upper layer. Otherwise the function calls the general retransmission function **SCTPsendRetransmits()**, which will recognize the early state of the association and resend just the cookie. Note that on a retransmission of a cookie, the code will not perform any bundling of data. This was a design choice made while implementing the retransmission function. It is perfectly legal to retransmit the cookie with DATA chunks bundled to it, but it was felt that it was better to cut back on the size of the SCTP packet being sent when an *RTO* timer had fired.

Our other alternative is the arrival of the COOKIE-ACK. This will follow the same control path leading into the **SCTP_handleControlPortion()** function. Once there, the *Verification tag* is again validated, and the control chunks contained in the SCTP packet are processed. The COOKIE-ACK should be the first chunk within the message, but the implementation does not place this requirement on the processing. In fact a SACK could arrive ahead of the COOKIE-ACK and the association would still process both the SACK and the COOKIE-ACK correctly. No additional function is called when the COOKIE-ACK is detected. The state is set to ESTABLISHED and the upper layer is notified about the new association. At this point the association is considered completely established and normal data transfer can proceed (see Section 14.5). Figure 14–6 illustrates the call flow just described.

We have looked at the procedures surrounding the initiation of an association by an endpoint. We will now turn our attention to receiving and responding to an INIT.

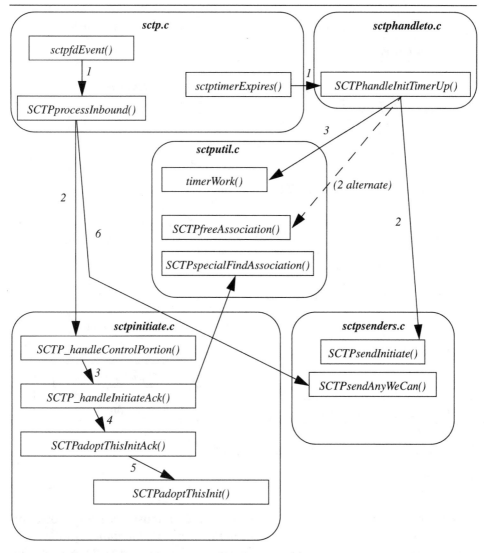

**Figure 14–5** *INIT-ACK processing call flow*

### 14.4.2   When a Peer Sends the SCTP Endpoint an INIT

When an SCTP endpoint receives an INIT message from a potential peer, many of the code paths we have discussed previously are followed. The message is read in by **sctpfdEvent()**, which hands off the message to **SCTPprocessInbound()**. **SCTPprocessInbound()** performs the same functions as mentioned in the previous section, resulting in a call to **SCTP_handleControlPortion()**. One notable

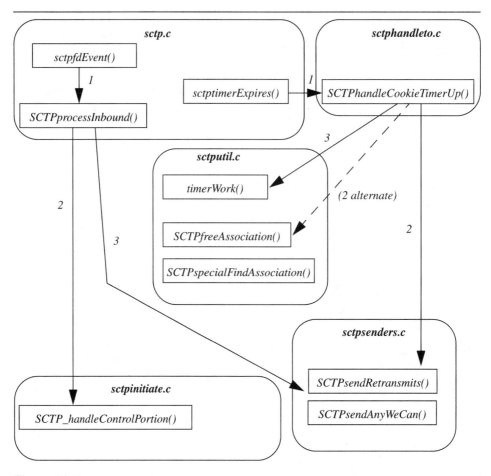

**Figure 14–6**   *Final association setup*

difference in the handling of an INIT is that, here, in most cases no association TCB exists. The control processing does not expect a *Verification tag* other than the value of zero in the SCTP common header of the inbound SCTP packet. The control processing also expects the INIT chunk to be the only message within the SCTP packet. If previous chunks are found before the INIT, the INIT message and any other chunks contained within the SCTP packet are ignored. The control processing also verifies that the *Initial tag* in the INIT message is not zero; if it is zero, the control processing will send an ABORT and terminate processing of the SCTP packet.

If all is well, the function **SCTP_handleInitiateIn()** is called. This function does a number of tests and checks after first using the **SCTPspecialFindAssocia-**

**tion**() function to attempt to find any previous association that may exist. If a previous association is found and is in the shutdown state, a SHUTDOWN-ACK is sent by calling the **SCTPsendShutdownAck**() function. After sending a SHUTDOWN-ACK, the function returns, ignoring the INIT and depending on the sender's retransmission timer to resend the INIT after responding to the SHUDOWN-ACK. Note that this is different than what was described in the previous chapters, but it is a shortcut that was taken within the implementation and is quite harmless.

After this special case test is done, the following tests are performed upon the new INIT:

- Does the initial *rwnd* meet the minimum required *rwnd*?

- Does the sender of the INIT allow at least one stream in its MIS value?

- Does the sender of the INIT ask for at least one stream?

If any of these conditions are not met, an ABORT is sent to the peer and processing of the SCTP packet is terminated. After passing all the tests, the function calls **SCTPbuildACookie**() (found in *sctputil.c*) to build a cookie using the inbound INIT. When building the cookie, if a previous association exists, the routine populates the tie-tags with the values of the current association's tags, and it also saves the base address of the previous association. If no previous association exists, these fields are set to zero. A special examination is then performed on the parameters of the inbound INIT. We carefully look for the *Cookie preservative* to see if the cookie life needs to be extended. The utility call **findAParameter**() is called to look for this parameter. This function also returns a special value to indicate if an unrecognized parameter was seen that requires the processing to be aborted. If so, the cookie building module will return a NULL value to indicate that the SCTP packet needs to be dropped.

The extended cookie life is added to the cookie life (if present) within a set limit of no more than double the normal cookie life. If a previous association exists and is in the early stages of association setup (that is, just having sent the INIT or waiting for the COOKIE-ACK), some of the values are copied from the old association. Otherwise, all new values are created for the *Verification tag* and other values in the cookie. After the complete cookie is prepared, the MD5/SHA-1 algorithm is run on the cookie by calling the **sctpMd5Digest**() function. This utility is precompiled with one of the two hashing algorithms, using SHA-1 as the default[5].

After the cookie is built and signed, the allocated cookie is returned to the caller, where it is placed into the outbound message by being passed to the send-

---

5.  A simple compile-level switch can be added to the makefile to change the algorithm to MD5.

ing module. After the successful building of the cookie, the **SCTPsendInitateAck**() function is called to create and build the complete INIT-ACK. The values to be placed in the INIT-ACK, that is, the mandatory parameters, are retrieved from the cookie by this routine to ensure that the COOKIE-ECHO and INIT-ACK contain the same information. Note that no association TCB is created in this process and that any existing TCB is left untouched. It is only when the COOKIE-ECHO arrives that an association TCB will be allocated and any necessary changes will be made to any existing association (if one exists). Figure 14–7 depicts the function flow just discussed.

Once the INIT-ACK is sent, nothing will occur until the COOKIE-ECHO arrives. The COOKIE-ECHO is the *State cookie* parameter changed into a COOKIE-ECHO chunk type, as you may remember from Chapter 4. With the arrival of the COOKIE-ECHO, the cookie is unpacked and verified. The usual functional flow occurs through to **SCTP_handleControlPortion**(). Again, due to the nature of this special case, no association TCB is expected to exist. The cookie is expected to be the first chunk in the SCTP packet; if it is not, processing is terminated and the SCTP packet is discarded. Otherwise, the function **SCTPunpackCookie**() is called (in *sctputil.c*).

**SCTPunpackCookie**() does the following validations:

- Verify that the cookie is of the minimum cookie size.

- Verify the signature to ensure that the cookie has not been changed. In verifying the signature, a choice of which current secret key to validate the cookie with is made. The secret key changes every hour by default. In some rare cases it is necessary to validate with both secrets (for example, when the time of the secret change exactly corresponds to the time of this cookie's creation).

- Verify that the cookie is not too old, that is, that it is not stale.

Only if all of these checks pass, is the cookie accepted, at which point one of two types of processing will be applied. If no previous association exists, we call the function **SCTPplainCookie**(). If a previous association TCB exists, the function **SCTPcomplexCookie**() is called. Complex cookie processing is described in Section 14.4.2.1.

Processing a plain cookie entails the following steps:

1. Allocate an association TCB.

2. Set up all the local association parameters within the TCB to correspond to those sent in the INIT-ACK message.

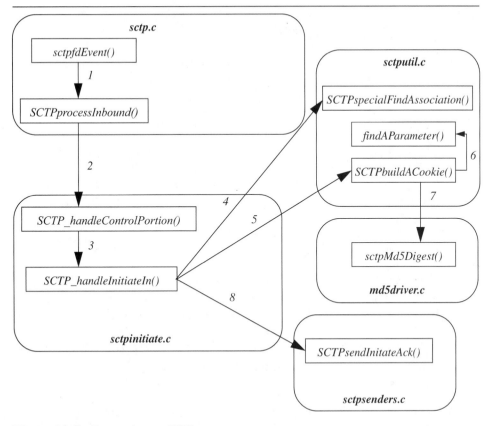

**Figure 14–7** *Processing an INIT*

3. Call the function **SCTPadoptThisInit()** to pull in all the parameters from the INIT chunk contained within the cookie.

Upon the successful completion of these steps, the association is brought into an ESTABLISHED state and a COOKIE-ACK is sent by calling the function **SCTPsendCookieAck()**. Two additional timers are started, one for PMTU discovery and the other for heartbeating. These will be discussed in Section 14.6 and Section 14.7, respectively.

### 14.4.2.1 Handling the Duplicate Association Case
When a previous association exists, the SCTP specification directs us to use special procedures to handle "a COOKIE-ECHO when a TCB exists." This special

handling is performed by the function **SCTPcomplexCookie**() and occurs as follows in the complex cookie processing:

1. First check that the previous association is not shutting down. If it is shutting down (that is, awaiting a SHUTDOWN-COMPLETE), the cookie is ignored and a new SHUTDOWN-ACK is sent.

2. Convert all integer values within the cookie to host byte order.

3. Check to see if the existing association tags match those found in the cookie. If they do, check the state of the association. If the state is COOKIE_WAIT or COOKIE_ECHOED, stop all timers, notify the upper layer that the association is up, move the association to the ESTABLISHED state, and send a COOKIE-ACK. Otherwise, the association is already in the ESTABLISHED state so no action is needed except to send a COOKIE-ACK to the peer.

4. Check to see if the local association's tag matches the tag found in the cookie but does not match the peer's tag. If this is the case, a duplicate INIT case is occurring and the COOKIE-ECHO sent will be discarded. The values from the cookie are adopted, and, if the association has not reached the ESTABLISHED state, it is set to the ESTABLISHED state, and all the correct timers for the association are set. Upon completion a COOKIE-ACK is sent to the peer.

5. Check to see if a restart has occurred. The restart case is indicated by the tie-tags within the cookie matching the old association tags. If this is the case, the peer has restarted. A verification is performed to ensure that the endpoint is not adding any additional addresses via a call to **sctpVerifyNoNewAddresses**(). If new addresses have been added, the cookie is discarded. Otherwise, the cookie is accepted. A restart notification is given to the peer, and all outstanding DATA chunks are rejected back to the upper layer. Once all the reporting is completed, the internal values of the cookie are adopted into the association and the appropriate timers are started.

6. If none of the conditions in steps 1 through 5 hold true, the cookie is dropped.

These final steps of cookie processing are depicted in Figure 14–8.

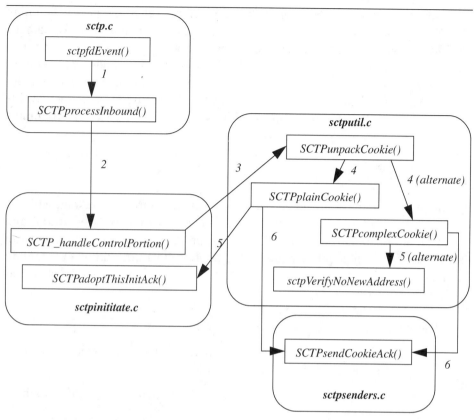

**Figure 14–8** *Final cookie processing*

## 14.5   Data Transfer

Data transfer generally occurs in the ESTABLISHED state. The notable exception to this is when data transfer happens within the SHUTDOWN_PENDING state. Data transfer may also happen on both the COOKIE-ECHO and COOKIE-ACK, but because the transfer will happen after the COOKIE-ECHO or COOKIE-ACK is processed, the association will have technically entered the ESTABLISHED state before the data portion of the SCTP packet is processed.

The reference implementation processes data and SACKs through a set of function calls similar to those you have seen so far. A few new functions are added, which are all contained within the *sctpinbound.c* file. There are two cases we will examine in the "data" path of the reference implementation: processing a SACK and processing data. Even though we describe these two actions separately, they may happen sequentially on the same SCTP packet (if the peer is bundling SACKs and data together). At the end of the processing of control and/or data the **SCTPprocessInbound()** function will make the appropriate calls to send data (and/or SACKs) to the peer (as you shall see). We will first address the control processing of SACKs, and then examine data processing of inbound data elements. We will conclude this section with a brief discussion of the outbound side of the function **SCTPprocessInbound()**, which is executed after all chunks within an SCTP packet are processed.

### 14.5.1  SACK Processing

SACK processing happens much the same as other control processing, with the now-familiar function calls **sctpfdEvent()**, **SCTPprocessInbound()**, and **SCTP_handleControlPortion()**. After the appropriate tag checks in the control processing function, a call is made to **SCTP_handleInboundSack()** (found in *sctpinbound.c*). This function contains the SACK processing that performs the following checks and procedures:

1. Pull the value of the updated *a_rwnd* from the SACK.

2. If the *Cumulative TSN* value from the SACK is less than the last *Cumulative Ack* point, discard the SACK; it is old.

3. If there is no pending outstanding data, use the updated *a_rwnd* from the SACK to set the local peer's *rwnd* value.

4. Determine if the *Cumulative Ack* point has advanced and record this fact. Also note how many fast retransmits have been completed.

5. If the *Cumulative TSN* point moved, stop all timers so that they can be restarted with a new timer at the end of processing (if needed).

6. Process all Gap Ack block reports in the SACK, marking any acknowledged TSNs, and noting any chunks that were revoked as well. Do this by marking all DATA chunks acknowledged by Gap Ack blocks with a special *Marked* flag. TSNs that remain "acknowledged" and that are not covered by the *Cumulative TSN* are revoked.

7. During Gap Ack block processing, track the largest or highest TSN that has been acknowledged; you will use this value later.

8. Go through and track the totals acknowledged and remove any pending chunks that were acknowledged by the *Cumulative TSN*. In this process,

also change any revoked DATA chunks back to the "Sent" but not "Acknowledged" state.

9. This major step is related to congestion control and *RTO* time calculations. We will defer this discussion until the next section.

10. After all processing is complete, if the output queue is empty, resynchronize the peer's *rwnd* to the *rwnd* contained in the SACK.

11. Go through and count all still-pending unacknowledged DATA chunks that were covered by the Gap Ack block reports (that is, stroked as missing or revoked), and increment their individual fast retransmit states. Also count exactly how many DATA chunks are ready for fast retransmission, and track the number of fast retransmits that were done on each destination address for congestion control purposes.

12. Restart timers, if necessary, and adjust the *rwnd* based on the *flightsize* and the *rwnd* values included in the SACK.

As you can see, SACK processing is quite intensive and somewhat complicated. Figure 14–9 depicts a functional flow of how we reach the SACK processing module.

### 14.5.2 Inbound DATA Chunk Processing

After all control processing is performed by **SCTPprocessInbound**(), the focus then turns to the DATA chunk processing. The control processing validates the *Verification tag*, but it is always possible to receive an SCTP packet with nothing but DATA chunks. For this reason a check is made to determine if control is present. If it is, the control processing is called; otherwise, this SCTP packet holds only DATA chunks. For this case the association is checked and possibly passed to OOTB handling, and, if the association is found, then the *Verification tag* is verified. If the *Verification tag* does not match the expected value found in the TCB, the SCTP packet is silently discarded. After all verifications, **SCTPprocessInbound**() processes each DATA chunk by calling **SCTP_handleDataPortion**() on each individual chunk. The first call is passed in the *TOS* bits for ECN handling (which is discussed in the next section). Subsequent calls are still passed in the *TOS* bits, but any ECN bits are cleared after the first call.

**SCTP_handleDataPortion**() begins by verifying that the association is in the correct state to receive data. If it is not, the function returns, causing the inbound

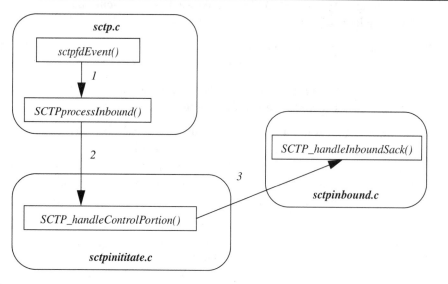

**Figure 14–9**  *Reaching SACK processing*

DATA chunk to be discarded. At this point **SCTP_handleDataPortion**() performs the following actions:

1. Verify that the TSN that has arrived is within the range of the mapping
   array (by default, 10,000 chunks). Use a simple array of bytes with a fixed
   size to indicate if a chunk has arrived or not. The TSN is always translated
   into an offset into this array. Anytime the value exceeds the array size, discard the DATA chunk.

2. If you do see a duplicate, set up the internal SACK generation variable so
   that you will SACK after processing this SCTP packet. This is done by
   forcing the value of the SACK generation variable (*needToAck)* to 2.

3. Examine the mapping array itself. If you find a "1" in the array, this chunk
   is a duplicate, and you must then record it and again set the SACK generation variable, *needToAck*, to the value 2 and return.

4. If the mapping array indicates the chunk has not been received, mark the
   array to 1 to indicate that the TSN is now received. Along with setting the
   mapping array, you also update the largest TSN value inside the array if the
   new chunk holds a higher TSN value than you have earlier recorded. This
   is done to optimize the memory copies when you juggle the array around.

5. Move the mapping arrays (if possible) and reset the mapping array's base TSN (using the variable named *mappingArrayHigestTSN*) to the newly updated value.

6. Finish by calling **SCTPinqueueData()** to queue the DATA chunk into the association and endpoint data queues.

The function **SCTPinqueueData()** pushes the data into the SCTP association. It first copies the data into an appropriate data structure and sets up a link so that the data can be put onto one of the possible linked list queues. After building this link structure, **SCTPinqueueData()** performs the following:

- If the DATA chunk is a piece of a fragment, the chunk is queued into the single linked list that holds all pending fragments. This list is then examined and possibly a new reassembled DATA chunk is obtained by calling **SCTPreasmData()**. If no reassembly is performed, the function returns.

- If a DATA chunk is considered complete (this includes newly reassembled chunks), the appropriate stream is determined. If an invalid stream is found, then the function **sendStreamError()** is called to send back the appropriate operational error.

- If the data is unordered, it is immediately queued into the receive path of the SCTP endpoint and made available for delivery by a subsequent API read call.

- If the DATA chunk is ordered, it is placed in the appropriate position within the stream's inbound queue.

- Once the data is placed in its stream queue, an attempt is made to deliver data from the stream to the endpoint's queue. All DATA chunks that are in order (not just the one arriving) will be transferred to the endpoint's queue.

This functional flow is illustrated in Figure 14–10.

### 14.5.3   Finishing Off by Sending

As noted above, upon the completion of processing all inbound chunks (control or data), an attempt is made to send data. This all takes place within the function **SCTPprocessInbound()**, through the following steps:

1. A SACK timer is possibly started, if one is not running, and the SACK generation variable *needToAck* is incremented. This flag normally tracks the number of inbound SCTP packets received.

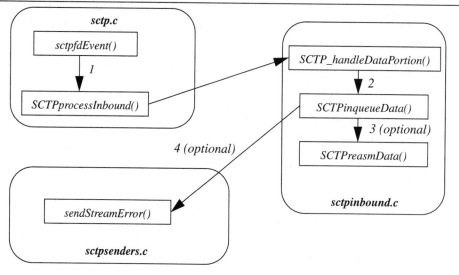

**Figure 14–10**    *Inbound data flow*

2. If you did not receive a cookie and there are DATA chunks that need to be retransmitted, attempt to send them using the function **SCTPsendRetransmits()**. Note that when a retransmission is performed, only one SCTP packet will be output (that is, only one IP datagram will be generated).

When no retransmission is performed, if the output queue has data and some of that data is unsent, repeated calls are made to **SCTPsendAnyWeCan()** to send out data. The function **SCTPsendAnyWeCan()** will return a nonzero value if it succeeds in sending one SCTP packet. A limit is imposed on the number of calls to **SCTPsendAnyWeCan()** if a fast retransmit has just been completed. In this case the association's *maxBurst* is applied to keep the association from transmitting too many SCTP packets.

Otherwise, when no retransmission is performed and no data is in the queue, if you did receive a cookie or if we have an operational error to send, call the send function **SCTPsendAnyWeCan()** one time. This one send function will send out a SCTP packet with either the cookie and/or an operational error.

3. After attempting to transmit data, the SACK generation variable, *needToAck*, is checked. It is possible that the data sending routines may have sent a piggybacked SACK out and thus cleared this flag. If the flag is larger than 1 (indicating the reception of two SCTP packets or the immediate need to SACK), a SACK is sent out and any running SACK timer is

stopped. Note that a SACK will also be sent by this check if you are in the shutdown state or if this is the very first SCTP packet received that contained DATA chunks.

4. At the end of all processing the **SCTPprocessInbound()** function returns the number of user messages that are awaiting reading on the entire SCTP endpoint.

## 14.6    Congestion Control, PMTU, and RTO

Congestion control, PMTU discovery, and *RTO* calculation are scattered among several routines. We will review each of these in separate subsections.

### 14.6.1    Congestion Control

Congestion control adjustments occur in the inbound processing of an SCTP packet (as noted previously). Congestion control restrictions are performed as part of the sending routines **SCTPsendAnyWeCan()** and **SCTPsendRetransmits()**. We will first examine the congestion control adjustments made within the function **SCTP_handleInboundSack()**. As data is acknowledged, counts of the number of bytes acknowledged on a destination are maintained on each network. These are kept in an array, *netAckSz*. A secondary array is maintained, *netAckSz2*, which tracks the amount of non-retransmitted data. To adjust the *cwnd*, each array element is examined. Anytime an element in the *netAckSz* array is zero, it indicates that the element's destination address (indexed by the same array variable) had no DATA chunks acknowledged. Thus if *netAckSz* is zero, we skip to the next element. Otherwise we set up a pointer to the actual network destination address maintained as part of the association. If *netAckSz2* is not zero, we clear the destination's error count and possibly announce that the address is reachable. Next, if the cumulative acknowledgment has moved, we apply the *cwnd* updates. Note that no update will be performed if the cumulative acknowledgment did not move. If the cumulative acknowledgment did move forward, we perform the following:

1. Gather the *flightsize* for the destination address at which we are looking.

2. Determine if we are in slow start or congestion avoidance.

3. If we are in slow start (that is, *cwnd* on this destination is smaller than the destination's *ssthresh*), we check first to see if the *flightsize* plus the amount being acknowledged is larger than or equal to the current *cwnd*. If

it is, we increment the *cwnd* by either the size of the data being acknowledge or one PMTU, whichever is smaller.

If we are in congestion avoidance, we add to our partial bytes acknowledged variable (for the destination) only if we are using all of the current *cwnd*. After possibly advancing the *pba*, we then see if the *cwnd* should be advanced by determining if *pba* is larger than the current *cwnd*. We also validate that the full *cwnd* was being used. If all of this is true, we subtract from *pba* the value of *cwnd* and advance *cwnd* by the destination PMTU.

The *cwnd* itself is enforced by the sending modules **SCTPsendAnyWeCan()** and **SCTPsendRetransmits()**. These functions are contained within *sctpsenders.c*, and in both sending modules the *cwnd* of the destination gates transmission of more data. When a decision is made, the current *flightsize* is always compared to the current value of *cwnd* on the destination selected for transmission. If the *flightsize* is less than *cwnd*, then transmission is allowed. This means that an effective "slop-over" of a PMTU minus 1 is allowed. Note also that there is one exception to *cwnd* gating retransmissions: by default (via a compiler switch), if the first DATA chunk up for retransmission is in the process of doing a fast retransmission, the *cwnd* value is ignored by not calculating *flightsize* and, instead, setting the internal variable to zero.

### 14.6.2   PMTU Discovery

PMTU discovery happens in two distinct ways. On each outbound DATA chunk, the lowest-level sending routine will set the *IP_DF* bit (for IPv4). This is all done within the file *sctpmtu.c* and function **SCTPlsendto()**. For the case in which a PMTU change leaves an individual TSN too large, a special flag is also given to **SCTPlsendto()**. This flag will be set when the upper-layer sending routines recognize a chunk as having exceeded the PMTU after the original fragmentation and TSN assignment are performed. It recognizes this condition via a special flag that is set on the DATA chunk bookkeeping structure by the other piece of the PMTU code, ICMP processing.

When an IP datagram arrives in **sctpfdEvent()**, the IP protocol type is examined and, if it indicates ICMP, then the function **SCTPhandleICMP()** (which is also found in *sctpmtu.c*) is called. This function will decode the ICMP packet. If it is the appropriate ICMP code, if the association can be found, and if the *Verification tag* of the SCTP packet matches that of the peer, then the ICMP packet is accepted. As part of accepting this ICMP packet, the function will do the following:

1. Stop the PMTU timer and restart it again.

2. Lower the PMTU of the destination.

3. Change the *smallestMTU* value if the new size is smaller than this. The *smallestMTU* is the fragmentation size used for all TSN fragmentation. This is kept on an association basis. (The PMTU is kept on a destination basis.)

4. If the *smallestMTU* size changed to a smaller value, the function marks any of the pending TSNs that exceed this new value to allow the special flag to override the *IP_DF* bit.

5. Restart the PMTU timer.

One other piece of the PMTU puzzle is contained in the timer handling routines. Here once every ten minutes the timer routine will try to raise the PMTU. First the *smallestMTU* value is raised, if possible. If this does get raised, then all destinations that have an MTU smaller than the new MTU are also raised.

### 14.6.3  *RTO* Calculation

The *RTO* timer is calculated in one of two ways in SCTP:

- When a heartbeat response is processed
- Once every *RTT* time during data transmission

In both instances the same function, **calculateRTO()** (which is found in *sct-putil.c*), is called. This function uses the exact methods described in Stewart et al. (2000), with floating point calculations to obtain the *RTO*. Jacobson's (1988) integer algorithm is also in the code but has been commented out.

In order to obtain an *RTO* measurement during data transfer, every time a transmission of new data occurs (not a retransmission), a flag is checked to see if a TSN is marked with a timestamp. If it is not, the TSN currently being sent is marked with a timestamp (if successfully sent), and the flag is then set to indicate that an *RTT* calculation is pending.

When the TSN is acknowledged, the **calculateRTO()** function is called using the time the TSN was sent and the time the SACK arrived. Note that Karn's rule is applied to this calculation (that is, you must not use a DATA chunk you have retransmitted for such a calculation). If a TSN has been retransmitted, it will *not* be considered, and the *RTO* calculation will be skipped. In fact, at the time a DATA chunk is recognized as needing retransmission, if the timestamp is present, it is cleared, and the pending *RTT* calculation flag is cleared so that the next new transmission will once again attempt to make an *RTT* estimate.

HEARTBEAT responses are used in *RTO* calculations very easily because the time that the HEARTBEAT was sent is included in the actual information within the HEARTBEAT. When the response arrives, it is a simple matter to call the **calculateRTO()** routine to update the *RTO* timer for the particular destination.


## 14.7   Fault Management

Fault management is derived in two ways. First, periodically a timer expires and a HEARTBEAT is sent to a destination. At this time, if the last HEARTBEAT sent was not responded to, then the destination that the HEARTBEAT was sent to is stroked with an error, as is the overall association error count. Anytime a destination's error count exceeds its threshold, the destination is reported as being "out of service" to the upper layer. Anytime the association error count exceeds its threshold, the association is torn down and reported as such to the upper layer.

The second stroking of errors will occur when a send timer expires and DATA chunks get marked for retransmission. When such a timer event occurs, both the association and the destination are stroked with an error, and again the thresholds are checked for possible action.

Of course, error counters that were raised and never cleared would result in a very unstable association to say the least. To avoid this, when a valid SCTP packet arrives on an association, the association error counter is cleared. Individual destination addresses are only cleared when data that was sent to that destination is acknowledged. Furthermore we also apply the optional Karn's rule[6] to clearing a destination's error count. This error-counter clearing can be found in the function **SCTP_handleInboundSack()** and is the reason that the variable *netAckSz2* is maintained. The other case in which an individual destination address error counter will be cleared is when the HEARTBEAT-ACK that was sent to a particular destination arrives.

Heartbeat processing happens on a periodic basis. When an association enters the ESTABLISHED state, a heartbeat timer is begun. When this timer expires, the **sctptimerExpires()** function is called. Upon recognizing the timer type as "heartbeat," the function **SCTPhandleHeartBeatTimerUp()** is called. This code will handle three cases in its processing of the heartbeat timer:

- A HEARTBEAT was sent but no response was received. In this case the error counters for the overall association as well as the error counter for the individual destination are incremented. Threshold management is then performed to see if either the association or the destination is unreachable.

---

6. Applying Karn's rule to error counter clearing simply means that no retransmitted DATA chunk will cause a destination error counter to be cleared. It will, however, cause the association error counter to be cleared.

If the association is unreachable, the association will be torn down. If just the destination is unreachable, a report is sent to the upper layer; however, HEARTBEATs will still continue to this destination.

- A HEARTBEAT was sent and a response has since been received. In this case the *cwnd* is decayed on this destination.

- A HEARTBEAT was not really sent. This case can occur due to transmission error by the sending module or the realization by the HEARTBEAT-sending code that no destination needs to have a HEARTBEAT sent to it. If this occurs no penalties or changes are made to the association. Note that transmissions that fail due to unreachable destinations (due to unroutable addresses) are marked directly into the "out of service" state and reported to the upper layer.

Upon the completion of the individual cases listed, a call is made to **SCTPSendHBReq()** to send out a new heartbeat. **SCTPSendHBReq()** will select the destination address that has been idle the longest and send a HEARTBEAT to that destination. It may also decide that no destination was idle, in which case no HEARTBEAT will be sent. Upon return from **SCTPSendHBReq()**, the appropriate flags are set up to indicate whether a HEARTBEAT was sent or not and whether a new heartbeat timer is started. Figure 14–11 shows the call flow we just described.

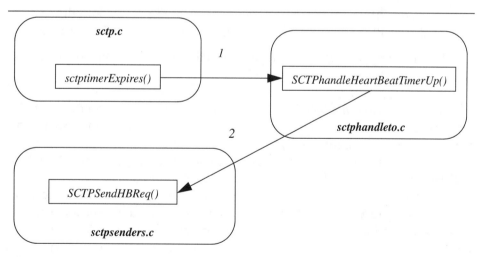

**Figure 14–11** *Heartbeat functional flow*

## 14.8    Tag and Out-of-the-Blue Handling

Tag and out-of-the-blue (OOTB) processing are interrelated because they both work together to respond to unexpected SCTP packets. There are three basic cases in which this occurs within the reference implementation.

In **SCTP_handleControlPortion**() special consideration is given to a SCTP packet that has control chunk(s) within it. An SCTP packet containing a control chunk that is *not* an INIT, INIT-ACK, or COOKIE-ECHO is validated in the very beginning in the following way:

- If no association exists, the OOTB handling module (discussed later in this section) is called.

- If the first chunk in the packet is an ABORT or SHUTDOWN COMPLETE, it is verified that the *Verification tag* in the packet's common header matches the local endpoint's tag (contained within the TCB). Alternatively, if the special *T flag* in the ABORT or SHUTDOWN COMPLETE chunk is set to 1, it is verified that the *Verification tag* in the packet's common header matches the peer's tag (which is also contained within the TCB). If both checks fail, the SCTP packet is discarded.

- If the first chunk is a SHUTDOWN-ACK, the tag is checked against the association; if it matches, processing proceeds. If this check fails, then a SHUTDOWN-COMPLETE is generated with the special *T flag* set to 1.

- Otherwise, the *Verification tag* must match that of the association; if it does not, the SCTP packet is discarded.

The second case in which *Verification tag* processing may occur is when the inbound SCTP packet contains no control chunk information. In this case the function **SCTPprocessInbound**() will either call the OOTB handling (if no association is found) or validate that the tags are correct. If the *Verification tag* does *not* match the expected value, then the SCTP packet is discarded.

The final case to examine is the actual OOTB handling function, **SCTP_handleOutOfBlue**(). This function is called when no association exists. This function performs a number of necessary operations if no association is found. It first examines the entire inbound SCTP packet for the following conditions:

- Does the SCTP packet contain an ABORT? If it does, the function silently returns, causing the SCTP packet to be discarded and not responded to.

- Does the SCTP packet contain a SHUTDOWN-COMPLETE? If it does, the packet is silently ignored again, and the function returns, causing the SCTP packet to be discarded.

- If the SCTP packet contains a SHUTDOWN-ACK, a special SHUTDOWN-COMPLETE is sent to the peer with the *T flag* set to 1. After sending the SHUTDOWN-COMPLETE, the function returns, discarding the SCTP packet.

After finishing a close examination of the SCTP packet, if no special processing was performed, the function will send to the peer an ABORT with the special *T flag* set to 1. The SCTP packet itself will be discarded and no further processing will be performed.

## 14.9 Association Close-Down

The close of an association happens in one of two ways: either the upper-layer user requests that the association be closed, or the peer endpoint sends a SHUTDOWN chunk. We will examine each scenario separately.

### 14.9.1 At the Upper Layer's Request

When the upper layer requests a shutdown, one of two things will occur. If data is still pending to be sent to the peer, a special flag is applied to the association state, indicating that a shutdown is pending. This flag, once in place, will cause all further transmissions of data by the upper layer to fail. At the end of SACK processing, this flag is checked. If the flag is present and all data has been acknowledged (that is, none is left pending), then a SHUTDOWN is sent to the peer, the SHUTDOWN_SENT state is set in the association, and the *Shutdown* timer is started.

If no data was pending to the peer when the shutdown was requested, then the state of the association is immediately moved to SHUTDOWN_SENT, a SHUTDOWN is sent to the peer, and the *Shutdown* timer is started.

Once an endpoint enters the SHUTDOWN_SENT state, every time an SCTP packet arrives containing DATA chunks, the local endpoint responds with both a SHUTDOWN and a SACK. This is accomplished by setting the *needToAck* flag to 2, thus causing a SACK for every SCTP packet that is received. The **SCTPsend-SackFlag()** function is "shutdown-aware" and will bundle a SHUTDOWN in every SACK sent if the state of the association is in the SHUTDOWN_SENT state.

At this point one of three things will happen: the peer will send more data, the peer will send a SHUTDOWN-ACK chunk, or the *Shutdown* timer will expire. If the timer expires, the shutdown will be resent and the timer will be restarted with the appropriate error counters incremented and with threshold management performed to see if the association should be terminated. This all occurs within the **SCTPhandleShutdownTimerUp()** function.

If more data arrives it will be treated as just described; that is, it will be processed normally and a bundled SHUTDOWN and SACK will be sent back to the sender. If the peer responds with a SHUTDOWN-ACK it will be processed by **SCTP_handleControlPortion()** by calling the function **SCTPhandleShutdownAck()**. **SCTPhandleShutdownAck()** will first verify that the association is in either the SHUTDOWN_SENT state or the SHUTDOWN_ACK_SENT state. If the association is *not* in either state, the SCTP packet is discarded and the message is ignored. If the association is in one of these states, the upper layer will be notified that the association is down and a SHUTDOWN-COMPLETE will be sent via a call to **SCTPsendShutdownAck()**. This function serves the dual purpose of sending both SHUTDOWN-COMPLETEs and SHUTDOWN-ACKs. After the SHUTDOWN-COMPLETE is sent, any running shutdown timers are stopped and the association is freed with a call to **SCTPfreeAssociation()**. Subsequent SHUTDOWN-ACKs will be responded to as described in Section 14.8.

### 14.9.2  Reception of a SHUTDOWN

The other possibility is the peer sends a SHUTDOWN to our endpoint. In this case the control processing function **SCTP_handleControlPortion()** (called through our normal sequence) will call the function **SCTPhandleShutdown()**. This function will play a trick on the rest of the SCTP code by calling the function **SCTPudpateAcked()**. This function will change the SHUTDOWN into a SACK with no gaps to run the normal SACK processing code. This may cause the implementation to think a chunk has been reneged, but if this is true, then one of the next chunks processed (presumably a SACK) should correct this view. After processing the SHUTDOWN chunk as a SACK, the function will do one of two things. If the output queue still holds pending data, then an attempt will be made to send any data that is marked for retransmit and any data that will fit into the congestion window by calling **SCTPsendRetransmits()** and **SCTPsendAnyWeCan()**. The other possibility is that no pending data is left. If this is the case, a SHUTDOWN-ACK will be sent to the peer and a *Shutdown-Ack* timer will be started.

Whenever the *Shutdown-Ack* timer expires, the function **SCTPhandleShutdownAckTiemrUp()** will be called. This function is very similar to the *Shutdown* timer expiration. It will check error threshold and possibly terminate the association; otherwise it will send another SHUTDOWN-ACK (after incrementing the error counters) and restart the timer.

Eventually a SHUTDOWN-COMPLETE message will arrive, or the association will be terminated by the error thresholds. If a SHUTDOWN-COMPLETE arrives, the control processing code will call the function **SCTPhandleShutdownComplete()**. This function will verify that the association is in the SHUTDOWN_ACK_SENT state. If it is not, the function will return, ignoring the SHUTDOWN-COMPLETE. If the association is expecting a SHUTDOWN-COMPLETE, then the upper layer is notified that the association is now terminated, all timers are stopped, and the association is freed.

## 14.10   Summary

We have tried to follow through on some of the mainline processing functions of the reference implementation. Many of the recent changes, such as the addition of IPv6 processing and the kernel daemon are left for you to explore on your own. For more details consult the source code that is on the CD accompanying this book. With this chapter and the code you should be able to follow all of the processing and get a clear idea of how an SCTP implementation functions.

# References

Allman, M., and V. Paxson. 1999. On estimating end-to-end network path properties. Presentation. SIGCOMM '99.

Allman, M., V. Paxson, and W. Stevens. 1999. *RFC2581: TCP congestion control*. Internet Engineering Task Force (IETF).

Bellovin, S. 1996. *RFC1948: Defending against sequence number attacks*. Internet Engineering Task Force (IETF).

Braden, R. 1989. *RFC1122: Requirements for Internet hosts—communication layers*. Internet Engineering Task Force (IETF).

Bradner, S. 1996. *RFC2026: The Internet standards process—revision 3*. Internet Engineering Task Force (IETF).

Deering, S. 1989. *RFC1112: Host extensions for IP multicasting*. Internet Engineering Task Force (IETF).

Deering, S., and R. Hinden. 1998. *RFC2460: Internet Protocol, version 6 (IPv6) specification*. Internet Engineering Task Force (IETF).

Droms, R. 1993. *RFC1531: Dynamic Host Configuration Protocol*. Internet Engineering Task Force (IETF).

Elz, R., and Bush, R. 1996. *RFC1982: Serial Number Arithmetic*. Internet Engineering Task Force (IETF).

Egevang, K., and P. Francis. 1994. *RFC1631: The IP Network Address Translator (NAT)*. Internet Engineering Task Force (IETF).

Ferguson, P., and D. Senie. 1998. *RFC2267: Network ingress filtering: defeating denial of service attacks which employ IP source address spoofing*. Internet Engineering Task Force (IETF).

International Telecommunication Union (ITU). 1996. *Error-correcting procedures for DCEs using asynchronous-to-synchronous conversion.* Recommendation V.42, section 8.1.1.6.2. Geneva: International Telecommunication Union.

Jacobson, Van. 1988. Congestion control and avoidance. *Computer Communications Review* 18, no. 4: 314–329.

Karn, P., and C. Partridge. 1987. Improving round-trip time estimates in reliable transport protocols. Presentation. SIGCOMM '87.

Krawcyk, H., M. Bellare, and R. Canetti. 1997. *RFC2104: HMAC: Keyed-hashing for message authentication.* Internet Engineering Task Force (IETF).

McCann, J., S. Deering, and J. Mogul. 1996. *RFC1981: Path MTU discovery for IP version 6.* Internet Engineering Task Force (IETF).

Mockapetris, P. V. 1987. *RFC1034: Domain names—concepts and facilities.* Internet Engineering Task Force (IETF).

Mogul, J. C., and S. E. Deering. 1990. *RFC1191: Path MTU discovery.* Internet Engineering Task Force (IETF).

Nagle, J. 1984. *RFC896: Congestion control in IP/TCP internetworks.* Internet Engineering Task Force (IETF).

National Institute of Standards and Technology (NIST). 1995. *FIPS PUB 180-1: Secure hash standard.* Washington, D.C.: National Institute of Standards and Technology.

Postel, J. 1980. *RFC768: User Datagram Protocol.* Internet Engineering Task Force (IETF).

———. 1981a. *RFC791: Internet Protocol.* Internet Engineering Task Force (IETF).

———. 1981b. *RFC793: Transmission Control Protocol.* Internet Engineering Task Force (IETF).

Postel, J., and J. K. Reynolds. 1985. *RFC959: File Transfer Protocol.* Internet Engineering Task Force (IETF).

Ramakrishnan, K., and S. Floyd. 1999. *RFC2481: A proposal to add explicit congestion notification (ECN) to IP.* Internet Engineering Task Force (IETF).

Rivest, R. 1992. *RFC1321: The MD5 message-digest algorithm.* Internet Engineering Task Force (IETF).

Simpson, W., ed. 1994. *RFC1661: The Point-to-Point Protocol (PPP).* Internet Engineering Task Force (IETF).

Stevens, W. R. 1994. *TCP/IP illustrated.* Vol. 1. Reading, MA: Addison-Wesley.

Stewart, R., Q. Xie, K. Morneault, C. Sharp, H. Schwarzbauer, T. Taylor, I. Rytina, M. Kalla, L. Zhang, and V. Paxson. 2000. *RFC2960: Stream Control Transmission Protocol.* Internet Engineering Task Force (IETF).

Stewart, R., Q. Xie, L. Yarroll, J. Wood, K. Poon, and K. Fujita. Forthcoming. *SCTP sockets mapping.* draft-ietf-sctpsocket-sigtran-03. Internet Engineering Task Force (IETF).

Zweig, J., and C. Partridge. 1990. *RFC1146: TCP alternate checksum options.* Internet Engineering Task Force (IETF).

# Glossary and Abbreviations

**3GPP**          Third Generation Partnership Project, a forum formed by an international group of telecommunications operators and equipment vendors in the late nineties. It is one of the most important standardization organizations responsible for defining the next-generation cellular communications systems. See *http://www.3gpp.org* for more information.

**API**          Application programming interface.

**association**          A relationship established and maintained by two communicating peers. An association in SCTP is semantically equivalent to a connection in TCP.

**association PMTU**          A protocol variable maintained by an SCTP data sender. This is generally set to the smallest PMTU of all available transport addresses of the data receiver.

**BOF**          Birds of a Feather, a meeting format used in IETF to gauge the technical interest of the engineering public on a specific topic. Normally when a new idea of development is brought forward to the IETF, a BOF will be held first. Only if the feedback from the engineers participating in the BOF is positive will a formal IETF working group then be formed to carry out the actual development.

**bundle or bundling**          The act of placing more than one chunk within an SCTP packet. See Section 5.8.4 for more details on how this is performed.

| | |
|---|---|
| **byte-oriented** | *See* **message-oriented.** |
| **chunk** | A unit of information within an SCTP packet. A chunk consists of a chunk header and chunk-specific content. For more details see Section 3.1. |
| **chunk header** | A self-describing format used by SCTP to identify each chunk in an SCTP packet. The first four bytes of each chunk can uniquely identify the type of information being presented to the SCTP stack and its size within the SCTP packet. For more details see Section 3.1.2. |
| **chunk parameter or parameter** | These refer to either a variable-length field or an optional filed of a chunk, defined with the TLV format. |
| **fragment** | A smaller piece of a message being sent. At the SCTP layer, a single user message may be split into multiple DATA chunks for transport over an association. (See Section 5.8 for more details.) At the IP layer, one larger IP datagram may be split into several smaller IP datagrams. |
| **fragmentation** | The act of splitting messages into smaller pieces. |
| **IAB** | Internet Architecture Board, an international technical advisory organization that has been overseeing the research and development of the Internet for almost two decades. |
| **IANA** | Internet Assigned Numbers Authority, a division of IAB. IANA serves the Internet by providing the central coordinating functions for the global Internet. These include assigning, maintaining, and bookkeeping port numbers, protocol identifications, and other commonly assigned identifications associated with the global Internet. |
| **IESG** | Internet Engineering Steering Group, the technical advisory committee inside the IETF. |
| **IETF** | Internet Engineering Task Force, the engineering arm of IAB, consisting of a number of technical working groups |

working on various aspects of Internet technology. IETF is responsible for defining and issuing all·the Internet-related standards, including all the IP protocols. See the IETF Web site, *http://www.ietf.org*, for more information.

**IP broadcast address**  A special type of IP address used to address all the host machines connected by a local IP link. When a message is sent to an IP broadcast address, all the machines connected to that link will receive a copy of the message.

**IP datagram**  The unit of data delivery across an IP network. This includes an IP header, any transport header, and the data being carried to the remote endpoint.

**IP header**  The header used in IP networks to route the data across it, usually from a local host to a remote host. For IPv4 (Postel 1981a) the IP header is at least 20 bytes long.

**IP multicast address**  A special type of IP address that identifies a group of host machines in an IP network. When a message is sent to an IP multicast address, all the machines that are members of that multicast group will receive a copy of the message.

**IP unicast address**  An IP address that uniquely identifies a single host machine in an IP network.

**IPv6 header**  An IP header specifically for IPv6 (Deering and Hinden 1998). An IPv6 header is at least 40 bytes long.

**ITU**  International Telecommunications Union, one of the major international telecommunications standards bodies. ITU has defined many of the important global telephone standards, including SS7.

**message-oriented**  Refers to the concept of passing a complete block of user data, called a user message, across the user interface to the transport layer. This is in contrast to the byte-oriented concept in which all data passed across the user interface to the transport layer is considered one continuous byte stream. SCTP is a message-oriented transport protocol, while TCP is byte-oriented.

**NAT**                              Network Address Translator, a device put into the Internet to automatically translate one IP address to another for the purpose of address reuse, etcetera. See more details in Egevang and Francis (1994).

**optional chunk
parameter or
optional parameter**                 An optional field of a chunk, defined with the TLV format.

**permanent chunk
parameter or
permanent parameter** A variable-length permanent field of a chunk, defined with the TLV format.

**PMTU**                             Path Maximum Transmission Unit, the maximum number of bytes of an IP datagram that can be transferred in a single unit over a specific path in an IP network. If an IP datagram exceeds the PMTU, normally it will be either fragmented into smaller pieces by the network en route to its destination or dropped by the network. See Mogul and Deering (1990) and McCann, Deering, and Mogul (1996) for more details.

**PMTU discovery**                   A mechanism used by an IP endpoint to discover the current PMTU of a particular path. This is useful because the PMTU of two given endpoints in an IP network is not guaranteed to be a constant; it may change over time. See Mogul and Deering (1990) and McCann, Deering, and Mogul (1996) for more details.

**PPP**                              Point-to-Point Protocol, a line protocol for setting up an IP connection that is commonly used by dial-up Internet service providers. PPP is defined in the IETF in Simpson (1994).

**protocol parameter**               A protocol variable with a preset recommended value. Most protocol variables can be set so that either an application or an administrator can configure the parameter to a different value.

**PSTN**                             Public Switched Telephone Network.

**RFC**                          Request for Comments, the name that the IETF and IAB use for all of their official publications.

**RTT**                          Round-Trip Time, the time needed for a datagram to make a round trip from one node in the network to another and back.

**SCTP common header**           A header placed on every SCTP packet being sent. The SCTP common header contains information that can be used by the receiving SCTP stack to route the information to the correct association. See Section 3.1.1 for more details.

**SCTP packet**                  The unit of data transmission across an association. This includes the SCTP common header and one or more chunks.

**SSN**                          Stream Sequence Number, the stream-specific message sequence number that an SCTP data sender assigns to an outbound message. Note that this is not the same as the TSN. For instance, if a large user message is fragmented and being transported in multiple DATA chunks, all the DATA chunks will carry the same SSN.

**ssthresh**                     The Slow Start Threshold, an SCTP congestion-control protocol variable that a data sender needs to maintain for each destination address of the data receiver.

**TCB**                          Transmission Control Block, an internal data structure containing a set of information that a communicating endpoint must maintain in order to operate and manage an SCTP association with a peer. The actual structure and content of a TCB are implementation dependent.

**TCP segment**                  The unit of data transmission across a TCP connection. This includes the TCP header and possibly some data bytes.

**tie-tags**                     A special set of integers used to discriminate cases of association restart. See Section 4.2.2.1 for details.

**TLV**                  A data structure format that is always composed of three fields—Type, Length, and Value.

**transport header**     The header attached by a transport protocol (such as TCP or SCTP) to an outbound IP datagram. The transport header precedes any other data in the IP datagram and is used by the transport protocol to perform various identification and validation procedures. The SCTP common header is the transport header used by SCTP.

**TSN**                  Transmission Sequence Number, the sequence number assigned to each DATA chunk by an SCTP data sender. Unlike the SSN, this is not assigned on a per-message basis. For instance, if a large user message is fragmented and being transported in multiple DATA chunks, each of the DATA chunk will be assigned a unique TSN number.

# Index

## Numerics

3GPP (Third Generation Partnership Project) 329

## A

a_rwnd (advertised receive window credit) 145–146
    calculating 145
    for INIT messages 46
ABORT chunk 33
    description of 40
    fields of 72–73
    receiving 249–250
    in SCTP packets 233–234
    sending 248–249
    using 248
abortive shutdown 248–250
accept() function 259
acknowledgment
    cumulative 138
    delayed 138–139
    generation of 28
    revoking 146–148
    to SCTP sender 131
additive increase multiplicative decrease
    (AIMD) 180
ADDRESS_ADDED state 274
ADDRESS_AVAILABLE state 274
ADDRESS_MADE_PRIM state 274
ADDRESS_REMOVED state 274
ADDRESS_UNREACHABLE state 274
addresses 2–3

ambiguity in detecting the reachability of
    208–208
broadcast 22
heartbeat period of 205
hostname 48, 48
inactive 160
multicast 22
source 161
unicast 22
unreachability detection algorithm for
    205–206
unreachable 201–204
unresolvable 69
use in association set-up 97–101
address-unreachability detection algorithm
205–206
Adler-32 checksum 37
    generation by data senders 171
    validation by data receivers 172
advertised receive window credit (a_rwnd) 46
    calculating 145
AF_INET 259
AIMD (additive increase multiplicative de-
    crease) 180
ancillary data 268
API (application programming interface) 24, 297
application programming interface. See API
ASSOCIATE primitive 30
association 21, 24–25
    asymmetric multi-homing configuration of
        220–221
    between single-homed and multi-homed
        endpoints 220–221
    chunk rejections during setup of 101–102

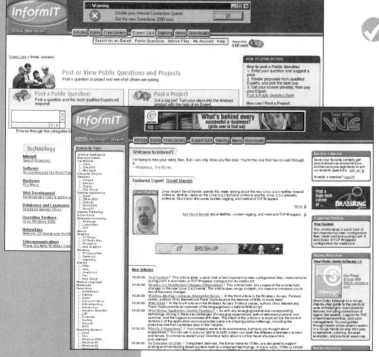

## CD ROM WARRANTY

Addison-Wesley warrants the enclosed disc to be free of defects in materials and faulty workmanship under normal use for a period of ninety days after purchase. If a defect is discovered in the disc during this warranty period, a replacement disc can be obtained at no charge by sending the defective disc, postage prepaid, with proof of purchase to:

Editorial Department
Addison-Wesley Professional
Pearson Technology Group
75 Arlington Street, Suite 300
Boston, MA  02116
Email:  AWPro@awl.com

Addison-Wesley and Randall Stewart and Qiaobing Xie make no warranty or representation, either expressed or implied, with respect to this software, its quality, performance, merchantability, or fitness for a particular purpose. In no event will Randall Stewart or Qiaobing Xie or Addison-Wesley, its distributors, or dealers be liable for direct, indirect, special, incidental, or consequential damages arising out of the use or inability to use the software. The exclusion of implied royalties is not permitted in some states. Therefore, the above exclusion may not apply to you. This warranty provides you with specific legal rights. There may be other rights that you may have that vary from state to state. The contents of this CD-ROM are intended for non-commercial use only.

More information and updates are available at:
http://www.awl.com/cseng/titles/